FOOLS
AND
JESTERS
AT THE ENGLISH COURT

Two Fools, c. *1600, Netherlandish School (Kunsthistorisches Museum, Vienna/
Bridgeman Art Library, London)*

FOOLS
AND
JESTERS
AT THE ENGLISH COURT

JOHN SOUTHWORTH

SUTTON PUBLISHING

First published in 1998 by
Sutton Publishing Limited · Phoenix Mill
Thrupp · Stroud · Gloucestershire · GL5 2BU

British Library Cataloguing in Publication Data
A catalogue record for this book is available from the British Library.

ISBN 0-7509-1773-3

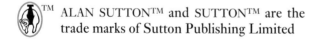
Typeset in 11/12pt Ehrhardt.
Typesetting and origination by
Sutton Publishing Limited.
Printed and bound in Great Britain by
Butler & Tanner Ltd, Frome and London.

Contents

Preface   vii

1   *King and Fool*   1

2   *The Elusive Dwarfs*   10

3   *Warrior Fools*   17

4   *Norman Buffoons*   29

5   *Minstrel Fools*   35

6   *The Innocents*   48

7   *Tudor Innocents*   61

8   *William Somer*   70

9   *The European Dimension*   81

10   *Fools to Jesters*   89

11   *'Jugler' and Jester*   94

12   *Jane: a Female Innocent*   100

13   *Elizabeth's Fools*   107

14   *The Player Fools*   121

15   *The Last of the Jesters*   138

16   *Jeffery Hudson: Court Dwarf*   153

17   *The Fools' Motley*   163

18   *Mr Nobody*   175

Abbreviations   185

Notes   187

Further Reading   209

Index   211

Preface

In the pages that follow I attempt to answer a series of straightforward historical questions. Who were the fools and jesters who are said to have served a succession of English kings and queens in their courts throughout the Middle Ages and up to the time of the Stuarts? If they were real people, and not just a retrospective invention of later poets and playwrights reflecting a now discredited romantic view of the past, what were their names and dates? Secondly, what was the nature of the relationships they are supposed to have enjoyed with their patrons? And, if such relationships are found to have some basis in historical fact, how did they vary, if at all, from age to age and from person to person? Thirdly, what did the fools actually do or say (and what costume did they wear) in fulfilling the role attributed to them?

At every turn of such an investigation, a stereotypical answer leaps out at us from an abundance of familiar images deriving from folklore, emblematic art (most of it continental in origin), and more recent stage traditions. Most turn out to be wrong or, at best, misleading. The truth, of course, is more difficult to find and altogether less simple.

The obstacles I have encountered in separating fact from various kinds of fiction may be readily imagined. The thing would not be worth doing at all if one did not exclude, as I have tried to do, all but contemporary evidence. For this reason, the matter of the jest-books – written for the most part long after the death of those fools whose names were attached to them, often quite arbitrarily – and much else that is of literary rather than historical interest has been left to one side. Nor have I concerned myself with folly as a literary or philosophical concept, but only with the persons of professional fools as they practised their particular skills at the English court.

Though the information I have come up with may disappoint those who are looking for simplistic answers to the questions I have posed or merely for confirmation of their preconceptions, I console myself with the belief that even the smallest facts are inherently more interesting than large but unsupported generalities. But facts of themselves – especially of the historical kind – tell us nothing unless they are placed in context and we know something of the background from which they have come. It is for this reason that I have devoted a first, introductory chapter to the king/fool relationship itself, and prefaced those early chapters in which I distinguish the various categories of fool – the dwarfs and the warriors, the clever and the truly foolish – with some background information from earlier and more distant cultures. Thereafter, I limit myself to the English court.

In the course of my research and writing, I have accumulated many debts of gratitude to those who have helped me in various ways. Firstly to Richard Barber of Boydell and Brewer who commissioned an earlier book on the minstrels which led me directly to my present subject, and for allowing me to make use of material from *The English Medieval Minstrel* that is equally, perhaps more, pertinent here. To the many librarians throughout the country who have aided my research by providing facilities to an itinerant performer, I can only express my thanks in general terms; but I must make a special mention of the librarian and staff of my home library, the Suffolk County Library in Ipswich, for their unfailing and friendly assistance over a long period. Thanks are due also to those institutions which have allowed me to reproduce illuminations, paintings or other artefacts in their collections and, in most instances, have supplied me with photographs of them. These are acknowledged severally in the captions. A final word of thanks to my Ipswich neighbour, Dr J.M. Blatchly, for finding time to read several of my chapters and for his valuable suggestions for their improvement. Responsibility for the whole of my text, especially its mistakes, remains of course mine.

JS
Ipswich, September 1997

CHAPTER 1

King and Fool

Clowns, fools – comedians of one kind or another – have been a feature of virtually every recorded culture in the history of civilisation and have made significant contributions to the development of early theatre and literary drama. This is certainly true of western European culture, and nowhere more so than in England, where the fool in various disguises is found at the heart of popular dramatic activity from its earliest recorded beginnings.

The history of the fool in that more general sense makes a fascinating story that has already been told, and will remain in the background of all that follows. But my subject here is with a particular type of fool, separated from others by the special relationship that he enjoyed with king or ruler as his personal retainer. He commonly goes by the name of 'jester', though that is a term that in its present usage dates only from the Tudor period. I shall call him simply a court or king's fool.

In some of the earliest European records he is designated *nebulo*, a word expressive of clerical contempt but which nevertheless conveys an accurate assessment of his social standing; he was seen as a paltry, worthless fellow, a nobody. It was not merely that his position in the feudal hierarchy was low; like the minstrels, he was altogether excluded from it. Being neither lord nor cleric, freeman nor serf, he existed in a social limbo. Even in his natural habitat of the court, he remained apart, almost as if he belonged to another species. In this, his situation was more extreme than that of the minstrels. Though obliged to sit at a separate table (when not performing), they at least had the companionship of their fellows; he was alone in his separation. In fifteenth-century scenes of court life (Plate 1) he occupies otherwise empty spaces or is shown flitting from one group of courtiers to another, a barely corporeal presence.

It was only in relation to his master that he was able to gain identity. By definition, he was someone on whom the king could bestow his favour without giving rise to any of the jealousies or counter-claims on the part of competing court factions that normally accompanied the exercise of royal patronage. Indeed, his office was a gift of the dubious kind that few would regard as a favour at all; it was one that 'none but he that hath wit can perform, and none but he that wants wit will perform'.[1] And whatever position at court the fool might obtain through a successful performance of his role over a period of time, he remained wholly and

A fifteenth-century Dutch fool, dancing and playing (Bodleian Library, Oxford: MS Douce 248, f. 212, detail)

permanently dependent on that favour. It could be withdrawn at any time and frequently was; and when that happened, he could usually be relied upon to disappear from the scene as though he had never existed. Yet, for as long as it lasted, the bond between the king and himself might be close, even intimate, and in those circumstances he could come to have a real, if incalculable, influence on his master's policy and decisions. Again, the fool's nebulous status at court enabled him to act on occasion as confidential informant or spy – as the fool Golet is said to have done for William of Normandy, warning him of the approach of intending assassins and thus saving the future Conqueror's life. It was the source and pre-condition of whatever freedom of action he enjoyed.

We now tend to picture the court fool – the traditional jester in cap and bells – as belonging in a special way to the Middle Ages and to western European culture. But his origins, though hidden in unrecorded antiquity, may be as old as kingship itself. For wherever forceful and ambitious men or women have attained a position of autocratic power over others, there is often found at their side an insignificant person of obscure origins who, whether given the formal title of 'fool' or not, is seen to fulfil an equivalent function.

The 'trickster' figure that anthropologists have identified in myths and legends across a wide range of early cultures as chaos-maker and sower of discord, but who at the same time is able to win boons for mankind from the creator-gods,[2] is here bound and contained in a mutually advantageous partnership with tribal chieftain or king; advantageous to the ruler because it provided him with necessary recreation, for putting aside the rituals and prerogatives of kingship in simple enjoyment of the humour and companionship of a fellow human being who carried no weight of social and political debt; advantageous to the fool because it gave him a privileged haven for the practice of his eccentric skills for so long as he could keep his patron amused and retain his interest.

In the course of its long history, the partnership was to take a variety of forms. In what follows, I focus on English records from the medieval, Tudor and Jacobean periods; but that it was known to much earlier cultures is evidenced by writings from ancient Egypt, the *Historical Records* of Sima Qian ('father of Chinese historiography'), and by the classical, Celtic and Islamic texts that Enid Welsford drew upon in her more general account of the fool's history.[3]

The curious double-act of king and fool, master and servant, substance and shadow, may thus be seen as a universal, symbolic expression of the antithesis lying at the heart of the autocratic state between the forces of order and disorder, of structured authority and incipient anarchy, in which the conditional nature of the fool's licence ('so far but no further') gives reassurance that ultimately order will always prevail. The fool, though constrained, continually threatens to break free in pushing to its limits whatever freedom he is given. He is the trickster of myth in an historical strait-jacket from which he is forever struggling to escape. And if the king, as the dominant partner, sets the tone of their exchanges and the fool has everything to gain from a willing acceptance of his subservient role, his participation can never be forced. If, for whatever reason, he should come to feel that his master has reneged on the unwritten contract between them (the rules of the game), it is always open to him to refuse to play, however costly to himself the refusal might prove to be. He thus retains – and needs to retain if he is to achieve the full potential of his role – a degree of independence. Like the actor on stage in a live performance, success is inevitably accompanied by the possibility of failure, and the higher the stakes that are played for, the greater the possible failure. It is only the successful fool who lives on in the remembrance of later generations to find his way into the jest-books. The sycophantic, flattering fool produces an inferior type of humour and is soon forgotten; those who take too high a risk and fail in the attempt face a grimmer fate in prison or madhouse.

But there was danger on both sides of this balancing act. If the fool risked going too far in his banter and tricks, the king was also vulnerable to the fool's abuse of the licence he was given. In the case of a foolish king and an unscrupulous fool, the danger could be very real. The classic example here is that of the eleventh-century Byzantine fool Romanus Boilas, who exploited the privileged position he had gained at court to plot against the life of his patron, the Emperor Constantine IX. Romanus had fallen in love with the emperor's mistress and aimed, not only to eliminate his rival, but take over his throne. According to a contemporary historian, he came within an ace of success.[4]

In medieval psalters, Psalm 52 (beginning 'The Fool says in his heart/There is no god') was usually illustrated by a depiction of King David the Psalmist in

*The Suicide of Saul
(Bodleian Library,
Oxford: MS Barlow
22, f. 67, detail)*

company with his fool, or, more rarely, the suicide of Saul. In the fourteenth-century Barlow Psalter, these two subjects are juxtaposed in a telling image of the potentially destructive power of the fool as perceived by clerics: the fool's bladder-stick mimics the thrust of Saul's self-directed sword.

It is in the infinitely varied nuances of the relationship between king and fool, and the widely differing tone of their exchanges, that the greatest interest may be found to lie. At one extreme, the fool – in St Chrysostom's definition, 'he who gets slapped' – is a more or less complicit butt in the low but universal comedy of the banana skin and the custard pie. At the other, their partnership may be so close as to allow an identification, even a voluntary exchange of roles, in which the fool becomes an *alter ego* of the king, and the king assumes his fool's identity in religious ritual or actual combat. We shall encounter instances of both.

But it is remarkable that in nearly all medieval illustrations of the court fool that have survived, he is represented as armed with a weapon – club, marotte (stick with a miniature fool's head at the top), bladder, dagger or sword. The club may be padded and the dagger or sword (like that of the Roman actor) made only of wood, but the hint of aggression – or, at the least, of preparedness for an active defence – remains. The coxcomb, familiar in Renaissance art and literature as an emblematic badge of fools and of folly, gives warning of similar assertiveness. The madman-fool of the mentally unstable Charles VI of France was named Haincelin Coq.

At this point, however, it is necessary to make a basic distinction between two broad categories of fool; between the natural and the artificial; those who were regarded as fools 'by nature' and those who pretended folly to fulfil a professional, comedic role. It is a distinction that in Europe was understood and applied from as early as the twelfth century, but, in a wider context, goes back to the earliest recorded beginnings of the fool's history. A subdivision of the first of these categories (the naturals or 'innocents', as I prefer to term them) should also be made between the madman-fools who were congenitally or spasmodically insane and those who would now be described (in politically incorrect but plain language) as 'slow-witted' or 'mentally retarded'. Of this latter group, a few rare individuals – of whom Will Somer, the fool of Henry VIII, was a notable exemplar – might be further distinguished as 'wise innocents'.

The relations that these several categories of fool normally enjoyed with their patrons naturally differed from each other greatly, as did the costume and 'props' with which each was associated in succeeding periods. In later pages I have detailed information to offer on the complex subject of costume, and this will be summarised in a concluding chapter; but to illustrate the distinctions that were made between the clever and the innocent, the mad and the simple, it may be useful here to pursue a little further the related matter of their 'weapons' as these were depicted in contemporary psalters. This will enable me also to indicate the plan of my subsequent chapters in which their histories – insofar as these have required separate treatment – are told.

The medieval Latin word for fool, *follis*, had the original, classical meaning of a leathern sack or air-filled bag; hence the bladders or 'baubles' of the innocents. Such visual clues to their identity would have been essential to illiterate lay users of the psalters. But the phallic suggestiveness of the clubs and branches of wood wielded by the clever or 'counterfeit' fools (Plates 2 and 3) carried an additional, more ominous message; not only were these elegantly dressed figures to be identified as fools (a fact not otherwise apparent in their appearance), they were to be regarded by the layman as fools of an especially dangerous kind. They are unlikely to have been drawn from life. The artists who painted them were not so much concerned with individual fools as in making a general, admonitory point about the wickedness and folly of the secular world of their time, and in warning of its moral dangers. In the Eadwine or Canterbury Psalter of 1147, which derives from a Utrecht original of ninth-century date, the situation described in Psalm 52 –

> God is looking down from heaven
>   at the sons of men . . .
> All have turned aside,
>   all alike are tainted . . .   (vv. 2–3)

– is given a literal interpretation (Plate 4a). Here, the fool appears as an evil prince, installed on a dais, surveying with evident complacency a scene of universal disorder, rapine and slaughter. A sword rests in readiness across his lap, while above the figure of Christ appeals in vain for peace to be restored.[5]

We know, however, that fools of the mentally competent kind existed from an early date and were often armed with real weapons. For these, we shall look first (in Chapter 3) to Ireland, where a unique body of oral lore, comprising praise poetry, annals and pseudo-historical myths and legends, survived the coming of Christianity to provide what one distinguished scholar has described as a 'window on the Iron Age'.[6] In this Irish Celtic tradition, kings were little more than tribal chieftains in constantly shifting warfare with their rivals; and the fools who are said to have accompanied them were expected to take an equal share in the fighting with their lord's other attendants. The *riogdruth* (king's fool) was thus required to combine the gift of eliciting laughter with prowess as a warrior; his aggressive potential was fully absorbed in defence of his lord and the defeat of his enemies. Norman *joculatoris*, literally 'jokers', are also found to have been active on the field of battle; and one of them, Taillefer, is credited with initiating the decisive charge of the French cavalry at Hastings and decapitating an opponent.

It is only with his domestication in the more settled courts of the Angevin and Plantagenet kings (as evidenced in Chapter 5) that the clever fool forfeits his right to carry arms. It is a process whereby the joculator – along with his old companions, the wandering *mimi et histriones* of early Latin documents – takes shelter under the new, umbrella term of *menestrel* in its original meaning of 'little servant', combining a talent to amuse with utilitarian skills of huntsman, waferer or messenger.

In the thirteenth century, he is given the title of *Magister*, a horse to ride and a servant to attend him at the king's expense, and may be rewarded with a plot of land to cultivate on his retirement. We are not deceived by such royal favours. The Celtic chieftain, when he realises that his defeated opponent in personal combat is not the kingly rival he had taken him to be but merely his rival's 'double' with the 'shameful haircut' of a fool under his crown, feels insulted and disgraced. To medieval clerics, especially the king's chaplains, the presence of such people at court was never less than an embarrassing nuisance. It was against that continuing social and religious prejudice that the fool was to achieve his modest apotheosis as *Mr* Nobody. (His subsequent history, culminating in his emancipation as itinerant entertainer and stage fool, will be traced in Chapters 9–11, and 13–15.)

The hefty clubs and marottes carried by the psalter fools of disordered mind (Plate 5) were in part representative of the threat that the fool of the psalm (who 'says in his heart, There is no god') was seen to pose to the people of God. But their weapons were not merely emblematic in kind. Though rare at the English court, 'frantic fools', as they were termed in the Middle Ages, made regular appearances at the court of France. The madman Sibelot, armed with a marotte, is said to have attacked on sight everyone he encountered at the court of Henri III with the sole exception of the king himself, 'whom a marvellous instinct obliged him to respect'.[7] Though doubtless contained to tolerable limits by the restraining hands of their keepers, such fools come closest in character to the anarchic tricksters of myth.

Fool in cart drawn by apes balances a bowl of wine. Flemish, fourteenth century (Bodleian Library, Oxford: MS Douce 6, f. 136ᵛ, detail)

The sticks and bladders of those fools who were accounted 'simple' rather than mad were probably used as much for defence as attack. For the closer the bond between king and fool – and with the innocents this might reach to mutual affection – the more the fool was resented by other court servants. However, Master Guillaume, a seventeenth-century Mantuan fool, was described as a 'mortal enemy to Pages and Lacqueys', and as carrying under his coat a 'short Stick, which he call'd his Bird, and when he beat them he was always the first that cry'd out *Murder*'.[8] The stubborn little fellow shown in Plate 6a, with cudgel resting conveniently on his shoulder, is giving as good as he gets in his argument with David. A near-naked fool from another psalter (Plate 6b) carries what appears to be a dagger or sharpened stick in one hand and a large wafer in the other. The 'targe' or small shield bought by Edward II for one of his innocents called Robert was probably for a play fight of some kind, as was certainly the cardboard armour with which Will Somer was equipped for the Christmas revels of 1551 (Chapters 6–8). The 'mock combat' was to be a popular turn in the repertoire of English court fools, both innocent and clever, throughout their history.

I have said that the king/fool relationship was advantageous to the kingly patron in that it provided him with recreation and the companionship of a person with whom he could establish rapport at the basic level of one human being to another; but there was always something more to it than that. A medieval bishop is reported to have said on the occasion of his election, 'I have heard the truth for the last time'. For the more powerful men become, the more isolated they tend to be as their channels of communication with the real world outside the artificial ambience of the court are progressively impeded by the desire of their courtiers to please; to tell them what they like to hear rather than what they need to know. The king's need for truth, especially of the unpalatable kind, and the fool's ability to communicate it in a uniquely acceptable form as humour was a crucial factor in the relations between them from which the fool derived much of his *raison d'être*. Part of the fascination of Shakespeare's handling of the king/fool relationship in *King Lear* lies in his reversal of what is often thought to be the typical slapping order, in which the king becomes a target for the fool's truth-bearing shafts. Far from distracting Lear from his grief (as is sometimes supposed), their effect is to confront him with the unbearable reality of the situation in which he finds himself, a painful but necessary stage in his progress to self-knowledge and ultimate redemption.[9] Shakespeare's dramatic treatment of this theme is wholly in accord with an ancient historical tradition.

The innocent speaks the truth because he can do no other. He blurts it out and (more often than not) escapes retribution because of his transparent honesty. It was not so much for his folly as for his 'wisdom' – that special gift he possessed for hitting the nail of truth on the head – that the innocent was so greatly valued in the medieval and Tudor periods. As Cardinal Perron said of Master Guillaume, 'he lives of a Profession he does not understand'.[10]

The clever fool understands only too well the risks he is taking in the communication of hard truths, and is obliged to adopt more subtle approaches. He is most effective (and funny) when he contrives to hold a mirror to the king in which his patron can see a magnified image of his own attitudes and decisions, and recognise for himself the folly in them. In the old legend, when Zeus announces in the busy market-place of the world that he will send down a torrent of rain but that only fools will be wetted by it, it is the one wise man there who hurries indoors to fetch an umbrella. When the rain descends and he alone remains dry, the others turn upon him in fury. In a world of fools, it is the person who realises (or who can be brought to realise) his own innate folly who is truly wise. This is the universal message of the clever fool.

When the Second Emperor of Qin (209–207 BC) proclaimed his intention to lacquer the Great Wall of China, his counsellors stood speechless, appalled by the economic and human cost of the project but too cowed to express opposition. According to Sima Qian in his *Historical Records*, it required the intervention of a fool named Twisty Pole to deflect the emperor's purpose; and he did it, not by contradiction, but by a show of agreement. 'That's a splendid idea', the fool promptly enthused. 'Lacquer the Great Wall all smooth and shiny, then it will be too slippy for any invaders to climb over it. Now let's get down to the practical side of the job. The lacquering is easy enough, but building a drying room may present a problem or two.' A long, tense silence ensued. Then, as the penny dropped, a slow smile was seen to spread over the emperor's face. The bizarre, impossible project was buried in laughter.[11]

In a court dominated by fear and hypocrisy (as many were) it might be necessary for truth to be represented as folly in order to be heard. When no one at the French court of Philip VI was brave enough to inform the king that most of his fleet had been destroyed by Edward III at Sluys in 1340, it was left to an unnamed fool to break the news. Entering the royal presence, he was heard to mutter, 'Those cowardly Englishmen, those chicken-hearted Britons!' 'How so?' Philip asked. 'Why, because they had not courage enough to jump into the sea like your own sailors, who went headlong from their ships, leaving them to the enemy who did not dare to follow them.'[12] As Erasmus was to claim of the Renaissance fools of his time, 'They can speak truth and even open insults, and be heard with positive pleasure; indeed, the words that would cost a wise man his life are surprisingly enjoyable when uttered by a clown. For truth has a genuine power to please if it manages not to give offence, but this is something the gods have granted only to fools.'[13]

Humour consists essentially in a surprising juxtaposition of opposites. As Thomas Fuller said in the seventeenth century, 'It is unnaturall to laugh at a Naturall';[14] but we may smile and be touched by his wisdom because (like that of the child) it is unpredictable and goes so often to the heart of truth. We laugh at the assumed folly of the clever fool or comedian because we see in it a reflection of our own foolish attitudes and behaviour.

Humour has been described as potentially one of the finest forms of thought and perception. It is a human necessity. The delicate and often dangerous task of the court fools was to supply that humour in the place where, for the greater part of our history, it was most needed: the centre and hub of supreme political power, the court of the king. As that power was gradually eroded and finally lost, so the fools were to take their departure, or be excluded to other, more promising fields of activity. The humour with which they had humanised the courts of the king in the days of his power, being mainly of the spontaneous kind dependent on personal idiosyncrasy and the mood of the moment, can never be wholly recaptured. But the fools themselves, though accounted nobodies in their own time, surely deserve rescue from the distortions or complete oblivion into which so many have fallen. This I attempt in the pages that follow.

CHAPTER 2

The Elusive Dwarfs

I have written in my opening chapter of the distinction that needs to be made between two broad types of fool, the natural and the artificial or counterfeit, the simple and the clever.

But there is a third category that evades this distinction, and, so far as available records go, claims precedence over both, in England as elsewhere. As the trickster of anthropology emerges from the shadows of myth and legend to become the court fool of history, he is usually found to assume the diminutive stature of a dwarf. There can be little doubt about the earliest of his appearances in the historical record.

In the time of the Sixth Dynasty of the Old Kingdom of Egypt (*c.* 2323–2150 BC), an official called Harkhuf wrote to the boy pharaoh Neferkere (Pepi II) to report the discovery of a 'dancing dwarf' in the course of an expedition to a mysterious region somewhere to the south of Egypt. It is Neferkere's reply that survives: 'Thou hast said in this thy letter that thou hast brought a dancing dwarf from the land of spirits, like the dwarf which the treasurer of the god Burded brought from Punt in the time of Isesi . . . Come northward to the court immediately; thou shalt bring this dwarf with thee . . . for the dances of the god, to rejoice and gladden the heart of the king of Upper and Lower Egypt, Neferkere, who lives for ever.' 'To rejoice and gladden the heart of the king': a classic definition of the role of the court fool in all succeeding ages and cultures.

Evidently, Harkhuf's dwarf was not the first of his kind to have found his way to the pharaoh's court; an earlier dwarf from Punt – a region thought to have been located along the Red Sea, comprising what is now eastern Sudan and Eritrea – had preceded him by a hundred years. The Egyptian word used to denote both these small people was *dng* or 'danga'. They were probably African pygmies, renowned then as now for their dancing, who in antiquity are known to have inhabited an area further north than the forests in the Congo where they have since taken refuge. Before 1933, they were still to be seen in the marshlands of the White Nile in southern Sudan.[1]

But who was the god with whom Harkhuf's dwarf was associated, whose dances he was expected to perform? Miss Welsford, following Maspero, believed it to be the dwarf-god Bes, a genie of foreign importation who was the buffoon among the minor deities of Egypt. Though normally depicted immobile, hands on hips, he is sometimes shown in a clumsy dance, brandishing a broad dagger with a menacing air. But these depictions of Bes belong to a much later period of Temple art, a thousand years on from the reign of Neferkere. Véronique Dasen has recently put forward a more persuasive hypothesis. She suggests that the dangas' dancing had a solar significance, and that the god in question was the far more important sun-god, Re. If this were so, the dances would indeed have 'gladdened the heart of the king because they celebrated his power as son of Re'.[2]

However that was, there can be no question as to the value that the young pharaoh placed on his official's discovery. His letter to Harkhuf continues, 'When he [the danga] goes down with thee into the vessel, appoint excellent people, who shall be beside him on each side of the vessel; take care lest he fall into the water. When he sleeps at night appoint excellent people, who shall sleep beside him in his tent; inspect ten times a night.'[3] Unless the utmost care is taken, the letter implies, the precious find could prove elusive.

Moreover, in a pyramid text of the same dynasty, the pharaoh sought to propitiate the god of the dead, Osiris, and obtain a speedy passage to a celestial afterworld by proclaiming himself 'that pygmy of the dances of god who diverts the god in front of his great throne'.[4] Could mimetic identification between king and fool go further? The pygmies were welcomed at the courts of the pharaohs because, in their dancing, they celebrated the rising each day of the sun-god Re; the dead pharaoh presents himself to Osiris in the assumed identity of a dancing pygmy in the hope of receiving a commensurate welcome.

It was from Egypt that the practice of employing dwarfs in palaces and other wealthy households travelled westward into the Greek and Roman world, and, as it did so, was rapidly debased. The dwarfs' closeness to the gods as perceived in Egypt was forgotten, and they became, at best, buffoons or good-luck mascots; at worst, playthings and objects of prurient curiosity.

In Lucian's *Feast of the Lapiths* (*c*. AD 150), a dwarf called Satyrion, described as an ugly fellow with shaven head except for a few hairs that stood up straight from his crown, is brought in by the host to cover a delay in the service of the dishes, and ordered to do or say something funny. 'First he danced, doubling himself up and twisting himself about to cut a more ridiculous figure; then he beat time and recited scurrilous verses in an Egyptian brogue, and finally he began to poke fun at the guests.' The guests take the dwarf's railing in good part except for a cynic philosopher called Alcidamus, who becomes very angry on being addressed as a 'Maltese lap-dog', a pun on the Greek word for cynic. 'So, throwing off his philosopher's cloak, he challenged him to fight, or else, he said, he would lay his staff on him. Then poor Satyrion . . . stood up to him and fought. It was delicious to see a philosopher squaring off at a clown, and giving and receiving blows in turn. Though some of the onlookers were disgusted, others kept laughing, until finally Alcidamus had enough of his punishment, well beaten by a tough little dwarf.'[5]

In Rome, the demand for dwarfs among patrician ladies exceeded the number that nature could supply, and Longinus tells us that children were deliberately stunted to fill the gap in the market.[6] Martial gives an example of the distasteful uses to which they were put:

> Labulla has discovered how to kiss her lover in the presence of her husband. She gives repeated kisses to her dwarf fool; this creature, slobbered with many kisses, the lover at once pounces upon, fills him up with his own kisses, and hands him back to the smiling lady. How much bigger a fool is the husband![7]

Fortunately, these decadent traditions of the dwarf-fool (*morio*) had limited influence on the indigenous cultures of the various peoples occupying western Europe during the centuries of Roman decline. Ireland, which remained outside the Empire, was immune; and there, as we have already noted, a rich oral inheritance from the Iron Age was partially preserved in poetry and legend.

In this Celtic tradition, dwarfs are associated with learning and the creative arts, and seen as having links with a mysterious other-world inhabited by the Túatha Dé Danand (People of the Goddess Danu), who were believed to be only partly human and to make their home in the *Síde* – burial mounds of prehistoric origin. Like the Egyptian dangas, the Irish dwarfs were both rare and elusive. Their discovery was matter for congratulation, but could also bring conflict.

In the *Cath Maige Mucrama* ('Battle of Mag Mucrama') from the twelfth-century *Book of Leinster*, the finding of a dwarf-musician occasions a protracted tribal war between Éogan, son of Ailill, and his foster-brother, Mac Con, which has been dated to the third century AD. Travelling together, the brothers hear marvellous music coming from a yew-tree growing beside a waterfall. Going nearer to investigate, they discover a little man in the tree playing a three-stringed harp. Unable to agree as to which of them should take charge of the dwarf, whose name is Fer Fí, they return to their father, Ailill the king, for his judgement. Ailill asks Fer Fí to play for him.

> Then he played them a tearful melody so that they began to weep and lament and grieve. He was entreated to stop. He played them a laughter-provoking strain and they began to laugh . . . Then he played them a sleep-inducing air so that they fell asleep until the same time next day.

Meanwhile, Fer Fí makes his escape, leaving trouble brewing between the brothers.[8]

Cnú dheireoil ('diminutive nut'), the treasured dwarf of the heroic Finn, proves a more willing retainer. As the old pagan Caeilte explains to St Patrick in the eleventh or twelfth-century *Agallamh na senórach* ('Colloquy of the Ancients'), Finn meets with him while resting on a burial mound, from which Cnú emerges in flight from the jealousy of his fellow musicians of the Túatha Dé Danand. Cnú plays his harp for Finn, and his music is so superlatively sweet that when Finn's companions join him and hear it also, they tell Finn that 'this is the third best windfall you have ever had'. They go in search of a female dwarf as wife for Cnú, who has no taste for the huge women favoured by the Fianna, and find Little Bláthnait, 'the young maiden, who pledged her troth to no man beneath the sun excepting Cnú dheireoil'. The two dwarfs are said to have been greatly loved by the Fianna, and were able to foretell the future. When Finn goes to confront the invading giant, Laigne the Great, in the guise of a bard, he takes Cnú and Bláthnait with him, hidden in the folds of his cloak, to provide appropriately calming music. When it rained, he would shelter them in the same way: 'Cnú dheireoil in the king's bosom, good son of Lugh of comely form'.[9]

In *The Death of Fergus*, the dwarf Aedh, 'poet of Ulster', acts as intermediary between Fergus and the king of the Lupra-folk, who are said to be even smaller than he is. When Esirt, a Lupracan poet, brings Aedh to the court of his king, the king asks Esirt why he has brought a giant to destroy them. 'No giant,' Esirt replies, 'but Ulster's poet and man of science, and the king's dwarf.'[10] Aedh thus mediates between two worlds: the brutal, everyday world of Iron Age Ireland, in which competing waves of Celtic invaders battle for supremacy, and the ideal, primeval world of the *Sídhe* which was thought to underlie it.

That these mythical dwarfs had their counterparts in unembroidered historical fact is supported by the record of a Gaulish scholar who took refuge in Ireland during the continental Arian persecutions of the fifth century, and was welcomed to the court of a king as *fili* (or poet). Though he called himself Vergilius Maro, Grammarian, he was familiarly known to his friends as 'Fatuus Homunculus', the mad or inspired manikin.[11]

The Irish dwarfs are thus seen to have been characterised, firstly by their learning and skills as musicians or poets, and secondly by their comely appearance, with no hint of ugliness or deformity about them. They inspired respect, became the familiars of kings, and were thought to bring a blessing on those who found them – but only if their allegiance was willing, not forced. Insofar as their occurrence in myth reflects an actual presence among the Celtic peoples of pagan and early Christian Ireland, they are most easily envisaged as belonging to the rare category of proportionate dwarfs who, like the pygmies of Africa, are near-perfect replicas of full-sized men.

In contrast, the dwarfs of Welsh mythology – deriving, like the Irish, from Celtic sources but with less immediacy and distinctiveness – are usually described as ugly in looks and rude of character. Though their Celtic origin remains discernible in the magical powers that are attributed to them and the kingly status they are sometimes accorded, relations between them and the Arthurian heroes they encounter are initially hostile, and they are treated with scant respect. (When, in the *Mabinogion*, a dwarf and his wife foretell the future glory of Peredur, Kay rewards them with a kick in the pants and a box on the ear.[12]) Again, insofar as they have counterparts in real life, they appear to have been modelled on the more common type of achondroplastic dwarfs, who would certainly have been known to the fourteenth- and fifteenth-century authors who gave to these stories the final form in which they have come down to us.[13]

This brings us to the earliest of our English dwarfs. He is named as Wolstanet and makes his sole appearance in *Lestorie des Engles* by the twelfth-century poet Gaimar, which was written for the instruction of his patron, the wife of an East Anglian baron of Norman descent. But although Gaimar's history was composed long after most of the events he recounts, in French verse, and in a story form clearly influenced by the literary romances of his time, the episode of King Edward's murder, in which Wolstanet features, is well attested by the Anglo-Saxon Chronicle and other near-contemporary sources.[14]

Edward (*c.* 962–79) was a son of King Edgar by his first wife, Aethelflaed. After a reign of less than three years, the seventeen-year-old king was to fall victim to an assassin's knife at the home of his stepmother, Queen Aelfthryth, who, greedy of power for her own son by Edgar, the notorious Aethelred, was widely suspected of complicity in the crime. So much is generally agreed. But Gaimar is alone among the chroniclers in relating how Edward came to put himself so obligingly into the hands of his known enemies, enticed from hunting by the antics of a fool.

> He had a dwarf named Wolstanet
> Who could dance and play.
> He could leap and pipe,
> And play many other tricks.
> The king saw him, called him,
> And ordered him to play.
> The dwarf said he would not,
> He would not play at his order.
> And when the king asked him more gently,
> And he railed against the king,
> The king grew very wroth with him.
> Wolstanet then fled;
> He took his horse, he found him ready,
> He went to Aelfthryth's house,
> It was only one league off . . .
>
> (ll. 3991–4005)

Edward follows the dwarf to the house of his stepmother, who comes out to greet him and offers him a horn of wine. As Edward leans forward on his horse to take it, his assailant approaches unseen and stabs him to the heart.[15]

The sequel to the story need not concern us except to note in passing that Edward's contemporaries were so appalled by the murder of this young, anointed king that he was given the accolade of popular canonisation, and a shrine for his bones at Shaftesbury. His cult was already well established by the time that Gaimar wrote; the fact that he was not averse to depicting the putative martyr in a somewhat less than flattering light is perhaps a point in favour of the historicity of his account. The recalcitrant dwarf is heard of no more and may be safely assumed to have made himself scarce. Like his mythical Celtic precursors, Wolstanet, for all his ability to 'dance and play, leap and pipe', was not to be forced.

The presence of dwarfs in Anglo-Saxon and early Norman England and their employment about the court is confirmed by the appearance of a bearded, achondroplastic dwarf in one of the scenes of the Bayeux Tapestry. He is shown holding the reins of two horses belonging to William's messengers who have come to demand the release of Harold, intercepted on his way to visit William in Normandy. The dwarf is wearing an unusual outfit of hauberk and trews. As one of only four named, minor characters in the story of the Norman Conquest as

Turold from the Bayeux Tapestry, eleventh century (by special permission of the City of Bayeux)

depicted in the tapestry, we must assume that Turold enjoyed popular fame in his time, and perhaps lived on to serve at the English court under William.[16]

It is often presumed that the presence of dwarfs in medieval courts was virtually continuous; this may well have been so but it is not demonstrable from surviving records. We have to jump a hundred and fifty years to the reign of Henry III to find our next English example.

This was Jean, who is noticed by contemporary chroniclers in the retinue of Henry's much-loved queen, Eleanor of Provence, in 1249. Provence, of course, was the original home of the troubadours, whose poems and stories of chivalric love, combining with those northern myths and legends we have already drawn upon, gave rise in the twelfth and thirteenth centuries to a new genre of rhymed romances. Eleanor herself was a daughter of one of the last of the great troubadour poets, Raymond Berenger V, count of Provence. In this new type of popular literature – in its earliest, oral form the stock-in-trade of the minstrels – dwarfs featured in a variety of contrasting roles, as kings and servants, heroes and villains.[17] It is no surprise, therefore, to find an actual dwarf in Eleanor's company, or that she led him about with her as a 'prodigy'.

Jean is said to have been eighteen or nineteen years old but scarcely three feet tall. In a characteristic touch, Matthew Paris adds that 'the length of his tiny body is sixteen times that of this line'. He also tells us that he was found in the Isle of Wight, and that 'he was not a dwarf, for his limbs were of just proportions'. (In the Latin, he describes him as *homunculus*, a 'little man'.[18]) Clearly, Jean belonged to the category of proportionate dwarfs; that he was viewed as a prodigy of nature is confirmation of the rarity of such small people, then as now.

It will already have become apparent that the dwarfs were distinguished throughout the whole of their early history by a certain 'liminal' quality. Everywhere they are seen as belonging to, or having links with, that 'other' world that in the universal experience of humanity is felt to lie beyond the edges of what is ordinarily perceptible. Everywhere they are attributed with a degree of magical power, in which rulers are eager to participate by gaining their personal allegiance and attaching them to their courts.[19]

The coming of Christianity did little to lessen belief in their other-worldly associations. In spite of repeated warnings and denunciations on the part of the Church's *magisterium*, a residual belief in magic persisted (not least among kings and queens) to as late as the Tudor period, and, at a popular level, far beyond it.

Some of the superstitious awe the dwarfs continued to inspire may have had to do with the talents they commonly possessed as musicians and poets; and the recurring accounts in Celtic mythology of their ability to manipulate human emotions are an early acknowledgement of the potential power of the creative and performing arts to influence behaviour – not always in ways that those affected may anticipate or desire. It is used to effect escape from capture, and, in one instance, to lead a king to his death.

The strangeness of their small size, especially that of the proportionate dwarfs, was enhanced in many of those I have cited, and in others who have yet to appear, by the remoteness of their origins. They come on the familiar scene from islands and other distant places; the dangas from Punt and 'the land of spirits', the Irish dwarfs from the mysterious kingdom of the *Síde*. Calot Jean, a visitor from France to the court of Edward I, is said to have come originally from Sicily, and an unnamed dwarf in the service of Edward IV from Constantinople.

If we are not to get too far ahead of ourselves in the chronological survey on which we are embarked, I must now leave the dwarfs to trace the early history of the more usual types of court fool. (I pick up the story of the dwarfs in Chapter 9, where I shall have something to say of their role in the chivalric pageantry of the later Middle Ages; and again in Chapters 13 and 16.)

For the present, we shall need to retrace our steps a little. For if, on the basis of surviving records, the dwarfs may justly claim the precedence, their fellows of ordinary stature were only a few, short paces behind them.

CHAPTER 3

Warrior Fools

Though there is evidence of entertainers of various kinds including buffoons at the courts of the pharaohs, it was from ancient Greece and China that court fools of normal stature first emerged as individuals with a name and a face.

The truth-telling function of the philosopher-fools of Greece and the Hellenic diaspora is exemplified in the anecdote of Alexander's encounter with Diogenes (he of the barrel). After his defeat of the Greeks in the fourth century BC, Alexander is said to have visited the ruined city of Thebes and to have found the

Diogenes and his live-in barrel as depicted on the title page of Samuel Rowlands' Diogenes Lanthorne *of 1608 (Courtauld Institute of Art, London)*

philosopher, who had encouraged the Greeks in their resistance, sunning himself in a quiet spot. 'What favour can I do you?', Alexander asks, seeking his allegiance. 'Nothing', Diogenes replies, 'except to go away and leave me the sunshine so that I can warm myself.'[1]

Not all the philosopher-fools were as determinedly self-sufficient as Diogenes. Anaxarchus, described as Alexander's friend, appears to have accepted a degree of patronage from him without any loss of freedom of speech. When Alexander, who had pretensions to divinity, was wounded in battle, Anaxarchus was quick to point out to him that the blood flowing from his wound was all too obviously human. Alexander merely laughed; but Anaxarchus was to pay the price for his temerity after his patron's death when one of Alexander's generals, who had been present to overhear the remark, ordered his execution by pounding in a mortar. 'Pound away, pound away', the philosopher famously cried, 'you can kill my body, but not my soul.' It is the element of danger in such legendary encounters that makes them memorable. As William Dolby has pointed out in relation to the Chinese fools, it is 'difficult to order a man's decapitation just after he had made one laugh. Difficult to stand on the high-horse of inviolable majesty after having had one's leg pulled.'[2] But, of course, it is equally difficult to venture any kind of a joke when the cost of its failure may be to lose one's head!

Sima Qian's account of the court fools of China relates to the period 613–207 BC. There, the dwarf Twisty Pole, whose success in dissuading the Second Emperor of Qin from his intention to lacquer the Great Wall has already been reported, was preceded by a six-foot former minstrel called Meng, and by Baldy Chunyu.

Meng impersonates a long-dead Chancellor to awaken the conscience of the king of Chu in regard to the Chancellor's son, who was living in poverty, and was always offering 'useful advice in the guise of a good joke'. Baldy is described as having 'a sharp wit and a quick tongue'. In consequence, he was sent by his master, a king of Qi, as ambassador on diplomatic missions to neighbouring states. In the eighth year of the king's reign (348 BC), the kingdom of Chu mounted a massive campaign against Qi. The king sent Baldy to his ally Zhao to request reinforcements, and supplied him with a hundredweight of gold and ten four-horse chariots to give as inducements. Baldy looked up to the heavens and roared with laughter. 'Am I giving too little?' the king asked.

'Oh, dear me', said Baldy, 'I'd never think of suggesting such a thing.'

'Then could you perhaps explain why you are laughing?' asked the king.

'Just now,' said Baldy, 'as I was coming from the eastern part of our country, I saw a man by the roadside performing fertility sacrifices for a good harvest. He was holding just one pig's trotter and one single cup of wine as his offerings, but his prayer went as follows:

> Grant cartloads from the low ground
> and full hampers from the high,
> grain in ripe abundance
> and sheaves piled to the sky.

When I saw the niggardliness of his offering and the extravagance of his demand, I couldn't help laughing at him.'

The king took the hint and increased his gifts to a ton of gold, ten pairs of jade orbs and a hundred chariots. As a result, Baldy was successful in obtaining from Zhao a relief force of a hundred thousand crack troops and a thousand war chariots. When news of this reached Chu, its invading army was promptly withdrawn.[3]

In the west, the period of Roman dominance has few such illustrations to offer of the type of fool and the type of fooling we are concerned with here. Republican Rome, lacking kings and tyrants – the essential corollary to the relative freedom of the licensed fool – had no need of such people, and the rulers and patricians of the Empire preferred to surround themselves with human 'freaks' and half-witted slaves. The uglier and the more idiotic these were, the better they were pleased. 'He has been described as an idiot', complains the satirist Martial of a recent purchase. 'I bought him for twenty thousand sesterces. Give me back my money, Gargilianus; he has wits.'[4] Only in the presence of the slave who was required to accompany the early imperators in their triumphal chariots to remind them of the ephemeral nature of human glory (*sic transit gloria mundi*) do we find an echo of the admonitory function of the true jesters.

Early Christian scholars of the fifth century inherited, with the Latin language, the negative attitude to performers in general displayed by the Greek and Latin Fathers, whose condemnation of the comedians (*mimi*) in particular is understandable in view of the often obscene and sacrilegious content of their performances. The Arian heresy espoused by many of the Germanic kings who came to seize control in the western regions of the Empire inclined them to be the more suspicious of Roman 'luxuries'.[5]

It was not until the period of the Frankish Carolingian renaissance of the eighth and ninth centuries that allusions to entertainers at European courts occur with any frequency, and we find our first clear references to *scurrae* in the medieval sense of professional buffoons, and to *joculatores* or 'jokers'.[6]

Writing to Gregory of Utrecht in 750, Lull, the saintly archbishop of Mainz, lists among such other 'vain delights of this world' as costly garments, grain-fed horses, falcons, hawks, baying hounds, and the delicious flavours of food and drink, the 'wild merriment of the buffoons (*scurrarum bacchationes*)'; and, in similar vein, one of Charlemagne's ordinances of 789 forbids the clergy to own 'hunting dogs, falcons, hawks and jokers' – an association of hunting, feasting and fooling that we shall meet with again in thirteenth-century England. Three letters of the English monk Alcuin (Charlemagne's tutor), written about 800, warn of the danger of associating with entertainers, and the impropriety of bestowing food on such people that should properly go to God's poor – a line of reasoning that, again, we shall find taken up by later, clerical authors.[7]

It is striking, however, that most of these prohibitions and warnings are addressed by clerics to other clerics; the performers themselves are specifically condemned only when they commit the sacrilege of dressing in a 'priestly or monastic robe, or that of a nun, or any other clerical garb', for which they are to suffer corporal punishment and exile.[8]

Though contemporary records of court fools in England are wanting until the eleventh century, it is probable, in view of the close contacts that were then maintained between the English and Frankish courts, that fools would have found a place for themselves in the households of some earlier Anglo-Saxon and Danish kings.

William of Malmesbury, writing in the twelfth century, relates an anecdote of King Edgar (r. 959–75) that suggests as much. Though small in stature and slight of build, the king is said to have been possessed of a pugnacious spirit. At a banquet he was giving, one of the guests, Kinad, king of the Scots, remarked in a light-hearted way to his neighbour at table that it seemed extraordinary that so many provinces should be subject to 'such a sorry little fellow'. This was picked up by one of Edgar's fools and gleefully reported to his master. Edgar contained his anger until the next day, when Kinad was summoned, handed a sword, and challenged to demonstrate his superior strength.[9] Geoffrey Gaimar, writing a decade or so later, gives Edgar's son, Edward the Martyr, a dwarf fool as hunting companion with the unfortunate results we have already seen.

But William of Malmesbury was a monk and Gaimar probably also a cleric, and their anecdotes, written long after the events they relate, reflect the long-standing clerical view of court fools as parasitic trouble-makers. For a uniquely secular view of the 'jokers' – one that, for all its poetic exaggeration and legendary accretions, gives a fuller and more detailed account of their dealings with their kingly patrons – we must look once more to that ancient testimony of the Irish Celts that I have drawn upon in the previous chapter.[10]

The part mythological, part heroic tale of *Togail bruidne Da Derga* ('The Destruction of Da Derga's Hostel') survives in the form of a twelfth-century manuscript, but we know that it was already in written form by the eighth century, and its setting is clearly pagan.

An extraordinary gathering of warriors had assembled in the open-sided compound of the title in defence of a king called Conare Már, who, having broken the taboos imposed on him, was doomed to destruction. One of the attackers, a terrifying one-eyed Briton named Ingcél, describes to two others, Fer Rogain and Lomnae Drúth, what he has observed of the defenders. (*Drúth*, which is close in form and meaning to *druí* or 'druid', is the early Gaelic word for 'fool', and Lomnae Drúth, like the dwarfs Cnú dheireoil and Bláthnait, has the gift of second sight.)

'I saw three fools at one end of the fire', said Ingcél, 'all wearing dun mantles. If the men of Ériu were assembled in one place, and if the bodies of his father and mother were before each man, no one could help but laugh . . . When the king's eyes lights upon them, it laughs with each glance. Explain that, Fer Rogain.'

'Not difficult that,' replies Fer Rogain, the man of knowledge. 'Mlithe and Máel and Admlithe they, the three fools of the king of Ériu. A man will fall by each of them, and they will match the performance of any trio in the hostel, and they will escape afterwards'. 'Woe to him who carries out this destruction, if only because of those three', says Lomnae Drúth.

These are not the only fools to have been present, however. There is also a 'strapping fellow' with a 'shameful haircut', wearing gold ear-rings and a cloak of many colours, who is seen to be juggling with nine swords, nine silver shields and nine apples of gold. But, as the evil eye of Ingcél rests on him, swords, shields and apples all clatter to the ground. 'That one was Tulchaíne', Fer Rogain explains, 'the royal fool of the king of Temuir, Conare's trickster, a man of great power. Three nines will fall by him at the first onslaught, and he will match the performance of anyone in the hostel, and, though wounded, he will escape afterwards.' 'On his account alone,' says Lomnae Drúth, 'there should be no destruction. Happy the man who spares him.'[11] The 'performances' referred to here clearly have more to do with the fools' fighting ability than their skills as jokers and jugglers.

Cath Almaine ('The Battle of Allen') relates to the historically unstable political condition of eighth-century Ireland, when the northern Irish under a king called Fergal had invaded Leinster. On the eve of a great battle between the opposing armies, Fergal feasted his warriors and invited a famous story-teller, Donn Bó, to entertain them. Donn Bó, however, is said to have refused the honour in favour of a certain Úa Maigléine, who is described as a *riogdruth* or king's fool. Úa Maigléine accepted the commission and sought to inspire Fergal's men with stories of the heroic deeds of their ancestors.

But in the battle that followed the northern Irish were defeated, and both Fergal and Úa Maigléine taken prisoner and executed. Before his death, Úa Maigléine was invited by the Leinstermen to make a 'fool's shout', of which the saga relates that it was 'loud and melodious' and remained with the fools of Ireland from that time on.[12] There is much in the story that remains obscure, but the fool's shout can hardly have been anything other than a shout of laughter: an explosion of mirth in the face of death that echoes down the centuries.

There are indications here and in other sagas that the person of the *riogdruth*, though able to defend himself, was also protected by an aura of superstitious awe arising from his office, and that to kill him was regarded with particular horror. 'Happy the man who spares him', said Lomnae Drúth.

In 'The Battle of Mag Mucrama', which has already given us the story of Fer Fí and his finding by the sons of Ailill, Mac Con's fool is named as Do Déra, and is said to have been exactly like his master in form and appearance – his double, in fact. When Mac Con, the king, is challenged to personal combat by his brother Éogan and anticipates death at his hands, Do Déra offers to take his place: 'I will go against him', said the jester, 'with your diadem on my head and wearing your battle-dress so that all will say that it is you that will fall there. If it happen then that I fall, take yourself off at once . . .' This is just what occurs. Do Déra dies in the king's place.[13] In one of several textual 'doublets' of this episode, in which the name of Mac Con's challenger is given as Corpre Musc (one of Éogan's allies), Do Déra offers his own crown as *riogdruth* in exchange for that of the king. When, having killed Do Déra,

The Petrie Crown, ceremonial head-dress of bronze, AD first to second century (National Museum of Ireland, Dublin)

Corpre realises his mistake, he remarks, 'This was an unworthy deed . . . a king's diadem on a jester's head.'[14]

It is within the aristocratic core of the Celtic royal household – at the king's side as he entertains his nobles with gargantuan feasts or goes into battle surrounded by his war-band – that we find the *riogdruth*. Like his companions, he is a warrior, called upon to take his share in the fighting, or substitute for the king himself when the situation requires it. And though the word *drúth* is also used of other kinds of fool, including madmen, in early Irish literature, there is nothing to suggest that the *riogdruth* was anything other than mentally competent. But whatever honour he receives is strictly *ex officio*. Beneath the crown of his office, the haircut is 'shameful'; a king's diadem on a jester's head, 'an unworthy deed'.[15] Whatever the intimacy of his relationship with the king, however many honours are heaped upon him, and however great the awe that his office inspires, he remains a 'nobody'.

The precious gift of eliciting laughter is the *drúth*'s primary function; but, apart from prowess as a warrior, his versatility has been seen to extend to prophecy, juggling, and to the recitation of heroic tales as an inspiration to his fellow warriors on the eve of battle – if only as second string to a qualified bard.

If nothing else, the redoubtable, many-faceted figure of the *riogdruth* as portrayed in the Irish sagas may serve to dispel any lingering preconceptions we may retain of the court fool as an invariably effete person prancing about in cap and bells. It is this more ancient and interesting conception of his character and functions that we take with us as we return across the Irish Sea to consider the earliest documentary evidence for the English fool.

This dates from the eleventh century, prior to the Norman Conquest, and relates to a man called Nithard, who is described as *joculator* to King Edmund Ironside (*c.* 981–1016). After the death of his father Aethelred, and his coronation in London in the spring of 1016, and with Cnut and his invading forces already ensconced in Southampton and threatening to besiege London, Edmund set out to raise an army in his power-base in the south-west. It is possible that Nithard joined him then, or he may have been with him from an earlier, more settled time. The name is Frankish, but in the absence of any records of Nithard during Edmund's tumultuous reign of less than a year – or, indeed, until many years later – we can only speculate as to his origins.

A cathedral charter of 1051 in the reign of Edward the Confessor tells us, however, that he had been rewarded by Edmund with the town of Walworth in Surrey, but had then decided to donate this considerable property to the monks of Christ Church, Canterbury (Canterbury Cathedral), and to make a pilgrimage to Rome, from which, it appears, he had little expectation of returning.[16] There is something very touching in the picture of this old survivor of Edmund's brief but heroic campaign of resistance to the Danish invader laying his deed of gift on the high altar of the cathedral, as we are told that he did, before setting out on his final journey.

In the conditions of Anglo-Saxon and early Norman England, the *joculator*, like the Irish *drúth*, would have needed the resource of personal arms and the ability to use them. It would seem also that the ambiguity of both these terms may have had more to do with the versatility of the performers' skills than with any lack of precision in their use by the chroniclers.

Taillefer, the juggling Norman hero of the Battle of Hastings, is indiscriminately designated *histrio*, *mimus* and *ioglere*; the last a French derivative of *joculator*. Whether he was much of a 'joker' in the modern sense we do not know. The episode in which he features in the chronicles has been described as a 'serio-comic prelude to the battle', and there may indeed have been an element of satirical pantomime in the earlier part of his performance. He was certainly a professional entertainer who carried the stigma of social inferiority (of being a nobody) attaching to his profession. It was the remarkable nature of his actions in the battle that was to bring him notice and distinction. His fame is attributable, not to who he was, but to what he did.

A fifteenth–century French interpretation of the Battle of Hastings (Bodleian Library, Oxford: MS Bodley 968, f. 173, detail)

Taillefer is not mentioned in William of Poitiers' contemporary Norman account of Hastings; nor does he feature in the Bayeux Tapestry. These omissions, together with apparent inconsistencies in other, mainly later reports, have led some historians to doubt his existence as an historical person and to dismiss the actions attributed to him as retrospective, romantic invention. But, as we shall discover, there were good reasons for the Normans' neglect, and the inconsistencies turn out to be not so irreconcilable as first appears when we place them in context.[17]

The preliminaries of the battle are not in question. In the early morning sunshine of 14 October 1066, the English and Norman armies were drawn up in opposing formations along a ridge of the Sussex Downs; the Normans in an extended line of three divisions over half a mile in width, the English facing them in a more compact body across a narrow valley from the higher ground of Telham Hill. The English, on foot, were armed with spears and axes, forming a shield wall; the Normans comprised a mixed force of cavalry and foot.

According to the *Carmen* (song) *of the Battle of Hastings*, of disputed date and authorship but possibly written as early as 1068, Taillefer's intervention was preceded by a period of uncertainty on the part of the Normans; faced by the formidable sight of the English on their commanding ridge, whom they were required to charge uphill, their resolution faltered. While the battle thus hung 'in ominous suspense' (I quote from a prose translation of the original Latin verse), 'a player [*histrio*], whom his most valiant soul greatly ennobled, rode out before the countless army of the duke. He heartened the men of France and terrified the English, and, tossing his sword high, he sported with it.' One of the English emerged from the shield wall to engage him. But Taillefer, here named for the first time in the Latin as *Incisor-ferri*, 'pierced the Englishman's shield with his keen lance and hewed the head from the prostrate body with his sword'. He held it aloft to show to his comrades, who 'exulted that the first blow was theirs . . . and at once the men hastened to close shields'.[18] As the *Carmen*'s modern editors comment, the Taillefer of this account is 'a man with a job, not a figure of high romance. His ride is necessary because of the events which have preceded it. He heartens his own side and confounds the enemy, whom he insults by juggling with his sword – an invitation to the insulted to break ranks and chastise such impudence.'[19]

Geoffrey Gaimar, writing about 1140 in French, gives our redoubtable sword-juggler his more usual name of Taillefer ('hewer of iron') and describes him as *ioglere*. His account agrees substantially with that of the *Carmen*; but he elaborates it, bringing Taillefer's lance as well as his sword into play.

> One of the French then hasted,
> Before the others he rode.
> Taillefer was he named.
> He was a minstrel [*ioglere*], and bold enough.
> Arms he had and a good horse.
> He was a bold and noble warrior.

> Before the others he set himself.
> Before the English he did wonders.
> He took his lance by the butt
> As if it had been a truncheon.
> Up high he threw it,
> And by the head he caught it.

Three times he throws his lance in the air; then, advancing towards the English, hurls it among them, wounding an English soldier.

> Then he drew his sword, retreated,
> Threw the sword which he held,
> On high, then caught it.
> One said to the other, who saw this,
> That this was enchantment
> Which he did before the folk.

Three times he tosses his sword, then charges into the English line and is engulfed.[20] All this is expressed, of course, in the language of heroic verse, that of the *chansons de geste*, the jongleurs' own *métier*.

Henry of Huntingdon in his Latin *History of the English* (*c.* 1150) gives a briefer, prosaic version of what is basically the same story.[21] The apparent confusion that has led historians to dismiss the whole episode as romantic myth is created by two further accounts.

The Jerseyman Wace (writing in French between 1160 and 1174) has nothing to say of Taillefer's juggling with sword or lance, but, drawing on what is clearly a different source, reports that 'Taillefer who sang right well, rode mounted on a swift horse before the duke, singing of Karlemaine, and of Rollant, of Oliver and the vassals who died in Renchevals'. He seeks permission from the duke to strike the first blow in the battle and, on receiving it, 'put his horse to a gallop, charging before all the rest, and struck an Englishman dead, driving his lance below the breast into his body, and stretching him upon the ground'.[22]

More impressively, William of Malmesbury, who, as a youth (he was born before the turn of the eleventh century), may have been able to speak to survivors of the battle, tells us that a 'song of Roland (*cantilena Rollandi*)' was sung as an inspiration to the Normans as the battle began.[23]

Here is the key to a reconciliation of the apparent contradictions in the two sets of accounts. For if we look at the earliest surviving text of the famous *Song of Roland* – dating from the end of the eleventh century but generally acknowledged to have drawn on pre-existing, oral versions – we find this passage, where the dying and defeated Roland is addressing his sword, which is named Durendal.

> Oh Durendal, how dazzling bright you are –
> you blaze with light and shimmer in the sun.

(We may picture Taillefer's sword being thrown into the air as he sings.)

> King Charles was in the Vales of Moriane
> when God in heaven had His angel tell him
> that he should give you to a captain-count:
> the great and noble king then girded me.

(Again, the sword goes twisting and turning in the air.)

> With this I won him Anjou and Brittany,
> and then I won him both Poitou and Maine,
> with this I won him Normandy the Proud . . .

(Cheers from the Norman host as, for a third time, the sword is tossed and caught.)

> With this I won him Scotland, Ireland too,
> and England, which he held as his demesne.
> With this I've won him so many lands and countries
> which now are held by Charles, whose beard is white.
> I'm full of pain and sorrow for this sword;
> I'd rather die than leave it to the pagans.

And with a final –

> Oh God, my Father, don't let France be shamed!

– he launches himself at the English line.[24]

Could anything have been more likely to renew the resolution of the Norman knights than this particular passage of this particular poem? Of course, we have no proof that William of Malmesbury's *cantilena Rollandi* was indeed the *Song of Roland* as we now have it. The probability is that it was not; but, in view of the known importance of the *Song* to the whole tradition of French chivalry in the period, can we, on the other hand, dismiss the possibility that William's *cantilena* was an oral progenitor of the later written text, close enough to have borne the relevance to Taillefer's reported actions I have proposed?

Charlemagne, of course, had never conquered England or held it as his demesne. Was this an extemporisation of Taillefer's to fit the circumstances of the moment of the kind we know that jongleurs were accustomed to make? Or added later by Turoldus to take account of the great contemporary event of his time?[25] But either way, by putting the two versions of Taillefer's actions together into this poetic framework, we see how the inconsistencies between them disappear. Each is telling the truth of what had been heard and seen but neither account is complete. It is only when we put them together that they begin to make sense. And the partial nature of the observations on which they were based is explained by what we know of the conditions of the battle.

Taillefer's voice as he sings and juggles his sword and lance carries up Telham Hill to the waiting English; but, as he sings in French, the words are not understood by most of them. The Normans to his rear catch enough of the words to recognise their source and relevance; it is his singing that these will remember and report, rather than his juggling, which is the normal acting-out of his text expected of a jongleur. But those on the far wings of the Norman line – up to a quarter of a mile away – hear little or nothing. To them, and to the bemused English, Taillefer's actions, divorced from their poetic context, cast an incomprehensible spell of their own: an 'enchantment before the folk'. It is his juggling that these will remember and speak about afterwards.

As to William of Poitiers' failure to mention Taillefer and his absence from the Bayeux Tapestry, these are easily explained by the unavoidable implications of his exploit: that it took an *ioglere*, a *mimus* of all people, to spur the Norman knights into effective action; especially as those responsible for the 'official' version – William of Poitiers himself, a former knight who became the Conqueror's chaplain, and Bishop Odo, who is thought to have commissioned the tapestry – were clerics. However courageous and necessary, Taillefer's solitary, suicidal charge was also a clear infraction of the strict chivalric code that forbade men of inferior rank (let alone an *ioglere*) to advance against the enemy ahead of their betters; such behaviour was seen as a theft of honour from those who were properly entitled to it – in this instance, the nobles appointed by William to lead his divisions, Odo among them. (If Taillefer had really asked prior permission of the duke, as Gaimar, alone among the chroniclers, claims, it would surely have been refused.) According to the author of the *Carmen*, Taillefer was enabled to transcend his status as a 'nobody' through the bravery of his action – his 'valiant soul'; but this was not an argument that would have had much appeal to those who were put in the shade by it and made to appear less than valiant themselves.

Though written in French, Gaimar and Wace's accounts were composed in England, where it was possible to take a more objective view. For all their poetic elaboration, and though later in date, their accounts of Taillefer and his part in the battle carry conviction.

One other joculator of the eleventh century remains to be noted. This was Berdic, who has the unimpeachable authority of the Domesday Book behind him. Though included in the Gloucestershire volume, the property that Berdic is listed as holding in 1086 was in the marches of Wales. 'Berdic *joculator regis* has 3 villages; 5 ploughs there. He pays nothing.'[26] He is *joculator regis*, a king's fool; in Celtic terms, a *riogdruth*. But which king did he serve? Though his name is French, he is perhaps more likely to have been a retired retainer of Edward the Confessor's who, we should not forget, had a French mother and had been brought up in Normandy, than a serving fool of the Conqueror. The remoteness of his rural retreat, and the fact that no services of any kind were required of him, suggest retirement. 'He pays nothing', and nothing further would seem to have been expected of him.

The one thing we can say about Berdic with any certainty is perhaps the most significant. From the very beginning of the Norman domination of England, the office of *joculator regis* was already established, known to the Domesday surveyors, and duly recorded as one of those services to the person of the king on which all future claims to the possession of land were to depend.

CHAPTER 4

Norman Buffoons

The new Norman rulers of England were, as A.L. Poole put it, 'disagreeable men, masterful, stern, and cruel'.[1] Their households, as they progressed inexorably about the country, plundering and destroying, inspired justifiable fear. Consequently, as Eadmer recalls of Rufus's reign, 'when it became known that the King was coming, all the inhabitants would flee from their houses . . . taking refuge in woods or other places where they hoped to be able to protect themselves'.[2]

Along with the king and his immediate *familia* of knights and councillors, the household contained a crowd of lower servants and foot soldiers: archers of the royal bodyguard, scullions, hearth boys, keepers of hounds and hawks, stag and wolf-hunters. It was with these, and a disreputable following of whores, pimps and other hangers-on, that the jokers and buffoons who are the subject of the present chapter were classed by clerical authors of the time. But, on the same testimony, it appears that the king and his magnates had a different, altogether more indulgent attitude towards them, and the entertainers are more usually found in close companionship with their lay patrons, enjoying a familiarity which the clerics plainly resented.

Orderic Vitalis, an English-born monk who spent the whole of his religious life in the Norman abbey of Evroul (he arrived there as a ten-year-old boy in 1085), gives a brief glimpse into the nature of that relationship. In the course of a Latin account of the early history of his adopted abbey, he describes how a Frankish raiding party led by the Duke of Orleans had bivouacked in a wood, having sacked the adjacent abbey of its valuables, including relics. Among those present, grouped round a fire, were several joculators. One of them mockingly tells the duke that his chamberlain and chancellor 'have dug up the bodies of some peasants in Normandy and, deceived into thinking them holy relics, have placed them in your chapel and are reverently carrying them with them into Gaul'. The duke asks for the names of the supposed saints, and when the joker replies, 'Evroul, Evremond and Ansbert', they fall about with laughter at the unfamiliarity of the names, making coarse jokes about them. The point of the story appears in the sequel, which Orderic goes on to relate with grim satisfaction. In the course of the night, the joker and his fellows who had made such fun of the saints are struck by a thunderbolt and destroyed to a man.[3] Harsh retribution for a bad joke! But it is the picture of the duke sitting in company with his fools, passing the time in the kind of casual ribaldry that soldiers in all periods seem to enjoy, that stays in the mind.

An eavesdropper gathers news of Harold's capture by Count Guy. Bayeux Tapestry, eleventh century (by special permission of the City of Bayeux)

The Bayeux Tapestry, as well as providing a portrait of the dwarf Turold, also gives us what must be one of the earliest depictions in medieval art of a 'nobody'. He appears to the right of the dramatic scene in which Count Guy of Ponthieu (seated at centre) points accusingly at Harold and a Saxon companion who have placed themselves unwittingly into his hands. The 'eavesdropper', as he is usually described, is half-concealed by a pillar of the overarching canopy, and his identity is indicated by the vandyked edging to his tunic.[4] In the following scene of the tapestry (separated only by a decorative tree), Guy is confronted by the messengers from Count William, demanding Harold's release, in which Turold appears holding the messengers' horses (page 15). The implication of the fool's position between the two scenes, as well as his posture (he is about to set off), suggest he is intended as the duke's informant.

Interestingly, a similar instance of intelligence gathering is reported by the twelfth-century poet Wace of an earlier fool in the service of the duke, whose name he gives as Golet. At a time when the young duke was still struggling to assert his authority over a faction of rebellious counts, an attempt was made on his life in which the same Count Guy who appears in the tapestry was a prime mover.

William was then at Valognes in the west of his duchy, in bed asleep after a day's hunting, when the fool arrived at his door, crying out and beating on it with his staff.

> 'Open', he says, 'open, open
> or you are dead. Get up, get up . . .
> If taken, I know you'll be killed.
> Your enemies are even now arming.'[5]

Clearly, Golet had overheard something of what was afoot. Warned in time, the duke was able to escape to Falaise, where he appealed to his overlord, Henri I of France, with whose aid the revolt was crushed and his authority restored.

Though not contemporary, the story supports the evidence of the tapestry in suggesting that a fool of the kind that no one was accustomed to notice (a nobody) might use his invisibility to pick up vital information for which his patron would have good reason to be grateful.

William of Malmesbury describes the Conqueror's successor in England, Rufus, as 'thick-set and muscular with a protruding belly; a dandy dressed in the height of fashion . . .'[6] The outrageous fashions of his reign – tight-fitting shirts and tunics with flowing robes open at the front to reveal the thighs, the hair worn long at the back – were unfavourably compared to the more practical gear and short back and sides of the heroes of Hastings. They bring us our first documentary reference to a named fool in the period.

A particular fad of the young nobles who attended the dandified but dangerous Rufus was for shoes with long, tapering points like scorpions' tails. According to Orderic, a fool called Robert had stuffed the points of his own shoes with flax so that they could be curled back in the form of a ram's horn, and was consequently given the ribald nickname *Cornadus*, meaning 'Horner' – or perhaps, more explicitly, 'Horny'.[7] (The fashion persisted or returned; see the fourteenth-century Psalter fool shown in Plate 7a.)

No one, however, was more indulgent to the entertainers and fools who thronged his court than the Conqueror's eldest son Robert, who, on his father's death in 1087, inherited the duchy of Normandy. If William and his two younger sons deserved every word of the description with which I began the chapter – 'disagreeable, stern and cruel' – Robert Curthose was just the opposite: affable, good-natured, and temperamentally incapable of saying no to anyone. Though his courage was never in question, as a young man he had been in trouble with his father for giving away his portion of the family estates, and, when foreign relatives came to his aid, of scattering all that he received from them among 'histriones, parasites and courtesans'.[8]

As ruler of Normandy, Robert proved hopelessly incompetent, and was eventually to lose his patrimony to his more ruthless brother Henry, who, in 1100, succeeded Rufus in England. In a thunderous sermon preached to Henry's invading army of 1105, the turncoat Bishop of Séez attacked the profligate duke as squandering 'the wealth of a great duchy on trifles and follies, while he himself often fasts until noon for lack of bread'. Indeed, the '*scurrae* and harlots who constantly keep company with him steal his clothes at night while he lies snoring in drunken sleep, and guffaw as they boast that they have robbed the duke' so that, in the morning, 'he dares not rise from his bed, and cannot attend church, because he is naked and has no breeches, socks or shoes'.[9] (At the end of his harangue, the bishop is said to have produced a large pair of scissors and to have gone among the congregation shearing the flowing locks of the knights.)

The term that Orderic applied to 'Horny' Robert was *nebulo*, an utterly worthless person, a convenient butt for coarse humour and practical jokes; the *scurrae*, though equally unworthy as companions of the duke, were of a different breed. Though it has a classical origin and was used by Roman authors to denote an inferior type of *parasitus* or flatterer (one who 'lends himself out for his supper'), *scurra* distinguishes a category of medieval fools more reliant for the favours they received on innate cleverness and a talent to amuse. A somewhat less prejudiced view of their character and functions at court than that of the indignant bishop will emerge if we return to one of Rufus's unruly following; one who, in later years, was to distinguish himself in quite another capacity and so obtain more detailed notice than he would ever have done had he remained a buffoon. This was Rayer, or Rahere as he is sometimes called from the Latin form of his name, Raherus.

A twelfth-century biographer describes Rayer in his youth as haunting the 'housholdys of noble men and the palicis of prynces where, undir every elbowe of them he sprede ther coshyns [cushions] with iapys and flateryngis [jokes and flattery]'. Not content with that, he takes the lead in organising 'spectaclis', 'metys [banquets], playes and othir courtly mokkys and trifyllys'. He divides his time between attendance on the king and in 'proferynge servyce' to other 'grete men', with the aim of obtaining from both the 'peticions' he desired of them.[10]

The one element missing from this otherwise classic account of the *scurra*'s *modus operandi* (omitted perhaps out of consideration for Rayer's subsequent reputation) is the malicious gossip that we know from other sources to have been a normal part of his repertoire: saying 'scandalous and shameful things concerning those who were not present to delight the rest', as the author of a thirteenth-century penitential was later to put it).[11]

Rayer's biographer (whose original Latin text dates from about 1180) tells us that he was of 'low lineage', but the significance of the statement lies more in its claim of lineage than in the degree of its lowness. It follows from the nature of the activities attributed to him – arranging royal amusements and meals, at which he would have sat down to eat with the king and his guests – that in order to fulfil such a role he would have needed some minimal social standing; and this seems to hold true of the English buffoons we are to meet with later on. The occurrence of Rayer's name among the witnesses to several charters of the district of La Perche to the east of Normandy, lying within the lordship of one of the king's vassals Richard de Belmais, suggests that he belonged to a minor armorial family of that

Early fifteenth-century tomb effigy of Rahere in the Priory Church of St Bartholomew the Great, West Smithfield, in the City of London (by kind permission of the Rector and Churchwardens of St Bartholomew's; photograph by J.R. Southworth)

region, and furthermore was literate.[12] Indeed, during his early years at Rufus's court, Rayer may already have been in minor clerical orders. As Helen Waddell pointed out of the jongleur's profession, it was 'the most degrading a clerk could have, but it was also the most natural'; it was an important part of the business of both professions to sing, and the *scurra* was a type of *ioglere* or joker.[13] It is not altogether surprising, therefore, to find that when, in 1108, Rayer's feudal lord, Richard de Belmais, was appointed bishop of London by Henry I and, a few years later, the bishop's nephew became dean of St Paul's, Rayer followed them to London and, in 1115, was enjoying the stipend of an honorary canon of St Paul's.

The sudden death of Rufus, killed in suspicious circumstances by a stray arrow in the New Forest in 1100, and the very different character of his successor, may already have prompted a change of direction; but it was not until 1120 (the year in which the White Ship went down in the Channel with Henry's heir on board) that we find Rayer following in the footsteps of Nithard on pilgrimage to Rome; and it was in Rome that disillusionment with his former life came to a head. Whatever the exact course of events that followed, which is not at all clear in the only existing account, Rayer returned to London a year or two later a member of the reforming order of Austin Canons with a mission to establish at Smithfield a hospice 'in recreation of poor men'. He went on to become the founder of St Bartholomew's Priory and Hospital, and of the Fair associated with them. The later member of the priory community who wrote the account of his life from which I have quoted tells us that by adopting the playful manner of an 'ydiotte', he drew to him the fellowship of children and servants, and that it was with their assistance that priory and hospital were built.[14] Rayer's practice here of the ancient virtue of *eutrapelia* – that spirit of play that is seen to strike a mean between relentless buffoonery on the one hand and boorishness on the other – is of something more than biographical interest. It anticipates the teachings of both Francis of Assisi and Thomas Aquinas on the positive value of recreation which, in the course of the following century, was to open the doors of the Church to the art of the theatre.[15] For Rayer himself, it was the means by which he may be claimed to have achieved the true freedom of the *joculatoris Domini*. 'They that are fonnysch [foolish] and febill in the worldys reputacioun oure Lorde chesith [chooses] to confounde the myghte of the worlde.'[16]

Rayer was not the only 'joker' caught up in the great movement of religious reform that swept across Europe in the twelfth century; nor was he the first or the last to make the pilgrimage to Rome. But, though not unique, his mid-life change of vocation was of its nature personal and exceptional, and left the main body of his former colleagues – *mimi et histriones*, fools and jokers – in very much the same condition in which we found them: at the bottom of the heap, excluded by all but the highest and lowest in society, condemned as a morally pernicious influence by the clerical establishment of their day. The story of their gradual advance to a modest but generally accepted place in the courts of the Plantagenet kings is the subject of the following chapter.

CHAPTER 5

Minstrel Fools

Looking back from the last, troubled days of Henry II, the cleric Walter Map was able to describe the reign of the king's grandfather as 'the age of Saturn, ours of Jove', and to give a highly flattering account of Henry I and his court.

> The ripe in years or wisdom were always before lunch in the court with the king, and, by the cry of the herald, there were summoned to them those who desired a hearing in regard to business; after midday and the siesta those were admitted who sought amusement. Hence this king's court was a school of virtue and wisdom all the morning, of courtesy and decorous mirth all the afternoon.[1]

Even if we take this at its face value, the 'decorous mirth (*reuerende leticie*)' of Henry's afternoons does not sound an altogether promising atmosphere in which players or fools of the time could work. If that cruel and humourless king did employ any such entertainers, no evidence of them has survived.

In contrast, here is part of a letter written by another royal clerk, Peter de Blois, to some newly appointed chaplains, warning them of what they could expect to suffer in the court of Henry II.

> If the king has announced that he will go early next morning to a certain place, the decision is sure to be changed; and so you know he will sleep till midday. You will see pack-animals waiting under their loads, teams of horses standing in silence, heralds sleeping, court traders fretting, and everyone in turn grumbling. One runs to whores and pavilioners of the court to ask them where the king is going. For this breed of courtier often knows the palace secrets. For the king's court has an assiduous following of entertainers, laundresses, dice-players, flatterers, taverners, waferers, actors, barbers – gluttons the whole lot of them![2]

We are back on familiar ground. The entertainers and actors are our old friends the *histriones* and *mimi* of Rufus's disorderly following; the dicers clearly belong in their company; and the mention of whores (whether justified or not, and it probably was) falls into line with earlier clerical comments associating the entertainers with sexual immorality. But why are these dubious people so strangely mixed in Peter de Blois' list with others whose occupations appear on the face of it to have been both useful and morally innocuous: pavilioners, laundresses and barbers? What connection could there have been between these and the performers that would have justified Peter in lumping them all together in the indiscriminate and dismissive way that he does? What was the 'breed of courtier' to which they are said to belong?

A key to the answer lies in the emergence in contemporary literature of the term *menestrel*, first used by the poet Chrétien de Troyes in about 1164 of performers at a royal feast. This Anglo-Norman word derived from the Latin *menestrellus*, meaning 'little servant', and had no cognate connection with music-making or any other form of entertainment, but was rather an indication of status. To be a minstrel in the twelfth century was to be a minor court servant. That and no more.[3] It was a category that included all the people mentioned by Peter de Blois as well as many others.

The *mimi et histriones* of earlier times were coming in from the cold to form that inner circle of domestics combining performance skills with a dozen other crafts and functions which was to surround the person of the monarch throughout the whole of the Plantagenet period to as late as the Tudors. The waferers, for example, who were responsible for making the thin round wafers eaten as an accompaniment to sweet wine at the conclusion of meals, doubled as after-dinner cabaret artistes.[4]

How this linking of domestic service with entertainment came about in the first place is impossible to say; but such flexibility of function was a commonplace of the early medieval court.[5] And as mastery of an instrument was a basic requirement for every rank of courtier – as indeed it was for the educated class in general – and music the normal accompaniment to almost every type of medieval entertainment, it is hardly surprising to find that minstrels, whether listed primarily as craftsmen or performers of whatever kind, commanded at least one instrumental skill, and more usually several.

But it was not their performance skills as such that brought down on the minstrels the disapproval and contempt of clerics like Peter de Blois, but the professional use to which they put them; the fact that they were *paid* for their services as entertainers, receiving not only regular wages and grants of property on retirement, but occasional rewards of a kind regarded by the clerics as extravagant and out of all proportion to the performers' merits: 'robes of grey squirrel-skin and ermine, of rabbit skins and violet stuffs', horses and money.[6] The frequent indecency of their performances, especially those of the fools, added to the minstrels' offence; but the root of the clerics' objections lay in what they saw as the immorality of such people consuming resources which should properly have gone to the Church or the poor. It was for this reason that Peter describes them as 'gluttons – the whole lot of them!' In effect, they were regarded as eating the bread of the poor.

In the historiated initials of thirteenth-century English psalters (as in many later examples) that decorate Psalm 52 of the Latin Bible, we see fools doing just that, holding and eating large round wafers of the kind served at feasts by the waferer-minstrels and, in an especially refined form, consecrated and consumed by the faithful at Mass (Plates 2, 3 and 5a). 'The fool says in his heart, There is no God!'

Are they so ignorant,

the Psalmist goes on to ask,

> these evil men
> who swallow up my people
> as though they were eating bread,
> and never invoke God?[7]

What is depicted, therefore, in such fool illustrations is a kind of anti-Communion in which it is not the body of Christ in the form of the sacred host, but the people of God that is consumed.[8] Very occasionally, the round wafer in the fool's hands is replaced by what is clearly a rock or stone (Plate 7b) – a probable reference to Matthew 7:9, 'Is there a man among you who would hand his son a stone when he asked for bread?'

The range of entertainment offered by minstrels in the twelfth and thirteenth centuries was virtually unlimited. The poet Wace in his *Roman de Brut* – written in the year following Henry's marriage to Eleanor of Aquitaine and their joint coronation in 1154, and dedicated to Eleanor – depicts the coronation feast of the legendary Arthur in terms that may well reflect the contemporary event. Wace writes, not only of songs and a long list of *lais* for viol, harp, lyres, shawms and other instruments, but also of

> magicians,
> Performers, and jugglers;
> Some tell tales and fables,
> Others ask for dice and backgammon[9]

– the dice-players mentioned by Peter de Blois.

Chrétien de Troyes, who also had links with the Angevin court, is even more specific in his description of a royal marriage feast – the passage in which the term *menestrel* first occurs. We are told that after a blessing by the archbishop of Canterbury,

> There was not a minstrel in all the land
> Who could offer any entertainment
> Who did not flock to the court.
> Great was the joy in the hall:
> Each performed his service:
> One leaps, one tumbles, one conjures,
> One tells tales, the other sings,
> One whistles, the other plays tunes . . .
> Maidens carol and dance.
> All strive to make joy.[10]

Two conjuring minstrels form the letter 'H' in a twelfth-century manuscript of St Gregory's Moralia in Job *from the abbey of Cîteaux (courtesy of the Bibliothèque Municipale de Dijon: MS 173, f. 66, detail)*

We should not assume that Chrétien's minstrels who flocked from every corner of the land to be present at the royal wedding were itinerants; they are more likely to have accompanied their respective lords and patrons. The presence of the king's magnates and knights was *de rigueur* on such occasions.[11] As early as the Domesday survey, we know that magnates were following the king's example in retaining entertainers in their households, and granting them generous settlements of land and property on retirement.

In 1086 a *joculatrix* or female performer named Adelina was in possession of a virgate of land (about 20 acres) in Hampshire, given to her by Earl Roger, the Conqueror's cousin who had commanded the Norman right at Hastings.[12] And we have charter evidence from 1147–60 that Roger de Mowbray, earl of Warwick, rewarded several of his minstrels in the same way, including a man called Warin (referred to in the Latin as both *vielator* or viol-player and *joculator*) who received a life interest in a small estate in Yorkshire for an annual render of a pound of pepper.[13]

That such minstrels in the service of magnates also included joculators in the narrower sense of 'jokers' is suggested by a testimonial issued by the earl of Hereford before 1143:

Miles earl of Hereford to all his friends, French and English, of England and of Wales, greeting. You are to know that this Folebarba [Funny Beard?] is my *joculator* and my man. So I entreat all my friends that they look after him, lest harm happen to him. And if anyone does him good for love of me, I will know how to thank him.[14]

The document also confirms a grant of land to Folebarba.

In view of all this, we should expect to find Henry II treating his own regular following of minstrels ('this breed of courtier') with at least an equivalent generosity. We are not disappointed. Henry's personal waferer, a man named Godfrey, was rewarded by the gift of the manor of Liston Overhall in Essex, which, unlike Warin's estate, he was free to bequeath to his descendants. That is how we know about it; it was to remain in the same family for several generations.[15]

The term *follus* first emerges in Latin records as an occupational surname in 1179 as applied to a Roger Follus, who in that year was rewarded by Henry II with the office of keeper of the royal otter-hounds.[16] At the same time, he was given a *messuage* (a house and its outbuildings) with three virgates of land in Aylesbury, 'by the service of finding straw for the king's bed, and straw or grass for decking his chamber thrice a year, straw if he should come in winter and grass in summer . . .' along with a token contribution from his hunting bag in the form of geese and eels.[17]

But the only one of these royal grants to yield any clue to the nature of the performances or the kind of fooling for which Roger and his fellow jokers were rewarded is that in favour of a man named as Roland le Pettour, who received 30 acres from the king at Hemingstone, near Ipswich in Suffolk, which again he was free to bequeath to his heirs. The peculiar nature of Roland's speciality is indicated both by his surname and the serjeanty service enjoined on him. Instead of the usual pound of pepper or pair of spurs, he was to make an annual appearance at court on Christmas Day and to perform a 'leap, a whistle and a fart' (*saltum, siffletum et pettum*).[18]

The farters could claim a long history going back to the fifth century, when St Augustine of Hippo found legitimate matter for wonder in those who could 'produce at will such musical sounds from their behind (without any stink) that they seem to be singing from that region'.[19] Roland's remarkable feat was too good to be lost to the king's celebration of Christmas – even after the performer's retirement. We see that Chrétien was not indulging in poetic fantasy when he wrote that among the minstrels of the time, 'one leaps, one tumbles . . . one whistles . . .' There is nothing that can make joy/Which was not present that day at the wedding.'

Moving on into subsequent reigns, a man named William Picol, described as 'our fool' (*follo nostro*), was rewarded by King John with an estate in Normandy; and this by royal charter.

John, by the grace of God &c. Know ye that we have given, and by this present charter have confirmed to William Picol our fool *Fons Ossanne* with all the appurtenances to have and to hold to him and his heirs by doing therefore to us yearly the service of a fool as long as he shall live, and after his decease his heirs shall hold the same by rendering unto us yearly the service of one pair of gilt spurs . . .[20]

The charter is undated but, from the style of its opening phrases, probably belongs to 1199, the first year of John's reign, and before his coronation. It has the sound of another retirement grant, although as with Henry's gift to Roland le Pettour, William is required to continue his service once a year, probably at Christmas. Considerately, however, his heirs are allowed to substitute a pair of spurs. As William's estate was in Normandy (soon to be lost to King John) and there is no subsequent record of his name in the English rolls, it would appear that he was shortly succeeded in England by a huntsman named as John le Fol, John Stultus or John Fatuus – all meaning, of course, the same thing: John the Fool.

The earliest mention of John was in 1209–10, when, in partnership with an Irishman called Brian, he is found in charge of a hunting pack of forty-four dogs. In the same year, another fool called Ralph and a companion were paid for delivering twelve greyhounds to a certain Henry, son of Garin.[21] Ralph then disappears from view; but John makes repeated appearances in the Close and Liberate rolls over a period of thirty-seven years, extending from the eleventh year of John to 1247, the thirty-first year of Henry III, when he finally retired on a pension of 7½d a day.[22] It is obvious, then, that whatever the nature of the previous grants to fools I have mentioned, John's appointment as royal huntsman was a lifelong, seemingly full-time occupation. We know too that he had a groom to serve him and did not take kindly to insubordination because, in 1230–1, 'William, the groom of John Folli' was ordered punishment for striking his master.[23]

As huntsman, John had little to do with his employers' sporting activities; his primary function was as a supplier of meat for the king's great feasts at Christmas, Easter, Whitsun and All Saints (1 November). In 1227, for example, the sheriff of York was instructed to receive the venison that John and his then colleague, Master Guy, had taken in the forest of Pickering, cause it to be well salted and carried to York for the king's use at Christmas. In 1237 Christmas was kept at Winchester and three *venatores* including John were sent in advance to the New Forest to cull forty hinds. In 1245 John and his fellows were to take twenty-five boars and sows from Darnhal Park and 'carry them in the direction of Lilleshull [Shropshire] so that the king may have them on the vigil of All Saints to celebrate the feast'.[24] Many similar entries could be quoted. Most of John's time must have been spent away from the court; it was only on the occasions of the major feasts, when the required carcasses had been delivered to the cooks, that he would have been able to perform as a fool.

Normally then, John's two vocations were pursued independently of each other, though in tandem. As we have seen, there was nothing exceptional in this; the same was true of other minstrels, notably the waferers, who, having prepared and served their delicately flavoured confections were free to offer whatever performance skills they might also possess. (Not all of the waferers enjoyed such

With wafers on the table for the final course of a dinner, a waferer performs (engraving by F.W. Fairholt from a fifteenth-century French romance, reproduced from Thomas Wright, A History of Domestic Manners and Sentiments in England during the Middle Ages, *1862)*

additional skills; see the waferer Haukyn's complaint, quoted below. To describe those that did as 'amateur minstrels' would be a mistake, however. They may have been amateur musicians, amateur comics – whatever form their talents as performers happened to take – but as *minstrels* they were nothing less than wholly professional.)

The specific link between hunting and fooling, exemplified in the persons of Roger Follus and John le Fol, will be found to persist in subsequent reigns and at other courts (see Plate 8a). It is partly explained by the fact that both activities centred on feasts – for which entertainment and large quantities of game were equally in demand – and partly by the almost obsessive enthusiasm for the hunt shared by all the Plantagenet kings, which naturally involved those closest to them including minstrels and fools. (Interestingly, they were also linked by an unremitting antipathy to both on the part of the clergy; as Walter Map remarks of the foresters, 'They get no nearer to mirth than murder.'[25])

A rare example of the conjunction of a minstrel's varied abilities, and of fooling actually invading the hunting field, occurs in the later Wardrobe accounts of the luckless Edward II who, when stag-hunting from his lodge at Wolmer, was moved to reward Morris Ken of the kitchen with a pound 'because he rode there before the king and often fell from his horse, at which the king laughed exceedingly'. Edward, it seems (like Henry II), had a particular appreciation for the more ridiculous quirks of human behaviour; on another occasion he gave 50s to his court painter, James of St Albans, for dancing on a table top.[26] If the professional fools among the minstrels were expected to combine their seasonal fooling with other duties, it is clear that minstrels whose primary functions were of the utilitarian kind were not discouraged from occasionally 'playing the fool' if they had the bent to do so.[27]

Another way (apart from hunting and the keeping of hounds) in which fools are seen to have made themselves useful was as messengers. In 1240 Adam le Fol, 'coming to the king with certain letters', was rewarded with 5s by Henry III for his expenses and 2s 7d for a gift of salmon pasties (*pastellis de salmone*); and, in the following year, 'Robert le Sot, a messenger from our faithful and beloved W. Bisset', was tipped by the same king with a mark (13s 4d).[28]

The minstrel-fools who doubled as huntsmen and messengers were not, however, the only type of fools present at court in the thirteenth century. In the reign of Henry III, the *scurrae*, those buffoons of modest gentility we first encountered in the person of Rayer in the previous century, reappear in the records.

From 1251 a man named Fortunatus de Lucca, described as *miles istrio noster*, 'our player-knight', received liveries from the king which are specified as being 'just as for one of the king's knights', with the appropriate trimmings of squirrel-fur and other accessories. Then, in 1257, we learn that he was given a new robe to replace one that had been ruined when the king 'pushed him into the water'. Another *istrio regis* (literally, 'king's player') called John de Blavia was likewise rehabilitated in 1254 because Henry had 'torn up' the clothes from his back.[29] As a former Keeper of the Public Records (A.E. Stamp) surmised, both men may have gone a little too far in their fooling and occasioned one of those sudden, Plantagenet rages to which Henry was subject.[30] It may be significant that John de Blavia and Sir Fortunatus were succeeded by a man named simply as Jacomin *stultus et histrio regis* ('king's fool and player'), who had a special but unspecified outfit made for him in 1260.[31] As a fool of the humbler, minstrel kind, perhaps an innocent, Jacomin would not have been in any position to take objection to the kind of indignities inflicted on his knightly predecessors.

Outside the court, an entire subclass of popular entertainers, including jokers, continued the age-old traditions of the wandering *mimi et histriones*; travelling from fair to fair, seeking a bed for the night in monasteries where they would sing for their supper, performing in the market-places and churchyards of the towns. They constituted a continuing pool of talent and of performance skills on which kings and magnates could draw at will.[32]

By the end of the thirteenth century, the minstrels (the chosen few) had already come a long way from being dismissively classed among 'pavilioners and whores'. The best and more favoured of them were now given the title 'Master' or 'Monsire' and provided with a horse to ride and a servant to attend them at the king's expense. At the same time, their number had greatly increased, both at court and in magnate households, and there was then scarcely a country knight who would not have been able to boast at least a harper among his permanent retainers.[33] The same increase cannot, however, be claimed of the fools among them. Though, as we have seen, some jokers (such as Folebarba) and messenger-fools in the service of magnates are recorded from the twelfth and thirteenth centuries, the heyday of the household fool still lay in the future, and the *joculator regis* remained a solitary figure among the king's regular minstrel following. The situation may have been analogous to that pertaining in France, where the office of *fou de roi* is said to have been a unique and jealously guarded appointment, held by official patent. Though never formalised in England, it is remarkable that from the time of the Conquest onwards there never appears to have been more than a single person present at court at any one time to whom the title 'king's fool' was accorded.[34]

Eleanor of Castile (the beloved queen of Edward I) had a fool called Robert or Robin with whom she played dice, and for whom, in 1289, she provided an outfit of napped cloth, decorated with rabbit fur, and a woollen cape costing in total 31*s* 6*d*. After Eleanor's death in 1290, Robert was recruited by the count of Brittany and given a parting gift of 60*s* by the king.[35] But Edward's personal fool was a man variously named as Tom le Fol, Stultus or Fatuus, and, from the first appearance of his name on the royal payroll in 1286, when he received an advance of wages of 20*s*, he was rarely out of the king's company. In 1292 he is said to have been of Stratford St Andrew (a village in Suffolk) and to have acknowledged a debt of 40*s*. In 1295 he was with the king on campaign in Wales, where he is designated 'king's yeoman' and, along with some others of the household, granted respite of a tax that was due. In November 1296, Edward had recently returned from a successful campaign in Scotland to a stormy meeting of the Parliament of Clergy in Bury St Edmunds. Tom was there given a mark 'for his expenses in going with William de Lonbrugge from St Edmunds to Lord Edward, the king's son, leading a courser and two greyhounds from the king – an interesting recurrence of the hunting connection.[36] Perhaps, like Roger Follus and John le Fol before him, he had some additional responsibility, in tandem with his duties as fool, for the keeping of the king's hounds. A few weeks later, the king and his son came together in Ipswich for the marriage of Elizabeth, Edward's youngest daughter, to the count of Holland, and Tom le Fol was rewarded, along with thirty others, for 'making his minstrelsy before the Princess Elizabeth and her husband'.

The fee of 50*s* that Tom received for his Ipswich performance (a considerable sum at a time when the usual wage for a labourer was 2*d* a day) was one of the largest recorded, and places him among the senior men present, along with Edward's principal fiddler Richard Rounlo, Master John the lutenist, and three king heralds (*Reges haraldorum*), one of whom, Capenny, was famed as a harper. Among minstrels receiving lesser amounts were a female acrobat (Matilda Makejoy), four watchmen, two waferers, a bagpiper who doubled as messenger, and three performers known to the Wardrobe clerks only by the names of the characters they played, presumably in an interlude: *Griscote* (Greybeard), *Visage* (Face) and *Magote* (Ape).[37]

Sadly, the clerks had nothing to say about the content or nature of Tom's fooling; it was not their business, of course, to record such things but simply to make a financial statement of their disbursements of money. They do, however, tell us that Tom received an extra 20*s* for his outfit, which is in line with the cost of the twice-yearly issues of clothing to which all the minstrels were entitled. In 1305 each issue comprised seven ells (nearly nine yards) of cloth, divided into two equal lengths in varying colours, either blue and green or blue and striped, with a lamb's fur for trimming.[38]

It is possible, of course, that Tom (like the episcopal dog-handler of the Luttrell Psalter, illustrated opposite) assumed a 'character costume' on occasion. We know that minstrels of the period acted in plays, and if these were satirical farces – as was probably the Ipswich interlude featuring Greybeard, Face and Ape – it would have been natural enough for Tom to have taken a part in them.[39] But to judge by surviving records and also the pictorial evidence of contemporary psalters, the familiar *habit de fou*, with its eared hood, bells, and parti-coloured tunic and hose, was only then beginning to make its appearance in France and had not yet crossed the Channel – if it ever did, a point I shall take up later.

The probability is that for usual wear about the court, Tom wore a costume not dissimilar to that worn by colleagues among the senior minstrels and by other royal servants of comparable status: the enveloping *roba* of the period, with hood and trimmings of lamb or rabbit fur. As late as the second half of the fourteenth century, Langland's waferer Haukyn makes no sartorial distinctions in complaining of his own lack of qualifications as a performer.

> If you want to know, I'm a waferer, and work for many lords;
> But they furnish me with few robes or furred gowns.
> Could I lie to make people laugh, I should latch on
> To mantles and money among the lords' minstrels;
> But I play neither tabor nor trumpet, and cannot tell romances,
> Or harp or fiddle or fart in tune at feasts,
> Or tell jokes, or juggle, or pipe a jig,
> Nor tumble neither, nor dance, nor sing to the gittern,
> So I get no good gifts from those great lords.[40]

As we near the end of another chapter, it may be useful to look back over the detailed evidence I have presented from the twelfth to the fourteenth centuries to see if we can draw any general conclusions about the fools of the period. Though the surviving information is too meagre for us to extrapolate from it with any great degree of certainty, one or two general points may, I think, safely be made.

In the first place, it is clear that these Plantagenet fools occupied the status of minstrels or minor court servants, and were expected, along with their fellow minstrels, to combine their specialised, named calling with other duties. Apart from the evidence I have cited in relation to individuals (Roger Follus, John and Tom le Fol), it is striking that in the lists that survive of rewards given to entertainers on the occasion of feasts, the fools among them appear without distinction under the general heading of *Minstrelli*, 'little servants'. After 1328, a

Entertainer in costume of a bishop with performing dog. Luttrell Psalter, early fourteenth century (British Library: MS Additional 42310, f. 84, detail)

fool of Philippa of Hainault, the consort of Edward III, is specifically described as 'Master Robert le Fol, minstrel'.[41] Though still regarded with unease and suspicion by clerics, the disreputable companions of the Norman conquerors of England (joculators and 'nobodies') may thus be said to have found a modest place for themselves in the medieval court hierarchy where before they had no place at all, and that the price they paid for that acceptance was a loss of freedom consequent upon the additional duties with which they were saddled.

Of the minstrel fools I have named, only Edward I's Tom appears to have been associated with his patron's military campaigns, and his involvement, if any, in the fighting is left unstated; apart from his minstrelsy, the one specific act for which he received a reward was the conduct of hounds. When John le Fol was attacked by his servant, he resorted to the law. The process of domestication may thus have implied a progressive disarming. The swords with which their Celtic and Norman precursors were equipped in the camaraderie of military encampment, and put to effective use on the field of battle, were, in the hands of their minstrel successors, turning into mere tokens of a former function; the valiant deeds of the Celtic *riogdruth* and the Norman Taillefer into the mock combat.

From the nature of the additional duties they were required to perform as huntsmen, messengers or waferers, it follows that these minstrel fools were mentally competent. We shall be looking more closely at the whole question of the distinction made from an early date between 'natural' and 'artificial' fools in the following chapter. It is sufficient to point out here that the minstrel fools received wages and acknowledged debts, were rewarded with grants of property on retirement (instead of being sent off to monasteries, as usually happened to the innocents), and had grooms to serve them rather than keepers to look after them. It is possible, though not demonstrable, that the men named as 'Follus' or 'le Fol' (notably Roger, John and Tom) were dwarfs.[42]

One other general point may be made: the importance given to the Christmas season as the time of year when the minstrel fool – whatever other tasks he may have been required to undertake in the rest of the year – comes into his own precisely as *fool*. It was on Christmas Day that Folebarba received Hereford's letter of protection, and Roland le Pettour was called upon to perform his unusual serjeanty service. It was on the occasions of the major liturgical feasts, especially Christmas, that John le Fol was commanded to attend at court with his supplies of meat for the feast; and it was following hard on the twelve days of Christmas, on 7 January, that Tom le Fol was rewarded for his minstrelsy at the wedding feast of 1297. The significance of this concentration of fooling at a particular season of the year will again be addressed in the chapter that follows.

It has to be admitted that, at this early date, we have learned very little about the most intriguing aspect of the life of these performers: what they actually did or said to entertain and amuse their patrons on those occasions when they were able to put aside their other occupations and justify their title as fools; the nature of the fooling for which they were so richly rewarded. Apart from Roland's 'leap, whistle and fart', Morris Ken's repeated falls from his horse (which may, for all we know, have been involuntary) and James's table dancing, we are left in the dark. Of one thing we can be sure: that their fooling was as idiosyncratically varied, unpredictable and largely incommunicable as the few odd examples I have been able to give; for the essential characteristic of comedy in all ages is its capacity to surprise.

Finally, let me briefly return to the pictorial evidence of contemporary psalters. As we move forward into the fourteenth century, the unsympathetic, sometimes sinister, depiction of the court fool as feeder on the bread of the poor, typical of the previous century, begins to give place to a more approachable and amusing conception, in which the fool's formerly threatening club is replaced by a harmless bauble or marotte, and his costume becomes more fanciful. A Canterbury psalter of about 1320 (illustrated in Plate 8b) shows a fool of this new kind holding a flower in one hand and a flaccid bauble on a stick in the other, arrested in mid-performance by the warning finger of David. In Plate 9a a king kneels in prayer to God the Father as the fool dances heedlessly away from him. As the threat of the fool's appearance softens, the psalmist's attitude to him becomes more one of admonition or sorrow than of absolute condemnation, reflecting a significant shift in clerical opinion. At the same time, it becomes increasingly difficult to determine whether these more colourful figures are intended as representative of professional fools of the minstrel type or of innocent naturals fulfilling a similar role in return for their keep.

So far as the records are concerned, it is the innocents who come to the fore, and it is to these that we must now turn the focus of our attention.

CHAPTER 6

The Innocents

Though we have waited so long to meet with the natural fools, it should not be supposed that they were altogether absent from the courts of the Anglo-Saxon, Norman or early Plantagenet kings. Indeed, some of the individuals who have featured in earlier pages, such as William's Golet, the eavesdropper of the Bayeux Tapestry, and Henry III's Jacomin, may themselves have belonged to this category; but we are not told enough about them to determine whether they did or did not. And there were doubtless many others, both natural and artificial, who failed to achieve notice at all. If the artificial or counterfeit fools are assumed to have modelled their behaviour on genuine madmen or 'simpletons', the precedence of the latter may be taken for granted.

From the earliest times, natural fools, of whom the madman represents an extreme in his near-total loss or abandonment of reason, have provoked a strangely mixed set of responses comprising (in varying proportions) fear, pity, contempt, laughter and awe. In certain cultures, the madman is thought to be in communication with a world of spirits and is attributed with powers of clairvoyance and prophecy. As a fourteenth-century Muslim historian put it, 'The mad have cast upon their tongues words from the Unseen and they tell them'.[1]

In the Islamic tradition, a number of these djinn-inspired fools occupy a position close to, if not exactly that of, court buffoons. The way in which they combined the functions of saint and joker is nicely exemplified in an anecdote of Buhlul-al-Madjnun ('Buhlul the Madman') at the court of the powerful Haroun-ar-Rashid (c. 763–809). When Haroun went on pilgrimage to Kufa, he ordered that Buhlul should attend, dressed in black, to pray for him. Buhlul complied; but his prayer was so uncomplimentary as to be risible, implying that the Caliph cared only for money. The Governor of Kufa ordered that he be beaten, but Haroun merely laughed and countermanded the order. On another occasion, when rebuked by Haroun's courtiers for his frankness, Buhlul replied, 'You, and people like you, have spoilt the Caliph'.[2] Whether he was protected by his madness or his sanctity, or a combination of both, remains an open question.

In the West, treatment of the insane and of the mentally ill was, for the most part, surprisingly down-to-earth and pragmatic throughout the medieval period. While frequent recourse was had to prayer and pilgrimage, medieval doctors, such as the thirteenth-century friar Bartholomaeus Anglicus, inclined to physical diagnoses along the lines of the ancient Hippocratic theory of the Humours, and prescribed bleeding, dietary regimes and herbal remedies. The Old Beggar's advice to the poet Hoccleve in his *Regement of Princes* of 1412 to talk about the causes of his melancholia as a means of overcoming it anticipated Freud.[3]

In popular romances and plays ranging in date from the twelfth to the fourteenth centuries, love-crazed heroes are treated with a combination of magical potions and behavioural strategies in which common sense and kindness are shown as being most effective. In the early thirteenth-century romance of *Amadas and Ydoine*, the mind of Amadas gives way when the father of the lady he loves forces her to marry someone else. His embarrassed servants conceal him from view, and are obliged to bind him for his own and others' protection. Various medicines are tried without success. But Amadas escapes and wanders off to Italy, where, years later, his former sweetheart finds him naked, dirty and with shorn hair. She cures him over a period of time by talking to him and gently repeating his name and hers, which, she declares, 'is the best medicine, the most helpful and the finest'.[4]

The incurably insane were supported in and by the community to which they belonged, normally within their immediate family; but, in the absence of alternative, institutional arrangements for their long-term accommodation and care, those whose relatives were unable or unwilling to look after them and those, like Amadas, who had escaped the physical restraints imposed on them, joined the ranks of the vagrants – a constant but containable element in medieval society.

In accordance with a Celtic tradition going back to the seventh century, some of these sought refuge in the extensive wilderness and forests of the time to survive as best they could on wild berries and the occasional coney, providing some basis in fact for the persistent medieval myth of the *wodwoses* or 'wild men' with which mothers would scare their recalcitrant children.[5] But the majority of the drop-outs and escapees took to the road, travelling from one religious house to another, where their immediate needs would be met. In the larger monasteries, they were usually allowed to rest for two or three days before being sent on their way. There too, probably for hygienic reasons, their hair was cut short by the monastic barber, which accounts for the shorn heads and occasional tonsure with which these insane ('frantic') fools appear in the psalters. The tonsure may have been thought to have a therapeutic effect on their troubled minds; it would also have provided a degree of protection. It announced to the world at large, including less than sympathetic villagers they met on their way, that in contrast to the shaggy men of the woods, the Church had put its mark on them and claimed them for its own; members, however strange and repulsive in appearance or eccentric in behaviour, of God's kingdom on earth.

In an English, fourteenth-century version of the story of Robert of Cisyle, a proud king who derides the scriptural teaching that God has 'put down the mighty from their seats and exalted the humble', is punished by being transformed into a fool in his own household. His place as king is taken by an angel in his identical likeness, who calls for a barber and commands that Robert

> . . . schulde be schore
> Al around, lich a frere [friar],
> An honde-brede [hand-breadth] bove either ere,
> And on his croune make a crois [cross].[6]

Wodwose *between two lions as depicted in a fifteenth-century misericord in St Mary's church, Beverley (with permission; photograph Fred H. Crossley © Maurice H. Ridgway and Courtauld Institute of Art, London)*

A tonsure of this kind is found on the head of the near-naked madman shown in Plate 5b from a fourteenth-century bible. Another such fool from a Parisian psalter of slightly earlier date (Plate 9b) has the tonsure without the cross. The use of a hood by fools of the innocent kind as depicted in the psalters may also reflect a monastic influence, and, though the naked or semi-naked figure remains the commonest type of psalter fool, the hooded fool (with sometimes the hood thrown back) is almost as frequent in its appearance (Plates 4b, 9a and 10a).

Before what Michel Foucault has termed the 'Great Confinement' of the seventeenth century, when the insane were locked away in supposedly remedial institutions of one kind or another, the most striking feature of their situation was their visibility at every level of society, including the highest. Whether treated with kindness or cruelty (and there are plentiful instances of both), they were accepted as a normal thread in the social fabric.[7] When, in the twelfth-century *Tale of Tristan's Madness*, the hero disguises himself as a 'frantic fool' to gain access to his beloved Yseut, then wife to his rival King Mark, he changes his appearance by tearing his clothes, shearing his hair and scratching his face. He attacks everyone he meets on the road and is pursued by showers of stones, but is able to walk straight into the court and the presence of the king, for 'no door', we are told, 'was closed to the fool'. When, after some riddling exchanges between the two, the king expresses sympathy for him, Tristan tells him, 'What does it matter to me if you are sorry. I don't care a scrap.' And the attendant knights comment to the king, 'No one heeds a fool or argues with him.'[8]

But in the psalters, as we have already seen, no less a person than David the Psalmist is shown in argument with a whole succession of fools, both clever and frantic, in illustration of Psalm 52, and in some of them the figure of David is replaced by that of Christ himself (Plate 5a). Satan too is brought into play. The confrontation pictured in Plate 10b between an innocent fool and a demon remains in doubt. Is the demon repulsed? Or is he about to carry his victim away in triumph – the fool having said in his heart, 'There is no God'?

To St Anselm of Canterbury, commenting on this first verse of the psalm in the eleventh century, the denial of what was to him the self-evident truth that God exists was itself a symptom of folly that could be met and overcome by reasoned argument, his famous 'ontological' proof.[9] But for a long series of saints and mystics, beginning with St Paul and extending through Gregory the Great in the sixth century to Francis of Assisi in the thirteenth, the simplicity of the fool was seen and presented as the model for a spiritual ideal of detachment and humility in opposition to the intellectual vanity and acquisitiveness of the worldly wise. Paul tells his Corinthian converts that 'if any one of you thinks of himself as wise . . . then he must learn to be a fool . . . Why? Because the wisdom of this world is foolishness to God.' Gregory praises the honest directness of the fool in contrast to the expediency of those who seek to conceal the truth. Francis and his early followers were not afraid to assume the title and role of *Mundi Moriones*, 'Fools to the World'. And in Langland's dream of the 'field of folk' in his *Piers Plowman* (*c.* 1378), it is left to a 'leene lunatik' to instruct the king in his duty: 'May he grant you grace to be so just a ruler, that you may win the love of your loyal subjects, and the reward of heaven hereafter', a message that is seconded in the poet's vision by an angel.[10]

Here then is the paradox that lies at the heart of the medieval attitude to the insane, and to natural fools in general. Insofar as their mental incapacity was of such severity as to disable them from any true understanding of themselves or of the world around them, they are used as a figure or iconographic symbol for those who in their folly deny God; but in the world as perceived by Paul and later moralists – a world that has itself gone mad in its pursuit of material values and personal profit – the fool is looked to as a source of wisdom. The key to an understanding of the apparent contradiction here is theological, for not even those 'frantic fools' whose insanity was congenital were barred from baptism, or from the Eucharist if they were able to receive it with due reverence. As St Thomas Aquinas explained, 'Stupidity' (i.e. folly of the kind that leads men to deny God) 'implies a dull heart and blunted senses. Stupidity is opposed to wisdom, madness just its absence. Judgement can be blunted in two ways: by natural disposition as in the mad (and that is no sin), or from so burying our senses in earthly things that we cannot see divine ones, and such stupidity is a sin.'[11]

But among the gifts of grace that the sacraments were believed to confer was wisdom, which the Spirit 'distributes as He wills'. Though incapable of reason, and however recalcitrant and difficult their behaviour might be, the truly insane could not be held as morally responsible for their actions, and were thus, like children under the age of reason, incapable of sin. They were, in the strict theological sense, innocents, whose foolishness could act as a shield against the corruption of the world and the deceits of the devil.

This belief in the essential goodness of the fool, along with a current concept of worldly, even churchly, hierarchies as belonging to the purely temporal order and the expectation of a divine, apocalyptic re-ordering in which the 'first shall be last, and the last first',[12] provided initial inspiration to the Feast of Fools. Beginning in the eleventh century as part of the Christmas *tripudia* (the days immediately following on the great feast of the Nativity), this extraordinary annual celebration of folly was to reach the height of its popularity throughout Europe in the later Middle Ages.

On 6 December, the feast-day of St Nicholas, in a parallel affirmation of the innocence and wisdom of the child, a boy bishop was chosen from among the choir and altar boys, and on 28 December, the feast of the Holy Innocents, he was permitted to preside over the liturgy and to preach a sermon ('out of the mouths of babes and sucklings'). On New Year's Eve, in cathedrals and minsters wherever a sufficient number of clergy was present, the office of Vespers began as normally; but on reaching the words of the *Magnificat*, 'He has put down the mighty from their seats and exalted the humble' (the verse that Robert of Cisyle had been so unwise as to mock), the subdeacons and other junior clergy rose in a body from their usual lowly seats, and, chanting '*Deposuit*', 'Put down, put down, put down', proceeded to eject the canons and senior priests from their high stalls and take their places. At the same time, the *baculus* or staff of office properly belonging to the Precentor (the canon responsible for the ordering of the services) was handed over to the person chosen by the subdeacons to be their 'Fool Precentor', who might be one of their own number or an actual fool co-opted for the occasion. In cathedrals, he might be called the 'Fool Bishop' (Plate 11a) or 'Fool Abbot'; in churches under papal dispensation, even the 'Fool Pope'.

What followed over the next few days is commonly described as burlesque, a turning upside-down of the normal liturgy; it is more accurately seen and understood as a literal acting-out of the *Magnificat*, in which the 'nobodies' among the clergy, as represented by the fool and his assistants, were exalted as a salutary foretaste and prophetic anticipation of the Last Judgement.

One of the main events of the feast-day itself (the Circumcision) was the ceremonial entry into the church of that most humble of animals, an ass, bearing a young mother and her child in commemoration of the Flight into Egypt, while a special hymn was sung:

> *Orientis partibus*
> *Adventavit Asinus . . .*

('From Eastern lands the Ass is come, beautiful and very brave, well fitted to bear burdens. Up, Sir Ass, and sing . . .')

In the Mass that followed, its constituent parts each ended with an imitated bray from the celebrant, and in place of the final dismissal to the congregation of '*Ite, missa est*' ('Go, the mass is ended') the rubrics laid down that he was to bray three times, and that the people should respond in similar fashion. And yet this was a true Mass – celebrated not by the fool, but by an ordained priest – in which everything that happened was carefully prescribed and reverently carried through in a spirit of good-humoured enjoyment.[13] (In a sermon at Christmas, Francis of Assisi, who was never more than a deacon in ecclesiastical rank, is reported to have imitated the bray of an ass in his pronunciation of 'Bethlehem'.)

The Feast of Fools is now usually discussed in terms of its later abuses. Attempts at reform, it is true, specified that the shouts of '*Deposuit*' be limited to five, and that not more than *three* buckets of water be poured over the Fool Precentor at Vespers! There are reports of old shoes being burnt on the altar in place of incense, and of riotous assemblies in the streets at night. It was excesses such as these that led to the feast's suppression; in England by the end of the fourteenth century,[14] in France a century later. But everywhere it left behind it a rich and lasting legacy. In France and elsewhere on the continent, its potential for anarchic jollification and satirical comment on the abuses of government, both ecclesiastical and lay, was exploited by the *Sociétés Joyeuses*: secular fool societies of bourgeoisie, based in the towns, who came together wearing a uniform *habit de fou* at Christmas and carnival-time to take part in elaborate plays and processions.[15] In England, it survived in the form of secular celebration of the Twelve Days of Christmas, over which Lords of Misrule were appointed to preside at court, in magnate and manorial households, schools and universities, and the boy bishops were to retain their popularity until the eve of the Reformation. Fools of one kind or another, and comedy generally, have been associated with the Christmas season ever since.

But the message that the Feast of Fools was primarily intended to deliver was a spiritual one; and it deserves respect as a genuine expression of liturgical drama – as authentic in its origins and early history as the gentler ritual of the Three Marys, or the Magi making their way to the crib at the Epiphany.

Turning from the evidence of popular literature, of theology and the Christmas liturgy to court records of the later Middle Ages, we find that, in contrast to the situation in France where 'frantic' fools (Sibelot, Haincelin Coq, Triboulet) make regular appearances, the 'naturals' retained by English monarchs in their households are not so easily distinguishable from their artificial, minstrel colleagues, and were of a kind that we would now describe (in ordinary language) as 'simple-minded' rather than 'frantic'. It is only on the basis of the type of payments they received, and other contextual details, that we are able to separate them.

In 1311–12, for example, Isabella, Edward II's queen, was sheltering a certain Michael, described as 'the Queen's fool' in her household. As Michael was capable of handling money – he was given 4*s* 4*d* to buy shoes and other small necessities for himself at York in that year – and is termed 'fool' rather than 'idiot', he was clearly something short of insane; but the money he received was listed in the queen's accounts as 'alms', not 'wages', and he was thus in quite a different category to the minstrel-fools we have previously noticed, who were accorded the title 'Master' and provided with expensive outfits of imported cloth and squirrel-fur.[16]

From the admittedly fragmentary Wardrobe and other household accounts that survive, it would appear that Edward II was the first of the English kings to retain such innocents on a regular basis among his immediate following. For him, they filled a place in the odd assortment of 'inferior' people – actors, carters, ditchers and boatmen – with whom he was given to passing his time in preference to those younger members of the nobility who regarded themselves as his proper companions by right of birth and who were deeply resentful at being so excluded.[17] But it was as fellow gamesters that he kept the innocents about him, rather than as entertainers in the usual sense.

The earliest known to us, a man named Robert Bussard, is first mentioned in 1303, when Edward was eighteen and Prince of Wales (the first of that title) to his father, Edward I. Robert is recorded as having been paid 4s 'for the trick the Prince played him in the water that day'.[18]

In January 1316, a chronicler was to sneer over the fact that Edward (then king) had taken a winter break in the Fens 'that he might refresh his soul with the solace of many waters', and had had a narrow escape from drowning while 'rowing about on various lakes'.[19] If, as seems likely, his earlier expedition had been of a similar kind, and had ended in a ducking for Robert, his payment to the fool of a sweetener becomes readily understandable when we learn that the season was February and the place Scotland.

All we know of Robert thereafter is that some time between 1303 (the year of his watery misadventure) and 1307, he was sent off by the prince's father to the Yorkshire abbey of Meaux to pass the rest of his days in peaceful retirement. There was nothing unusual in this; it was a procedure (much resorted to by Edward I) whereby the king could secure a retirement home for former royal retainers and dependants, especially those too old or ill to fend for themselves, at minimum cost to a depleted Exchequer. Nor was it out of the way that he failed to consult with the abbot beforehand.[20]

After his accession in 1307, Edward acquired another fool called Robert; a nickname that confusingly was given to nearly all the royal fools in his own and the succeeding reign of Edward III, whether natural or artificial, and whatever their baptismal name may have been; an earlier Robert had served as minstrel-fool to Edward's mother, Eleanor of Castile, and may have set the precedent.[21] In 1312, Robert III was allowed 20s to buy a 'targe' or small shield for some kind of exhibition, perhaps a mock combat, in the king's presence, and there is mention also of a *garcio* to look after him. Five years later, Edward (and presumably Robert) received a visit from a lady named as Dulcia Withestaf, 'mother of Robert, the King's fool'.[22] It is good to know that, in spite of his adoption by the king, relations between the fool and his natural family had not been entirely broken off.

The Bernard le Fol and his fifty-four companions whom Edward encountered on a visit to Pontoise in 1313, 'coming naked before the king with dancing

Members of a fool society in 'dancing revelry' from the Romans d'Alexandre, *1338–44 (Bodleian Library, Oxford: MS Bodley 264, f. 84ᵛ, detail)*

revelry', were almost certainly members of one of the French fool societies with their paid professional, who had gone a stage further in their impersonation of actual fools by abandoning clothes altogether – or, at the least, stripping down to their underwear – like the madmen of the psalters.[23] These 'amateur' fools, wearing their normal uniform costume of eared hood and bells, and sometimes carrying their children with them in portable cots, throng the margins of fourteenth-century French and Flemish manuscripts, as in the Jehans de Grise miniatures of the *Romans d'Alexandre* (above and overleaf). They should not be confused (as they often are) with professional court fools of either the natural or artificial kinds.

In view of what is known of the character and interests of Edward III, which inclined more to the theatre of chivalry and war than to the play of minstrels or fools, it is no great surprise to find that of the three Roberts who appear briefly in the records of his reign, two are associated with other members of the royal family rather than with the king himself. Both of these were mentally competent.

A family of amateur fools on their way to a fête. From the Romans d'Alexandre, *1338–44 (Bodleian Library, Oxford: MS Bodley 264, f. 133ᵛ, detail)*

The 'Master Robert le Fol' (Robert IV), supplied by Edward's consort, Philippa of Hainault, with an elaborate outfit of striped cloth and furs at an indeterminate date after 1328, is specifically described as a minstrel;[24] and 'Robert le Fol' (Robert V), whose annual grant of '4 quarters of wheat, 4 swine, an ox, and 4 cartloads of hay' was restored by the Black Prince in 1362, following the prince's marriage to Joan of Kent, was then enjoying an independent life as country squire, and was probably a former minstrel retainer of Joan's in retirement.[25] Only 'William Chewepayn, otherwise called Robert Fol of St Albans' (Robert VI), who was sent to the abbot and convent of his home town in 1361 to have such maintenance as Robert Bussard had formerly enjoyed at Meaux, appears to have been an innocent. And though this Robert was to be the last of a long line of pensioners at St Albans, rather than the first as Robert II had been at Meaux, the abbot likewise protested, and, in return for certain lands that were ceded to the king in compensation, was successful in obtaining from Edward an undertaking to quit his claim to the corrody – but only after Robert's death.[26]

That Queen Philippa also kept an 'idiot' called Jakeman in her household we learn only from an Exchequer account of 1374 (five years after her death), which records the fact that Jakeman's keeper at Westminster was still receiving an allowance 'of the king's alms' for his maintenance. As the payments are designated 'alms', Jakeman is unlikely to have been one of those insane people who, having inherited land or property, became subject to the statute *de Praerogativa Regis*, and were known as 'kings' idiots'. By the terms of the statute, which is of uncertain date but usually attributed to 1323/4, such people became wards of the king and were kept, not out of charity, as Jakeman would have been, but for the value of their income. Like other wardships, these could be farmed out to any of the king's courtiers or servants whom he wished to favour; hence the later expression, to 'beg for a fool'. There is no evidence, however, to suggest that they were put on public display. Jakeman's position at court was probably similar to that of Isabella's Michael in the previous reign; both received alms; neither was designated 'king's idiot'.[27]

In the fifteenth century, William appears to have succeeded Robert as the usual name for court fools. It is through their clothing, as recorded in the Wardrobe accounts, that we know about them, and, quite often, this is the *only* information we are given. The 'William Fool' fitted out by Richard II in the early years of his reign (1377–80) with a 'long tunic, a long tabard and hood parted of short camlet and rayed caynet . . . faced with red, and two pairs of breeches'[28] was almost certainly a fool of the minstrel type. Though hoods were then in common use by all classes of society, 'ray' (striped cloth of various materials and colours) was reserved for the liveries of court servants, especially minstrels.[29]

But the 'king's fool', another William, who accompanied Henry V to France in 1417 (or, at the least, was made ready to do so) is more intriguing. For the making of 'apparel, gowns and tabards' for himself and his servant, William II was to be supplied with a long list of materials, including 31 yards of broadcloth, 30 yards of Flanders linen, smaller quantities of blanket and other cloths, along with 12 pairs of shoes and 2 pairs of boots and black spurs. But the most striking feature of the order is the great quantity of furs to be provided: no less than 5,470 skins of Calabrian squirrel (136½ timbers of 40 skins each, plus 10 bellies), 240 skins and 2 bellies of 'pured' (trimmed) miniver, 12 skins of ermine and 3 of black 'bong' – possibly *boug* or *budge*, an imported lambskin.[30]

All this was to be made ready against the coming feasts of both summer and winter – from Christmas through to Pentecost – which indicates that a protracted stay in France was anticipated, as indeed it proved to be. But it is the prominent mention of the servant, and the combination in the materials listed of colourful but relatively inexpensive cloths such as broadcloth and blanket (presumably to be worn by them both) with the abundance of rich furs including the royal ermine for the fool, that suggests an innocent in company with his keeper. That being so, William's appearance in France at the specified feasts would have been intended more as an impressive show than as an aid to his fooling. Certainly, his costume would have been more than a match for that of his opposite number in the French court, the fool of Charles VI.

The aged French king – who was himself subject to disabling attacks of mental instability – is known to have retained a notorious madman called Haincelin Coq, who was given to frenzied dancing and leaping, and, on the occasion of one such performance, is said to have torn his clothes into shreds. His usual wear was a long, loose gown known as a *haincelin*, from which he probably derived his name. The *haincelin* was already known in England; Richard II had had one made for him of embroidered satin costing over £10 in 1393;[31] but the material used for the fool's gown was of a reddish-brown colour that was also in use '*pour garnir la chaière nécessaire pour servir au retrait du dit seigneur, le roy Charles VI*' – the royal commode.[32] If William and Haincelin were ever brought together, there can be little doubt who would have taken the prize for sartorial splendour.

After Henry V's death in 1422, his widow Catherine (daughter of Charles VI) was to lead a retired life in England, latterly Wales, where she formed a liaison with one of her household officials, Owen Tudor; their eldest son, created earl of Richmond in 1452, was to be the father of Henry VII. It is interesting to find that in 1431/2, *uno stulto domine Regine* ('a fool of the Lady Queen') was rewarded by the City Receivers of Exeter with 20s.[33]

Few court fools of any kind, innocent or clever, surface in the reign of Henry VI or throughout the period of the Wars of the Roses, though whether this is attributable to the conditions of the time, to a change of fashion or loss of the relevant records is impossible to say. Henry VI (born appropriately enough on St Nicholas' Day) was himself something of an innocent, a pious one at that. When the king was seen as a fool, others may have been considered supernumerary. The door of Edward IV's privy chamber remains firmly closed. It is the more disappointing in that we know that fools of both kinds were then being kept by some of the king's magnates and officials; John Howard, duke of Norfolk, for example, kept an innocent called Tom Fole who, in 1482/3, was regularly supplied with clothes, shoes and, on one occasion, a 'pype'.[34]

A fool called Martyn is glimpsed in 1483/4 in the household of Richard III's seven-year-old heir Edward of Middleham, who was to disappoint his father's hopes by dying shortly afterwards; and we know that Richard's queen, Ann Nevill, had her 'Mr John' because there is a record of his burial at St Margaret's, Westminster, in 1485 – the same year as the death of the queen.[35]

It was left to Henry Tudor to bring back (if it had ever wholly lapsed) the ancient tradition of retaining innocents on a regular basis in the royal household; but for an adequate account of these, and of the more famous fools of his successor Henry VIII, we shall need two further chapters.

The fragmentary nature of published records from the Middle Ages has enabled us to do little more than establish a near continuity of the presence of innocents at the English court, and to retrieve a few of their names and dates.

From an early period, servants (in effect, keepers) were employed to look after them. Appropriate clothing, usually unspecified, was supplied by the Wardrobe on the king's warrant, and we have seen that in particular circumstances, as for Henry V's expedition to France in 1417, this could be of an extraordinary

An innocent fool at play. Flemish, after 1477 (Bodleian Library, Oxford: MS Laud Miscellaneous 751, f. 17, detail)

richness and cost, though probably more for show than for the comfort of the wearer – if not in inverse proportion to it. In old age or incapacity, they were sent to monasteries with or without the consent of the abbots.

Little, however, has so far emerged of the personality or activity of individual fools, or of the relations that such innocents enjoyed (or, in some instances, failed to enjoy) with their patrons. For this and more, we must proceed to the more personal and detailed accounts that follow.

CHAPTER 7

Tudor Innocents

In reviving the old custom of retaining innocents in the royal household, Henry Tudor may have been influenced by his long exile in Brittany, or was simply indulging an exceptional personal interest; whatever the motive, he was to more than make up for the apparent neglect of his immediate predecessors.

Among visiting fools to his court, or fools resident in the places where he was himself a visitor, were those of the 'Lorde Privy Seall' (Richard Fox, 1492), the 'King of Fraunce' (1493), 'Coltes fole', and 'a fole at Master Knyvettes' (1498).[1] We have no means of knowing whether these were of the natural or artificial kind.

Of his own naturals, one of the first to be recorded (in 1492) was Peche or Pache, always named as 'the fole' to distinguish him from his namesake, John Peche, one of the household knights. Though no keeper is mentioned and he was competent enough to receive rewards of 6s 8d and 3s 4d, his only recorded acts (in 1502/3) were to deliver gifts of fruit to the queen, Elizabeth of York.[2]

Another, named simply as 'Dik', who was clothed by John Flee of the Wardrobe in 1493, and again in the following year, at a total cost of £2 16s 7d, received neither wages nor rewards, and the only other references to him (in 1495/6) relate to the payment of wages to his 'master' – plainly a keeper.

Some light is thrown on the housing and clothing of these innocents by the queen's Privy Purse accounts for 1502/3. From these we learn that Elizabeth had her own fool, another William. He was boarded by a man whose proper name was William Worthy, but who, perhaps to avoid confusion with the fool, was familiarly known to the clerks as 'Phypp'. It appears that Phypp was in charge of an establishment separate from both sets of royal apartments where several of the innocents were accommodated together. He is the first person that we know about to be given the official title of 'Keeper of the King's fools'. He received 2s a month from the queen for William's board. When the fool fell sick, however, as happened in 1502, he was sent off to the care of a certain Rauf Wise in the healthier air of Greenwich, whose charges for 'diettes and othere necessaryes' amounted to 1s a week for a four-week stay.

William Worthy had also the responsibility of purchasing such personal items of clothing for the fool as 'hosyn' (breeches, rather than stockings) and socks, for which he was reimbursed separately. On one occasion, shoes were bought and 'cloughted' (reinforced) at a small extra charge; on another, a page was despatched to purchase a pair. Shirts and larger items, however, were ordered to measure from the queen's tailor, notably a long coat of green Kendal (a coarse

Historiated initial 'C' showing Henry VII and his court, 1499 (Bodleian Library, Oxford: MS Selden supra 77, f. 4, detail)

woollen cloth), of which I give some further details later. It is the earliest record I have come across of the long, skirted 'petycote' that was to remain the traditional wear of natural fools well into the seventeenth century.[3]

Henry VII was the first of the English monarchs who can be shown to have taken a natural fool with him on his formal progresses – a custom that was to be followed by all his successors down to James I. (Like the maypole and the morris dance, since promoted as distinctively English in origin, the custom may have been introduced by him from Brittany.[4])

The earliest innocent to be paraded in this way – at Sittingbourne, Kent, in 1492, and the Midlands in the following year – is of special interest because he is named simply as 'the folyshe Duke of Lancaster'; as head of the Lancastrian house, the king was himself, in effect, 'the Duke'. The latest editor of the household accounts on which I am drawing suggests that the fool was a legacy from one of Henry's Yorkist predecessors, and comments that 'if this were so, it says much for Henry VII that he could take in such good humour so spiteful a joke against his exalted House'.[5] It would indeed! But there is an alternative explanation for the fool's intriguing title: that he was a 'fool double' of the kind we last encountered in Ireland, exhibited by Henry as one of those marvels of nature in which he took such delight. Insofar as it invited a comparison that could hardly fail to be favourable to himself, his motive for including the 'folyshe Duke' in his entourage would have been less admirable than that proposed by Dr Anglo, but understandably human. In 1487, he had put the Yorkist pretender, Lambert Simnel, to work in his kitchens. (In the seventeenth century, Sir Thomas Browne was to include portraits of similar doubles, some dating from this time, in his *Musaeum Clausum*: 'Of King Henry the Fourth of France, and a Miller of Languedock; of Sforza Duke of Milain and a Souldier; of Malatesta Duke of Rimini and Marchesinus the Jester.'[6])

Two other innocents who are known to have accompanied the king on his progresses also enjoyed (successively) the distinction of bearing the title of 'the Kinges fole'.

It is first used of an unnamed fool in June 1498 at Hertford, where his costs (presumably for accommodation) were met, and he was supplied with two shirts, a coat and a pair of 'hooses' (breeches).[7] The coat was especially made for him and cost 15s 2d. On Christmas Eve 1500, he is named as Thomas Blakall and given a reward of half-a-mark (6s 8d). There are payments throughout this period to 'the foles master', meaning their keeper.

Then, at some date between Christmas 1500 and August 1505, Blakall was succeeded in his singular office by a 'Mr Martin', who on the latter date was provided with a horse. As the king was then preparing to set out on another progress that was to take him to Salisbury in September, it is clear that the fool was intended to accompany him. The only other journey with his royal patron that Martin is reported as making was in Henry's funeral procession to Westminster Abbey in 1509, where he was again described as 'the Kinges fole'. And if the 'Mr' before his name should suggest a superior mental status for Martin, it is belied by an added entry in the roll of 'Phypp hys master'.[8] Plainly, the need was felt for the restraining presence of his keeper on such a solemn occasion.

The young prince Henry, duke of York, was not considered too young at ten to have a fool of his own, who was rewarded by the king with half-a-mark in August 1501, and with 3s 4d in February of the following year. On both occasions he was simply named as 'the Duc of Yorkes fole'. Then, in March 1502, 'John Goose my

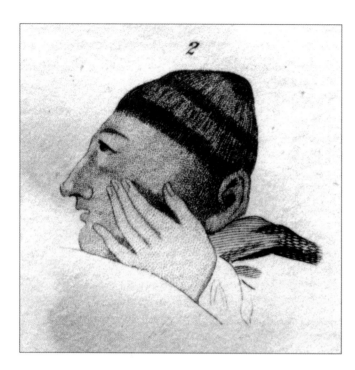

The Duke of Suffolk's fool in the reign of Henry VIII (from Francis Douce, Illustrations of Shakspeare, *1807, II)*

lord of Yorkes fole' was sent by his young master with the gift of a carp to his mother Queen Elizabeth, and came away with 1s.[9] 'Goose' has the sound of a boy's invention – a nickname given him by the prince. He was the first of a new series of court fools, both silly and clever, to have received the patronage of Henry VIII.

Unfortunately, neither Household nor Privy Purse accounts survive in any quantity from the early years of Henry VIII, and so we are dependent in this period on whatever scraps of information we can gather from the more formal of the State Papers.

William Worthy was succeeded as Keeper of Fools by John Devers or Devereaux, but in 1514 there was only one unnamed fool in Devers's care, for whom he was being paid 2d a day. In 1519, the 'king's fool' was included in a list of 'liveries', which, in this context, refers to the 'messes' of food to which the various members of the household were entitled to eat 'in hall'. The fool was allowed one such mess, 'once a day'. Presumably his other meals were provided by Devers. In the Eltham ordinances of 1526, provision was made for the stabling of a hackney for use of 'the King's Foole'.[10]

An innocent named Lobe, for whom we have an anonymous verse epitaph of the period, may well have been the one to have eaten the messes, if not to have ridden the horse.[11] The epitaph is too long to be quoted here in full, but three of its seven verses will suffice to convey the thrust of its meaning.

The losse of the[e], Lobe, maketh many sorye,
    Though ytt be nott alle for thyn awn sake,
Butt the kyng and the quene thou madyst so merye,
    With the many good pastimes that thou dydes make,
    Thy lyfe to be bought, I dare undurtake,
Gold nor sylver there shuld lake none;
Yet foolys be inoghe, thoughe thou be gone.

Thou wast a foole, withowten fraude,
    Shapte and borne of very nature,
Of alle good foolys to the[e] may be laude,
    For every man yn the[e] hade gret plesure:
    For owre kyng and quene thou wast a tresure.
Alas for them! wher shuld we have suche on?
Yet alle foolys be nott deed, thoughe thou be gone.

Now lobe Lobe, God have mercy on thy mery noole,
    And Lobe, God have mercye on thy folyshe face;
And Lobe, God have mercye on thy innocent sowle,
    Which amonges innocentes I am sure hath a place,
    Or ellys my sowle ys yn hevy case;
Ye, ye, and moo foolys many one,
For folys be alyve, Lobe, though thou be gone.[12]

The tribute speaks for itself. What is abundantly clear is the value that was placed on Lobe by his royal patrons, and that their attitude towards him was based more in affection and gratitude than the contempt which is sometimes unjustifiably assumed to have motivated the keeping of such innocents.

Returning to the State Papers, it becomes increasingly apparent that, typically, the royal innocents are not to be looked for in the Great Chamber and its adjacent offices, where the mass of such papers originated, but in that refuge of later medieval kings that was now in course of extension by their Tudor successors, the Privy Chamber. Once the king's more intimate Privy Purse accounts become available again, as they do from November 1529, the flow of more detailed information resumes.

This is another world to that we usually read about in history books; one in which great events such as the Reformation and the rise and fall of statesmen give place to a day-by-day record of the king's sporting activities and gambling debts, of his musical evenings, and the issue of hose to the more intimate servants and companions of his leisure hours. Among such ephemera, Mr Nobody is quite at home, and comes more clearly into focus. The earliest fool to be noticed (on 25 November) is an innocent called Sexton, and his name recurs prominently throughout the three years of accounts that follow.[13]

We have the authority of John Heywood, the contemporary minstrel and interlude writer, for the fact that Sexton had begun his career as fool to Cardinal

Wolsey, and was already known at that time by the nickname 'Patch'. Though undated, and not printed till Elizabeth's reign (in 1562), the following epigram clearly belongs to a time prior to Wolsey's fall from favour in 1529.

A saiyng of Patche my lord cardinals foole

Master Sexten, a parson of knowne wit,
As he at my lord Cardinals boord did sit,
Gredily raught at a goblet of wyne:
Drinke none (said my lord) for that sore leg of thine,
I warrant your grace (quoth Sexten) I provide
For my leg: For I drinke on tother side.[14]

Miss Welsford found this so feeble as to be 'not worth quoting'. Am I alone in finding its crazy logic amusing? In the circumstances of the moment, as a spontaneous riposte to a public rebuke, it would surely have raised a roar of laughter from the cardinal's guests.

The episode in which the once-powerful cardinal – stripped of the Great Seal and at the mercy of Parliament – 'donated' Patch to Henry VIII on receiving the king's assurance of a degree of protection is well known, but must be quoted from its original source in Cavendish's *Life and Death of Cardinal Wolsey*. Apart from its biographical interest, nothing else in the contemporary record speaks so eloquently of the mutual bond that sometimes existed between natural fools and their patrons.

The circumstances leading up to the gift are relevant to an appreciation of Wolsey's motive in making it, so must be briefly stated. He and his diminishing train were on their way from Putney to Westminster when they were intercepted by one of the king's gentlemen, Sir Henry Norris, with the gift of a ring and a message from the king to Wolsey that he was 'to be of good cheer, for he was as much in his highness's favour as ever he was and so shall be'. On hearing this, the cardinal had alighted from his mule and knelt down in the dirt upon both knees, 'holding up his hands for joy'. After a further exchange of compliments, Norris had begun to withdraw, when he was recalled by Wolsey.

'I am sorry,' quod he, 'that I have no condign token to send to the King; but if ye would at this my request present the King with this poor fool, I trust his highness would accept him well. Surely for a nobleman's pleasure he is worth a thousand pounds'. So Master Norris took the fool with him, with whom my lord was fain to send six of tall yeomen with him to conduct and convey the fool to the court; for the poor fool took on and fired so in such a rage when he saw that he must needs depart from my lord. Yet notwithstanding they conveyed him with Master Norris to the court, where the King received him most gladly.[15]

That Wolsey was prepared to sacrifice the fool to curry favour with the king, in spite of the value that he placed on him and Patch's extreme displeasure in the transaction, may be taken as a measure of his desperation; but he would also have had it in mind that Sexton's future was thereby assured. He must have known in his heart that for all Henry's reassuring messages, the days of his prosperity were over. If a contemporary Spanish account is to be believed, Sexton may have felt it too. We are told that in earlier days Wolsey had taken his fool with him 'to see a very splendid sepulchre which he was having made for himself', and the fool had said to him, 'My lord, why are you striving and spending so much money on this? Do you think you will be buried here? I tell you when you die, you will not have enough to pay the men to bury you.'[16] If it really took six 'tall yeomen' to remove him, Sexton must have been a man of considerable size and strength – notwithstanding his sore leg.

Cavendish is economical with dates, but the incident of Wolsey's gift of his fool to the king must have taken place towards the end of 1529: in late October or early November. Sexton's first appearance at court (as previously noted) was on 25 November, when he was rehabilitated with 'certeyne garments', probably including a royal livery coat with Henry's monogram embroidered on it. An additional doublet and hose of worsted, lined with sarcenet (a light silken material), and a 'perwyke' were given him before Christmas, and the total cost of his new wardrobe and wig amounted to the sizeable sum of £5 12s 9d. (Mention of the wig, and the later provision of a 'myllain bonet' and of several nightcaps, suggest that he was bald.)

He is usually described in the accounts as 'Sexten the king's fole', but on six occasions in the following year (1530) is referred to as 'Patch'. This has led Miss Welsford and others to suppose that Sexton and Patch were different people, but, as we have seen, the use of 'Patch' as a nickname for Sexton pre-dates his transfer to the king's household, so there is nothing surprising in the fact that the royal clerks occasionally reverted to its use; in view of the singular nature of the office, a reference to 'patche the king's fole' in November 1530 tends to confirm his identity, and there is nothing in other entries to suggest the contrary.[17]

Sexton, alias Patch, now takes his place in that intimate circle of royal servants who are specified as being 'of the Privy Chamber'; a term referring not just to the chamber itself but to a suite of rooms, galleries and a garden, to the whole of which access was strictly regulated. There are frequent visits by minstrels and other entertainers – including on two occasions in 1531 and 1532 a certain Thomas the Jester (of whom more later) – but none of these was in residence or regular attendance. However, in addition to the fifteen gentlemen and body servants appointed under the terms of the Eltham articles to render 'humble, reverend, secrett and comelye service' to the person of the king, we learn that, by 1529, Henry had also gathered around him in his private apartments a musical *schola*, of which the distinguished Flemish lutanist and composer, Philip Van Wilder, was the leading figure. It also included Henry's former page, Francis Weston, the virginals-player and dancer Mark Smeaton, and 'Phillip's children', boy musicians of whom the two Guillams, Guillam de Trosshis and Guillam Dufayt ('Great' and 'Little' Guillam), were the king's favourites. It was in combination with these that the fool is most frequently mentioned.

We know that Sexton had a man to look after him; in fact, three such keepers are named, Emson, Skinner and Grene. Taking their duties in turn, or in pairs, these received the usual pay of 2*d* a day, with frequent extra payments for monies 'laid out' on the fool's behalf; on one occasion in March 1530 for 'wasshing of his sherts, for shoes, for posset ale and other necessaries'. (Posset ale was a hot milk drink, curdled with ale and spices, taken as a remedy for colds.)

Payments to the Wardrobe enable us to describe the fool's clothing in these years with some exactness. In June 1530, a bill for a 'cote of kendall and a dobelet of fustian' (a twilled material with soft surface, known as 'mock velvet') along with lining and making, came to 15*s* 4*d*. Taking into account the many orders for 'hosen', it seems that Sexton wore the normal grooms' livery of doublet and hose, with the addition of a long coat of green Kendal. In the following month, Rydley the tailor was paid 19*s* 10*d* for another 'Cote of kendall' (also lined), and for a hat. In March 1532, a tailor of London received 8*s* for a 'doubelet and a pety cote'. Apart from those provided for him on his arrival at court, the materials specified for the fool's clothes were relatively inexpensive, and the usual cost of his outfits, including doublet and long-coat, did not even match the £1 2*s* 6*d* expended on a livery coat for his keeper. Not until May 1532 was he provided again with anything finer; no details are given, but the tailor's bill for his 'geyre' on that occasion rose to £3 2*s* 8*d*. This was probably in anticipation of his coming travels.

In August 1532, Sexton accompanied the king on a progress to Abingdon with Grene and Skinner in attendance, and in October of that year he was in Calais for the meeting between Henry and the French king, Francis I, where the costs of his lodging and other expenses came to a modest 7*s* 6*d*. Francis's jester received £9 6*s* 6*d* and Philip Van Wilder £4 13*s* 4*d* in rewards from Henry in Calais.[18] Though there is no record of Sexton receiving anything for himself in rewards or wages (on this or any other occasion), the recurring costs of his maintenance to the Privy Purse should not be underestimated. Including the wage of just a single keeper, in 1530 these amounted to £17 19*s* 0½*d*; in 1531, to £14 3*s* 8*d*; and in 1532, £17 18*s* 11*d*: an average of between 9*d* and 1*s* a day, which was more than the wage of a royal minstrel at 6*d* a day.

The Privy Purse accounts come to an end in December 1532, but we know that Sexton remained with the king for a further two and a half years. Though he must have given reasonable satisfaction to have kept his place for as long as he did, it is doubtful that his relations with Henry were ever so close as they had been with Wolsey, and certainly, were far less so than those to be enjoyed by his successor, Will Somer (to whom I devote the following chapter). But however they may have been at their best, they were to end in disaster.

Writing home in July 1535 to report on Henry's harsh treatment of Princess Mary, whose flight from England he was trying to arrange, Eustace Chapuys, the Imperial ambassador in London, added this postscript, written in cipher, to his letter.

He [Henry] the other day nearly murdered his own fool, a simple and innocent man, because he happened to speak well in his presence of the Queen and Princess [Catherine of Aragon and Mary], and called the concubine [Anne

Boleyn] 'ribaude' and her daughter [Elizabeth] 'bastard'. He has now been banished from Court, and has gone to the Grand Esquire [Sir Nicholas Carew, Master of the Horse] who has sheltered and hidden him.[19]

This was one occasion when an innocent telling the truth – the truth as he and many others saw it at the time – was *not* to be excused. Carew was to go to the block in 1539. We do not know what happened to Sexton.

CHAPTER 8
William Somer

The detailed Privy Purse accounts of 1529–32, which have yielded so many references to his predecessor Sexton, make no mention of Will Somer. A letter of 26 January 1536 from Thomas Bedyll, one of Cromwell's commissioners for the visitation of the abbeys, suggests that Sexton was still the king's fool at that date, and that Somer had not yet come on the scene. Reporting from Spalding in Lincolnshire of his visit to Croyland Abbey, a few miles away, Bedyll tells his chief,

> The King hath one old fool, Sexten, as good as might be, which by reason of age is not like to continue. I have espied a young fool at Croland, much more pleasant than Sexten ever was, not past 15, who is every day new to the hearer. Though I am made of such heavy matter that I have small delectation in fools, he is one of the best I have heard. He is very fit for the Court, and will afford the King much pastime, which he shall make both with gentlemen and gentlewomen.[1]

He goes on to recommend Cromwell to send for him to the abbot of Croyland.

Did Cromwell take up Bedyll's suggestion? Was the Croyland fool, 'not past 15', the young Will Somer? It is tempting to think so. But Bedyll was mistaken; the Visitation had already been in progress for several months when he wrote and he was out of date with his news of the court. As we have seen, Sexton had been banished in the previous summer, and, as early as 28 June 1535, a royal mandate had gone to the Keeper of the Great Wardrobe for a long list of new clothes required for the king and his servants, including

> a dubblette of wursteede, lyned with canvas and cotton . . . a coote and a cappe of grene clothe, fringed with red crule [wool embroidery], and lyned with fryse . . . a dublette of fustian, lyned with cotton and canvas . . . a coote of grene clothe, with a hoode to the same, fringed with white crule lyned with fryse and bokerham [buckram] . . .

– all for 'William Somer, oure foole'.[2]

The obvious inference is that Somer was recruited to fill the vacancy left by Sexton, and that the Wardrobe order of June 1535 represents his initial fitting-out as a royal servant. Bedyll's 'young fool at Croland' is thus a non-starter, and we must look elsewhere for a clue to Will's origins.

Leaving aside some scabrous and unreliable anecdotes that purport to tell of his former life as a country clown in a jest-book of the following century,[3] the only credible report of Will's previous employment is that given by Granger from an unknown source in his *Biographical History* of 1779. Though late in date, this does have the merit of connecting him with a verifiable historical person. 'Will. Sommers', he tells us,

> was some time a servant in the family of Richard Farmor, esq. of Eston Neston, in Northamptonshire, ancestor to the Earl of Pomfret. This gentleman was found guilty of a *praemunire* in the reign of Henry VIII for sending eight-pence and a couple of shirts to a priest, convicted of denying the king's supremacy, who was then a prisoner in the gaol at Buckingham. The rapacious monarch seized whatever he was possessed of, and reduced him to a state of miserable dependance. Will. Sommers, touched with compassion for his unhappy master, is said to have dropped some expressions in the king's last illness, which reached the conscience of that merciless prince; and to have caused the remains of his estate, which had been much dismembered, to be restored to him.[4]

The fact and circumstances of Sir Richard's impoverishment are confirmed in *Hall's Chronicle*; other authorities speak of a partial and belated restitution of his property, and it was not until 1550 in the reign of Edward VI that he was able to return to his home at Eston Neston.[5] But the part that Somer is said to have played in stirring Henry's conscience in Sir Richard's favour makes a good story that is consistent both with the facts as we know them and with Will's subsequent reputation, which was that of a simple, kind-hearted man who exercised a beneficent influence on his royal patron. There are many places from which Will's surname – variously spelt in contemporary records, but never with the final 's' that has since been added to it – might have derived. Summertown in Oxfordshire is one of them, and was the home of Sir Richard's brother William, a 'clerk of the crown'. It is a long shot, but it may have been William who recommended Somer to the king after Sexton's departure. (Bedyll would not have been the only royal official on the look-out for a suitable replacement.)

However he came there, Will's status at court was that of a maintained innocent. Though one of Cromwell's financial statements (of January 1538) records the purchase of a 'velvet purse for W. Sommer',[6] there is no mention in the State Papers of his receiving any money to put in it, either in the form of a regular wage or more occasional rewards. A bundle of undated bills – for his shaving and laundry, for '2 pair of black hose', '2 pair of summer buskins', etc. – indicates that he was dependent on the Privy Purse for his material needs; and a later warrant of Edward VI (in 1551), authorising payment of 40s to a man called William Seyton, 'whom his Majesty hath appointed to keape William Somer', puts him firmly (for that time at least) among the innocents, requiring supervision by a regular attendant.[7]

On the other hand, the way in which pithy sayings of his were quoted by his contemporaries show that he was something more than a token court natural, kept out of charity or custom, capable only of simple errands and a return of kindness with affection. Sir William Paget, Henry's commissioner at Calais, reporting back on his difficult dealings with the French in 1545, tells the king, 'I have lyed, sayd trouth, spoken fayre, roughly, and plaisantly; promised giftes, pensions; and don all that may be don or sayd for the advauncement of this mater, and *much more than I will abyde by* (as William Somer sayth) *if I wer asked the question*.'[8]

In Mary's reign, another ambassador, charged with negotiating terms of the queen's projected marriage to Philip of Spain, sends home 'a declaration whereby may appear the degree of consanguinity and affinity between her Majesty and the Prince of Spain; but remembering the saying of his friend Will. Somer's, *refers it to those who understand pedigrees better*'.[9]

In his *Arte of Rhetorique* (1553–60), Thomas Wilson quotes Will's remark to the king, then in want of money, that 'you have so many Frauditors, so many Conveighers, and so many Deceivers' – meaning 'Auditours, Surveighours, and Receivers' – 'that they get all to themselves'.

In these reported phrases, and the evident pleasure with which they are quoted, we glimpse the reflected image of a true eccentric; one of those rare people whose amiable character and ready turn of phrase give their sayings, however idiotic in context, the quality of catchphrases; and perhaps the more idiotic, the better they are remembered. But they also have that element of wisdom in them for which I have claimed the innocents were especially valued. Wilson gives a hint of this when he follows his 'money' anecdote with the observation that 'whether he sayd true or no, let God judge that, it was unhappely [inappropriately] spoken of a foole, and I thinke he had some Schoolemaster'.[10]

Later, unauthenticated sayings are legion, many plainly fictional. If he is judged by the frequency with which he has been quoted and misquoted, we may claim Will Somer as the best of Tudor court fools of the innocent kind.

For his relations with Henry, we have something other than anecdotes and reported sayings: a contemporary portrait in which king and fool are pictured together in one of the royal apartments (illustrated opposite, and in colour, Plate 11b); but its meaning is ambiguous in that both are shown as playing assumed roles in a mini-drama deriving from Scripture. It is from a psalter made for the king's personal use by the French artist and man of letters, Jean Mallard, in about 1540; that the psalter was actually used by Henry is proved by the marginal notes in his own hand that it contains. In line with the long-established tradition we have traced from its beginnings in the twelfth century and that is now coming to an end, the picture illustrates Psalm 52, 'The fool says in his heart, There is no God!'; but it is unique among such psalter illustrations in depicting, not only an identifiable, contemporary monarch (unmistakably Henry), but also an identifiable fool in the person of Will.

Henry, in one of the last of his portraits painted from life, appears with unusual realism as old, ill and overweight. He is shown in the guise of David, sitting to a Welsh harp – one of several instruments he is known to have played – that is resting conveniently to hand on the corner of a chest.[11] Will is standing in the foreground, turning his back to the king in an attitude of rejection, as the words of the psalm require, and looking a little bewildered and unhappy as if he had

Detail from Plate 11b (Henry VIII's Psalter)

been instructed by the artist to stand in that position without quite understanding why. The clothes he is wearing are exactly of the kind ordered for him in 1535. The 'coote of grene clothe with a hood to the same', specified in the Wardrobe account of that year, could well be the one he is seen wearing, except that it is edged with black and not white. Cromwell's purse (or one similar to it) is hanging prominently from his belt. There is nothing at all in his appearance to indicate his profession; and that too accords with the documentary evidence. (To put a bauble in his hands, as was usually done in psalter illustrations for purposes of identification, would not only have been factually wrong here, but unnecessary, as the person for whom the psalter was intended (Henry) did not need to be told that Will was his fool.) Will is shown to have been stocky in build, slightly deformed about the neck and shoulders, and of indeterminate age. (As he lived on into the reign of Elizabeth, it would be reasonable to suppose that in 1540 he was still a comparatively young man.) His brown hair is cropped short and he is in obvious need of a shave.

Several other alleged portraits of Somer exist but are of uncertain date and provenance. He can, however, be reliably identified in the background of the large family portrait of 1545 that is known to have once hung in the presence chamber at Whitehall[12] (Plate 12). Will hovers in the open archway to the right (as shown in detail opposite), wearing his usual outfit and purse, and with a pet monkey perched on his left shoulder; he is inclining his head to allow the monkey to search his scalp. (The female figure in the corresponding arch to the left is almost certainly Princess Mary's innocent fool Jane, of whom I shall have more to say in Chapter 12.) In what is intended as a reassuring public statement about the stability of Henry's dynasty, neither the king himself nor the members of his family appear as they really were at the time. Henry, as demonstrated by the psalter portrait of five years earlier, did not look at all like this in 1545. Jane Seymour (shown at his side) was long since dead, and, at the time of her death in 1537, Prince Edward (on the king's right) was a new-born infant. Mary and Elizabeth, who stand to either side of the central group, wear identical dresses and are virtually indistinguishable. It is sometimes called the 'fantasy' portrait. Curiously – but doubtless in deliberate contrast – only the peripheral figures of the two fools are represented by the unknown artist as having individual life and personality. Beyond them, through the archways in which they are framed, we see the newly planted Great Garden of Whitehall Palace. Will and Jane are shown as belonging to that wider world, into which the posed figures of the king and his children will return to a more approachable humanity when the artist has laid down his brush.

That Will was especially close to Henry during the final years of the king's life, and accompanied him on his frequent peregrinations between palaces, rather than being established at any one place, Whitehall or Windsor, is suggested by a ferryman's bill dating from Christmas Eve 1545 – within little more than a year of Henry's death.

The king and a small party of his usual companions and body servants were on their way from Westminster to celebrate the feast at Hampton Court. Included in a batch of sixteen horses ferried across the Thames at Lambeth – three of which were needed for the then grossly overweight and ailing king – was a mount for 'Wyllyam Somer', and in the new year he was supplied with spurs for his personal use.[13] Whatever specific contribution Will had made to it, Henry's Christmas would not have been complete without him.

Though he is unlikely to have enjoyed equally close relations with Henry's only son or his eldest daughter, Will Somer was to remain a popular figure at court

Detail from Plate 12
*(*The Family of
Henry VIII*)*

*Portrait of Edward VI, studio of
W. Scrots, 1546 (National Portrait
Gallery, London)*

throughout their succeeding reigns; and fortunately, the records from Edward VI's short reign throw a particular light on that aspect of Will's fooling that I have just touched on, his contribution to the court's celebration of Christmas and the New Year.

At Christmas 1550, he was provided with a painted costume to take an unspecified part in a revel requiring, among other props, three dozen 'fyne visars' (masks), two dozen pasteboard crowns, and thirty-two 'yrishe swordes'.[14] On Christmas Eve 1551, the young Edward, having removed to Greenwich the previous day, wrote in his journal, 'I began to kepe haule [hall] this Christmas, and continewed till Twelftyde'[15] – the normal pattern. This year, Will was cast as a fool-attendant in the train of the Lord of Misrule (George Ferrers), for which he was supplied with a gilded mace and chain, a 'sute of whighte and blewe bawdekyn [brocaded silk] garded [edged] with redd satten', and a 'ffrocke of tauny sylke stryped with gowlde, furred abowte the necke'.[16] Ferrers, a former page of Henry VIII's and, in 1542, Member of Parliament for Plymouth, when he had been famously liberated from imprisonment, was to make his ceremonial entry into the court with his train as from 'oute of the mone [moon]'.[17]

Most interestingly, there is record of a subsequent 'devise by the kinge for a combat to be foughte with Wylliam Somer', for which a 'harniss of paper boordes' (cardboard armour) was supplied.[18] If he did not himself take part in the proceedings, Edward, it seems, was involved in the planning, and Will's appearance here was by royal command. It is the first and only indication we are given that the nature of Will's fooling was anything other than verbal, and the clearest reference yet to what was to become a regular stand-by of the court fool's repertoire in succeeding reigns: the mock combat.

The festivities of 1552/3 were even more elaborate. According to Ferrers's prior announcement of his plans to the Master of the Revels (Sir Thomas Cawarden), he was to make his entrance with a long train of attendants ('Iuglers, tomblers, fooles, friers and suche other . . .') 'oute of a place caulled *vastum vacuum*, the great waste', where he and they were supposed to have spent the preceding year; and one whole day of the twelve was to be spent in a 'challeng performed with hobbie horsis where I purpose to be in person'. But the 'disard' or 'vice' is named as John Smith, a professional player, and although costumes and props were ordered for six other fools under the heading 'Children' (probably pages), there is no further mention of Somer.[19]

We are here, of course, in a tinsel world of deliberate folly and literary artifice in which fancy runs free – though at considerable cost to the Exchequer. It is not a world in which an innocent is likely to have been comfortable, and, by 1553, Will may well have been feeling out of his depth. These revels (of 1552/3) were to be the last of the reign, for in February of the new year, the fifteen-year-old king became seriously ill, and on 6 July he died.

In Mary's reign, Somer appears to have filled a largely ceremonial role as male partner to the queen's long-standing female innocent, Jane. Warrants to the Wardrobe for the expensive outfits provided for him mingle strangely in the accounts with the Dutch gowns and other garments ordered for her.

The elaborate furring of clothes of all kinds with squirrel and ermine was by then out of fashion at court, but for the queen's coronation, Will was supplied with a 'gowne of blue satten, the ground yellow stripping [striped] with a slight gold', and a 'jerkin furred, with sleeves of same, furred with conie [rabbit]'.

In the first year of Mary's marriage to Philip of Spain (1554/5), he was given 'twelve Handkerchevers of Holland', along with linen and knitted hose, 2½ ounces of green silk 'employed upon a grene coat for hym', and three dozen green buttons. (Though they may indicate a propensity for catching colds in the now ageing fool, the somewhat unusual supply of 'Handkerchevers of Holland', the finest linen, bear no relation to the 'muckenders' provided of necessity to slobbering idiots of a later period.) A coat of blue damask was to be embroidered with blue and yellow silk, and 'garded' (banded near the hem at the bottom) with yellow velvet – a sign of his liveried status. A gown of purple damask was to have three such 'gardes' of the same material.[20]

Damask, velvet and furs were for ceremonial use; whereas the three yards of red cloth 'to make hym a coate', and two of velvet to 'garde' the same, were intended for the livery embroidered with 'our Letters' (the royal monogram) that Will would ordinarily have worn about the court. But green was to remain the preferred colour for Will's coats and gowns. In October 1555, two such green coats, 'one garded with vellat, thother playne lyned with cotton', were supplied.[21]

The punning association of 'Somer' with 'summer' – to be taken up by Thomas Nashe in his *Pleasant Comedie called Summers Last Will and Testament* of 1592 – would not have been lost on Will's contemporaries, or on the fool himself.[22]

The plainness of the 'three yerdes of Russet Clothe to make a gowne for William Sommers his sister'[23] strikes a homely note. After twenty years at court, Will had not lost touch with his family; his sister was given a new dress when she came to visit him.

Will aside, John Heywood, the epigrammatist, is credited with being the only person at Mary's court who could move the melancholic queen to actual laughter. He was certainly a favourite of hers. And Heywood refers slightingly to Will in his earlier play of *Witty and Witless* as 'sott Somer', and as 'sotts not the best' who 'standthe . . . all day yn slomber', while those in other men's houses are treated like beasts of burden and whipped for faults they cannot help.[24] There may have been a touch of professional jealousy here. Heywood, the clever minstrel and wit, who had been exiled from court during the latter part of the old king's reign for his Catholic sympathies, may well have regarded the ever-popular innocent, Will, with mixed feelings.[25]

However that may have been, and however passive (possibly ailing) Will had now become, there can be no doubt of Mary's continuing kindness towards him. Within only a month of her own approaching end in November 1558, the queen was to order for 'William Somer our foole' a final bonanza of silk, linen, buttons, tassels, hose and handkerchiefs, with 'two canvas doublets for hym lyned with Bockram . . . a gowne of grene damaske garded with yellow vellat, and . . . a jerkin of same damaske lykewise garded with yellow Vellat'.[26] The young man of her father's reign in his plain suits of worsted or fustian had become a Summer Lord indeed! It is probable that Mary's half-sister Elizabeth had to pick up the bill.

Though present at Elizabeth's coronation in January 1559, Will Somer disappears from the scene shortly afterwards, along with Jane. On 15 June 1560 he died, and was buried at St Leonard's church, Shoreditch – the resting place of some later, much-loved players and fools including Tarlton.

A detailed study of Will's after-life in subsequent literature and drama would require separate, lengthy treatment. His earliest appearance in drama was in the school or university play *Misogonus* (of uncertain authorship and date, probably first performed between 1564 and 1577), in which he features as one of two identities assumed in alternation by a double-dealer called Cacurgas. 'Now will I go play Will Summer again', Cacurgus confides to the audience, 'And seem as very a goose as I was before.'[27] By 1592, when he resurfaces as the pivotal narrator of Nashe's charming pageant-play, *Summers Last Will and Testament*, his character had already undergone a fundamental twist from wise innocent to witty jester; a transformation that in 1605 Samuel Rowley was to take to completion in his chronicle play, *When you see me, You know me*. In characteristic disregard of historical chronology, Rowley brings Will and Patch together as a double-act, with Will as a loquacious 'cheeky chappie' and Patch as his stooge. None of these plays – nor the bogus *Pleasant History of the Life*

and Death of Will Summers of 1676, which is nothing more than a jest-book –
are of any historical value.

The best of the Jacobean accounts is by Robert Armin, the player of fools in
Shakespeare's company at the Globe and Blackfriars theatres, who was also a
competent writer of prose and verse, with several popular works to his credit. His
portrait of Will appeared in his *Foole upon Foole* of 1600, reprinted in an expanded
form as *A Nest of Ninnies* in 1608. Though he assures us of one of his anecdotes
that 'some will affirme it now living in Greenwich', a lengthy account of Will's
putting-down of Cardinal Wolsey, who had died five years before the fool's arrival
at court, does not inspire confidence. (When Armin wrote, Will had been dead for
forty-five years, and Henry VIII, to whose time his anecdotes are wholly
confined, for fifty-eight.)

One or two other stories he tells are more worthy of credence for their
originality (they are not paralleled in earlier jest-books) and because they do not
contradict the facts as we know them. We have seen that in Mary's reign Will
was visited by his sister at Whitehall. According to Armin, he received an earlier
visit at Greenwich from an uncle (at first unrecognised) up from the country.
Will lends him one of his coats, and they appear together in that way before the
king. It transpires that the uncle had recently been impoverished by an enclosure
of common land by his local lord, and Will's subtly worded appeal to Henry on
the uncle's behalf was successful in obtaining redress for the wrong done to him.
The anecdote of Will's encounter with a jester called Thomas may also have a
basis in fact; but I reserve it to a later chapter, where I shall have more to say
about Thomas. Interestingly, in several of the stories, Will is attributed with a
sickness that causes him to fall asleep in surprising places and at unusual times;
once when in the process of climbing a stile in Windsor Great Park. On that
occasion, a local woman is said to have found him and tied him to the stile with a
rope to prevent him from falling off when he woke. At the conclusion of a
riddling session with the king, he 'layes him downe amongst the Spaniels to
sleep'.[28] It will be recalled that Heywood describes him as standing 'all day yn
slomber'. (Like Shakespeare's Fool in *King Lear*, he goes 'to bed at noon'.[29]) If
the stories are true about this, the progressive nature of such an illness might
account for what appears to have been an increasing passivity in Will's later
years.

But the verse preamble to the section of *A Nest of Ninnies* devoted to Will
probably represents the sum of Armin's actual knowledge, as he himself goes on
to imply; the rest being more in the nature of imaginative illustrations to satisfy
public demand 'Insomuch as shee [the world] longed to heare his friscoes
morallised, and his gambals set downe.'

> Will Sommers borne in Shropshire, as some say,
> Was brought to Greenwich on a holly day:
> Presented to the King, which foole disdain'd
> To shake him by the hand, or else asham'd.
> How ere it was, as auncient people say,
> With much a doe was wonne to it that day.

Leane he was, hollow eyde as all report,
And stoop he did too, yet in all the Court
Few men were more belov'd then was this foole,
Whose merry prate, kept with the King much rule.
When he was sad, the King and he would rime,
Thus Will exiled sadnes many a time.

I could describe him as I did the rest,
But in my minde I doe not thinke it best:
My reason this, how ere I doe descry him,
So many knew him that I may belye him.
Therefore to please all people one by one,
I holde it best to let that paines alone.

Onely thus much, he was a poore mans friend,
And helpt the widdow often in the ende:
The King would ever graunt, what he did crave,
For well he knew, Will no exacting knave,
But wisht the King to doe good deedes great store,
Which caus'd the Court to love him more and more.[30]

Will's 'mellody', Armin tells us, 'was of a higher straine' than that of the other, more idiotic fools described in his book. To have kept his popularity and place with such a monstrous egoist as Henry VIII for so long as he did, and to have gone on, after Henry's death, to retain that popularity through two succeeding and highly contrasting reigns, Will must have possessed, along with simplicity and kindness of heart, an extraordinary degree of shrewdness. He was a fool of that rare and most highly valued kind, a wise innocent.

CHAPTER 9

The European Dimension

It is time to pick up the story of the clever or 'counterfeit' fools where we left it in Chapter 5.

Having been brought in from the outer darkness of their original condition as 'nobodies' among the wandering *mimi et histriones* and subjected to a process of domestication, we have seen that both minstrels and fools had gained in status at the cost of some of their former independence and freedom, and that the weapons of steel with which the fools had been armed in the camaraderie of military encampment and on the field of battle had been exchanged for an emblematic club or bauble in the illuminated pages of monastic psalters.

But we should not exaggerate the degree of their consequent dependence. Among royal minstrels generally a distinction had always been made between those whose particular duties required them to be more or less permanently resident at court and those who, in John Pecham's phrase, *vont et vi[e]nent*.[1] With the specialisation of minstrel functions and skills resulting from changes in the organisation of the household, the exigencies of the Hundred Years War and other factors,[2] the entertainers are increasingly found among those who 'came and went'. In contrast to the innocents, whose mental disabilities tied them to the person of their lords, whether at home or on progress, the clever fools and instrumentalists were soon spending more of their time away from the court than within it. The same is true of minstrels and fools in the service of the king's magnates.

In the higher reaches of the minstrel profession, where the royal fools occupied a privileged position and were accustomed to receive the most extravagant rewards, the touring circuit that came into being not only encompassed the more important provincial centres but was European in extent. And the evidence suggests that the best of the English fools, along with the more accomplished of their fellow performers, were as popular and well received across the Channel as their foreign counterparts were made welcome in England. In peacetime, both are seen to have moved freely between their own and friendly courts abroad.

I can now supplement the information already given about fools recorded at the English court with a further series of foreign visitors to it, and some English fools, on tour at home and abroad, whose names have so far escaped notice. It is interesting to find that several of these travellers (both domestic and foreign) were dwarfs or of diminutive stature.

Fool with Artesian cap, beard and bells, Artois, before 1302 (Bodleian Library, Oxford: MS Douce 118, f. 79, detail)

A fool of the Count of Artois had been present in England for the marriage of Edward I's daughter Margaret to John, son of the Duke of Brabant, in 1290. He was rewarded among 426 other minstrels who had gathered from every quarter to claim a share in the bonanza of £100 entrusted by the bridegroom to the king's harper, Walter de Stourton, for distribution among them.[3] In 1290, we know that the fool of Count Robert II of Artois was a dwarf called Calot Jean, whom his lord had recruited in Sicily. Jean took his nickname 'Calot' from a cap that he was in the habit of wearing as 'Haincelin' Coq took his from his gown. (It may have been of the grotesque kind shown in Artesian and Flemish manuscripts of the period; see illustration above.) In 1302, when Count Robert died at the hands of the Flemish weavers, he was succeeded as ruler of Artois by his daughter Mahaut, who bestowed on the dwarf a lifetime annuity and assured him a permanent place in her household. When away from their home base, fools and minstrels were sometimes referred to simply by the name of their patron. At the great Pentecost feast at Westminster in 1306, when Prince Edward (the future Edward II) was knighted by his father along with three hundred others, 'Artoys' was present with several other continental performers including Philip de Cambrai (a minstrel of the king of France), the herald 'Roy de Chaumpaigne', and, most intriguingly, by 'Adam Le Boscu', a nickname of the famous minstrel and playwright of Arras, Adam de la Hale.[4]

In 1299, Prince Edward was entertained at Carlisle by the fool Martinet of Gascony and, in the same year, rewarded Henry Stultus, fool of the count of Savoy, with 1*s* and a further 10*d* for dicing (*ad ludendum ad talos*).[5] We can only guess at the nature of Henry's performance in hall, but it is easy to imagine prince and fool settling down to a private gambling session afterwards with the fool coming off best. The prince's mother Eleanor had enjoyed similar relaxation with her fool Robin or Robert, who later entered the service of the count of Brittany.[6] In 1310/11, when Edward had succeeded to the throne, a certain Hugo de Helmeslaye, described as his fool – and, uniquely among Edward's known fools, of the clever kind – is recorded on tour at Durham Abbey, receiving 6*s* 8*d* from the bursar.[7]

The outbreak of hostilities with France did not altogether halt the cross-Channel flow. A fool accompanied the French king Jean le Bon into captivity in England after his master's defeat by the Black Prince at Poitiers in 1356.

King John, his son Philippe of Burgundy and their entourage arrived in England in July 1359. The entourage was considered by Edward III to be too large and thirty-five of the royal attendants were put on a ship and sent straight back to France. The fool, named as Maistre Jehan, along with his *valet* Girardin, were among those allowed to remain. A week after their arrival, a London goldsmith was paid by the French king for recasting and re-gilding a chalice of his own and a *gobelet* of Jehan's – perhaps damaged in transit.[8]

In early September, we find King John and the remnant of his household at the remote Somerton Castle in Lincolnshire. The king, it appears, was to meet all his own and his household's expenses. It is clear from the relevant *Journal* of the royal accounts that in this microcosm of the French court in exile Master Jehan was a highly privileged person. He had received special treatment before (as is apparent from earlier records from France); but at Somerton, in the exceptional circumstances of their shared captivity, king and fool were thrown into a more intimate relation, and Jehan was treated on a par with the king's son – as one of the family, rather than a servant. Orders and payments for Jehan's clothes mingle closely with those required for the king and Philippe and, if not of quite the same cost, are comparable in kind and quality. No other members of the household were treated in this way.

In December, a special *petite table* was ordered for Jehan, which indicates that he was of diminutive stature though he is never referred to as *nain* or dwarf. As the Lincolnshire winter closed in on them, the fool was allowed to take his meals in the warmth of the king's chamber, where a blazing fire was always to be found.[9] In the same month, large quantities of *menuvair* and *gris* (varieties of Baltic squirrel) were ordered from skinners in Lincoln and London, and used to line *robes, cote hardie, mantel* and hoods for the king; a house in Lincoln was rented for

Tassin, the king's tailor, to use as a workshop. He was ordered to make a *robe* of three garments for *maistre Jehan le fol*, comprising *cote*, *seurcot* (a long, outer coat) and *hosse* (breeches), all to be furred. Cloth was bought to make him a *cote hardie* (another kind of enveloping overcoat) and a *mantel* or cloak.[10] In February, the last two items were lined with four *pennes* (lengths of sewn furs, comprising on average 120 skins each) of black squirrel, trimmed with *bougueran* (black lamb) at a cost of 16s.[11] Boots and a total of thirteen pairs of shoes or slippers were bought for him during the course of the year he spent with the king in England. (Sometimes, such large quantities of footwear are taken to indicate hyperactivity on the part of fools, but were not in fact exceptional; in the same period, the king's son Philippe received forty-seven pairs.) There is nothing in any of the detailed descriptions of Jehan's wardrobe that would have marked him out as a fool.

We are not without clues as to how the king and Jehan passed their time together. (Whether Philippe, who had a separate chamber, was included in their recreations remains unclear.) Eleven skittles (*quilles*), a *tablier* and *jeu de tables* for games such as draughts, chess or dice were purchased.[12] The only minstrel to have survived Edward's earlier purge, *le roy des ménestereulx* himself, would have been in attendance. We even know the titles of some of the books the king was reading or having read to him, including the *Romans de Renart*.[13] On St Nicholas' Eve (5 December) a boy bishop and clergy from one of the neighbouring parishes were rewarded for singing *Ergo laudes*.[14]

When, in late March 1360, the king departed for London on the first stage of his journey home, it seems that Jehan remained behind for a time. To help or hinder the packing? Five carriages were hired to follow the king with his belongings: one for the furnishings of his chamber, one each for the contents of the chapel, the kitchens, and M. Philippe's chamber. The fifth was reserved for Jehan and his servant.[15]

The literary genre of romance enjoyed by King John, in which the figure of the dwarf deriving from Celtic sources had found a fictional home among Arthurian heroes, giants and other creatures of the medieval imagination, continued to exert a potent influence on contemporary culture. In a curious example of art imitating art and, in so doing, returning to its origins, actual dwarfs were recruited to add an element of mystery and of the picturesque to chivalric pageantry of the later Middle Ages.

In 1446, King René of Anjou sponsored an elaborate series of jousts extending over forty days, inspired by the traditions of Arthur's court as recorded in the romances. A wooden castle was built on the plain of Launay near Saumur, called *le Chasteau de la Joyeuse Garde*, to which the king and his knights were to return every evening. On the first day, an elaborate procession was seen to make its way from the castle, in which René was preceded by a dwarf dressed *à la turque*, riding a white horse, richly caparisoned, and carrying the armorial device the king had chosen for the occasion. Arriving at the jousting field, the dwarf sat cross-legged on a cushion placed at the entrance to a splendid pavilion, where he could see and comment on all that followed.[16] But at this period (the middle of the fifteenth

Joust from a fifteenth-century manuscript of the French romance, Le Petit Jehan de Saintré *(British Library: MS Cotton Nero D IX, f. 40, detail)*

century), the unrivalled trend-setters in the mounting of such pageants were the dukes of Burgundy, and perhaps the most spectacular of those for which they were responsible was *L'Arbre d'Or*, held in celebration of the marriage of Charles the Bold to Edward IV's sister, Margaret of York, at Bruges in 1468. It was there that an unnamed dwarf in the service of the English king made his only recorded appearance.

The pageant – which lasted nine days and included a whole series of elaborate processions, entries and jousts concluding in a tournament – was based on the typical legend of a lady who had been confined by magic to a mysterious isle, and had required her deliverer to undertake various labours to prove his devotion; one such task was to decorate a golden tree with coats of arms of the illustrious opponents he had fought and defeated.

Mention of the dwarf occurs in a description of the ceremonial entry of one of the competing champions, Anthony of Luxembourg, count of Roussy. Though 'belonging' to the English king, he is said to have come originally from Constantinople, which had fallen to the Turks fifteen years earlier. The bride had been escorted from England by a strong delegation of nobles. Presumably, Edward's Greek dwarf had come with them, and was borrowed by Roussy for his part in the show.

Leading the count's entry procession into the town square of Bruges at the head of a company of trumpeters, the dwarf was seen to be carrying a petition, and had a large key attached to his arm. A pageant-cart representing a citadel in which the count was imprisoned was then rolled in, and the dwarf read out his petition. '*Danger*', it ran, 'possessed the key to this prison and had entrusted it to him, *Petit Espoir*, his servant. The knight would only gain his liberty and take part in the *Pas* by the intercession of the noble ladies assembled there, for not even *Danger* could refuse such a request. The ladies having signified their approval, the dwarf flung open the great gate and out sprang the Count of Roussy in armour.'[17]

Among the English party at the marriage was John Paston. Of the Burgundian court at this time he was to write home to his mother in England, 'I herd never of non lyek to it, save kyng Artourys cort'.[18]

With the accession of Henry VII in 1485 and his restoration of peaceful relations with Spain, and a little later with France, visiting minstrels and fools of those nations reappear in the English records, and one of the fools is found to have entered his service.

Negotiations with Spain resulted in the Treaty of Medina del Campo of 1489. In June 1492, Henry rewarded a 'Spaynyarde that pleyed the fole' with a generous gift of £2.[19] The fact that the man in question *played*, rather than simply *was*, a fool indicates clearly enough that, unlike those innocents in Henry's service who have already been mentioned,[20] this was a fool of the clever, competent kind. (The same can be said of an English minstrel called Watt who, in October 1504, was rewarded as 'Watt the luter that pleyed the fole' but who, seven weeks later, returned to receive another reward as 'Watt the fole'.[21] At the end of July, the Spaniard, then named as 'Dego, the Spanish fole', was supplied with a saddle, bridle and spurs to accompany Henry to Dover. On 2 October he embarked with the king for France, where a large English army was assembling to oppose the French usurpation of Brittany. The scene that the records present of Henry Tudor sailing to war in a ship called *The Swan* with minstrels playing and a Spanish fool at his side would have appealed to Froissart in an earlier century, though from a romantic point of view the outcome was anti-climactic. An English siege of Boulogne had lasted only nine days when the Treaty of Étaples was signed with France, and by 22 November Henry was back in London and the cause of Breton independence abandoned.

Dego's last recorded performance at court was on 11 March of the following year (1493). Among other Spanish performers rewarded by Henry in the years that followed were a 'Spaynyard that tumbled' in 1494, and, in June 1501, a

'Spaynyard that pleyd on the corde' (a rope-dancer), who pocketed the munificent sum of £10. Spanish performers were soon followed by the French. At Christmas 1493, a company of French players was rewarded with £1 between them, and 'the King of Fraunce fole' (of Charles VIII) with £4.

Not all the foreign fools visiting England at this time came there intentionally. Master John, a French fool in the service of the Archduke Philip of Burgundy, was embarked with his lord in the Channel when their ship was caught by a sudden storm and driven to harbour at Melcombe Regis in Dorset. The archduke was on his way to Spain to claim the kingdom of Castile in right of his Spanish wife Juana, the daughter of Queen Isabella who had died two years previously. Though anxious to proceed on his way without further delay, Philip was persuaded into coming ashore and visiting Windsor, where Henry was able to resolve some outstanding differences between them to his own advantage. On the day their new agreement was signed, Philip was installed as a Knight of the Garter and reciprocated by bestowing on Prince Henry the Golden Fleece.

The name of Master John first occurs in an account of the feasting that followed when he and a party of the archduke's minstrels were rewarded for their entertainment, the minstrels sharing 20s and Master John – diplomatically described as 'the King of Castilles fole' – getting twice that amount for himself.

It was not until April that Philip and Juana were able to continue their voyage; but on arrival in Spain, the archduke suddenly died, precipitating Juana into a condition of demented grief from which she never fully recovered, and depriving John of his patron.

A bill of 15s 4d paid by Henry in December of the same year (1506) for 'master John, the King of Castilles fole' probably related to the fool's earlier visit; the expenses of the archduke's installation as Garter knight had to wait until 1510, when they were finally met by Henry VIII.[22] But by October 1507, John, left to his own resources in a foreign country, had somehow succeeded in making his way back to England, though by then in low water. Henry came to his relief with a donation of 10s for Master Hastings 'to bye certain thynges for Master John the Frenche foole'; with the loss of his patron, the fool sinks back into his own identity. It may have been at this point that he was able to make contact with the archduke's son and heir, Charles (the future emperor Charles V), who had then assumed the title, Prince of Castile. However that was, six months later, when the wages of an English servant were paid for him, his former title of 'the King of Castelles fole' had been restored to him.

Master John's next appearance was with a delegation from Charles to Henry VIII in July 1509, when he was given his highest-ever payment of thirty crowns (£6) as the prince's fool. And in England, it seems, he remained; for when, a year later, the young King Henry visited Reading and made his offering at the abbey, John was on hand to greet him and receive a final generous reward under his original title.[23]

The effects of political expediency are discernible here. So long as Henry Tudor and his son saw an advantage in being friendly to the fool's successive patrons – to the Archduke Philip and latterly, to Charles – his rewards remained on the highest, international scale. The footsore traveller who returned to

England patronless in 1507 merited only charity. For all their relative advances in social acceptability, the honour paid to such fools (as to their minstrel colleagues) was but a pale reflection of that properly belonging to their patrons, though to have achieved their position in the first place must have required a high degree of personal accomplishment. We are required by the nature of the records I have quoted to take the accomplishment for granted. The man himself and the idiosyncrasies of his fooling remain hidden behind the diplomatic niceties.

It is in turning from the European stage on which the more privileged fools were accustomed to move to its humbler, domestic equivalent at the level of provincial, manor and abbey (and from one type of record to another) that a clearer picture begins to emerge of what fools actually did to earn their bread. And if the rewards they could expect to receive in the course of this domestic touring were on a much reduced scale from the largesse of the court, they were perhaps the more regular and dependable. We must also take note of a series of significant changes of nomenclature, reflecting a gradual transformation in the character and functions of the clever fools which was to eventuate in the course of the sixteenth century in the emergence of the Tudor jesters, familiar to us from Shakespeare's plays.

Plate 1: At the centre of this court scene from a fifteenth–century Flemish manuscript, the stick-like figure of the fool flits from one group of courtiers to another (Bodleian Library, University of Oxford: MS Laud Miscellaneous 751, f. 127)

Plate 2: This cloven-footed but clothed fool from an English psalter of about 1200 may represent the clever type of fools, viewed by clerics of the time as more dangerous than the semi-naked madmen of other psalters. The wafer-bread he is about to eat refers to v. 4 of the psalm that follows: 'Are they so ignorant, these evil men who swallow my people as though they were eating bread and never invoke God?' (by permission of the Master and Fellows of Trinity College, Cambridge: MS M.102, f. 73)

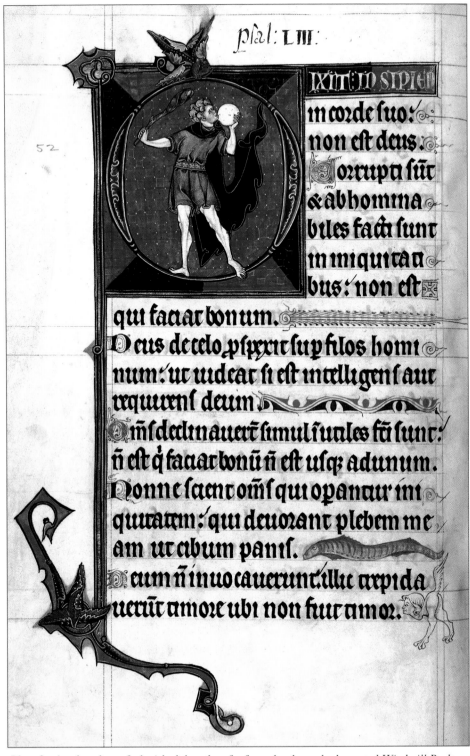

IXIT IN SIPIEN in corde suo: non est deus. Torrupti sut & abhomina biles facti sunt in iniquitati bus: non est qui faciat bonum. Deus de celo prspexit sup filos homi num: ut uideat si est intelligens aut trquurens deum. Omis declinauert simul inutiles facti sunt: ñ est q faciat bonum ñ est usqz adunum. Nonne scient oms qui opantur ini quitatem: qui deuorant plebem me am ut cibum panis. Dcum ñ inuocauerunt: illic trpida uerũt timore ubi non fuit timor.

Plate 3: Another clever fool with club and wafer from the elegantly decorated Windmill Psalter of late thirteenth-century date. Here, as in the other psalters illustrated, the fool occupies initial 'D' of the opening words of Psalm 52: Dixit insipiens in corde suo: non est deus, 'The fool says in his heart, There is no god' (Pierpont Morgan Library, New York: MS M.102, f. 53ᵛ)

Plate 4(a): In the twelfth-century Eadwine (Canterbury) Psalter, the fool is represented (top left) as an evil prince presiding over scenes of violent conflict. In the Celtic and Norman traditions, some clever fools are known to have been armed with real weapons and to have accompanied their lords into battle (by permission of the Master and Fellows of Trinity College, Cambridge: MS R.17.1, f. 22)

Plate 4(b): Early English psalters usually illustrated Psalm 52 by scenes from the Temptation of Christ. In the thirteenth century, under French influence, this subject began to be replaced by that of David, the psalmist, and his fool. The transitional York Psalter of about 1260 provides both (British Library: MS Additional 54179, f. 46, detail)

Plate 5: Madmen fools. While retaining club or marotte and wafer, the mad or 'frantic' fools are distinguished by their semi-nakedness and cropped or tonsured heads.

(a) The fool is confronted by Christ himself, holding a text of the psalm. Thirteenth-century English psalter (British Library: MS Add. 30045, f. 28, detail)

(b) A small dog looks up at his master in expectation of scraps while a worried Christ observes the scene from above. Note glum expression on the face of the marotte. Bible Historiale *of 1357 (British Library: MS Royal 17.E.VII, f. 241, detail)*

Plate 6: Two innocents. (a) A simple fool debates God's existence with King David, reputed author of the psalms. As will be seen from the scale of the calligraphy, the illumination is tiny. English Benedictine psalter of early fifteenth century (by permission of the President and Fellows of Corpus Christi College, Oxford: MS 17, f. 55, detail)

Plate 6(b): The fool's nakedness is concealed by a cloak. The point of the dagger or stick he holds ends in a decorative ring. Bible, 1250–70 (Bodleian Library, Oxford: MS Canon.bibl. lat. 11, f. 238ᵛ, detail)

Plate 7(a): A simple fool in white tunic, and shoes with curled toes, debates with a monk. The monk's words descend from above, inspired by Christ. A mini-drama is in progress – all within the letter 'D'. Fourteenth-century English psalter (Bodleian Library, Oxford: MS Rawl. G 185, f. 43ᵛ, detail)

Plate 7(b): A frantic fool in conversation with David holds what is plainly a rock; he is doubly deceived. Thirteenth-century English Dominican psalter (Bodleian Library, Oxford: MS Rawl.G.23, f. 57, detail)

Plate 8(a): An Italian Renaissance fool with large club and belled hood contemplates two hounds (Bodleian Library, Oxford: MS Douce 272, f. 43, detail)

Plate 8(b): A hooded innocent in striped tunic dances for David, holding a flower and flaccid bauble. Canterbury psalter, after 1320 (Bodleian Library, Oxford: MS Auct. D.2.2, f. 60, detail)

CHAPTER 10

Fools to Jesters

In the fifteenth century, when an increasing number of English borough and household records become available, we find royal and magnate entertainers beating a regular path in their tours of provincial towns and manors, a path that was to be followed in the Tudor period by 'interluders' and players. The problem is that town chamberlains and manorial stewards rarely recorded the names of their visitors; and the terms they employed to distinguish the fools and other types of performer varied so greatly from place to place, and from one individual clerk to his neighbour or successor, as to make them difficult to interpret and impossible to generalise. The change in the language of record from Latin to English or French in the course of the century compounds the confusion.[1]

Miss Welsford insisted that the only Latin words that can certainly be translated as 'fool' are *stultus*, *morio*, *follus*, *fatuus* and *sannio*.[2] This holds true of the innocents, but not of the clever, touring fools we are concerned with here, who might easily escape notice by inclusion in such loosely defined categories as *ludatores* or *lusores* or their equally slippery English equivalent, 'players'. For fools or 'vices' were often employed in the troupes of professional interluders we know to have been on the road from the fourteenth century, if not earlier. (For these, see Chapter 14.)

In domestic records, *fol* is rarely used of the clever fools, and *mimi* and *histriones* can sometimes refer to those who are clearly musicians or waits as well as to players. *Gestour* (however spelt) could denote an old-style singer of *gestes* or stories, its original meaning, or a joker on the way to becoming a 'jester' in the sixteenth-century meaning of the word. What, we may ask, was the nature of the entertainment provided by the *Garsioni vocata Geistour* ('boy called a geistour') who received a modest *2d* from the Chamberlains of York in 1449? Was Alexander Mason, minstrel to Edward IV, Richard III and Henry VII who is also described as a *geyster*, a survivor of the old tradition of *gesting* or a precursor of the new?[3] Many such questions arise to which there are no certain answers; only in the sixteenth century can we safely assume that the term denotes a joker. *Menestrellus* is no help to us either as it was used more as an indication of status than of occupation and thus embraces the whole range of performance skills.[4]

Fortunately, several other, more specialised terms come to our aid in separating the clever fools from both players and the older type of *gestours*. The earliest, and the one that retained its original meaning longest, was 'bourder', from 'bourd', meaning 'an idle tale, jest or joke' (OED). A court fool called Robert in the time of Edward III (probably Robert IV) is described in a contemporary document as 'Robert Foole, bourder',[5] which indicates a deliberate joker rather than an innocent. The clerical author of the fifteenth-century *Jacob's Well* warns that 'if thou be a menstrall, a bourdour, & schewyst bourdefull woordys and many iapys for wynnyng, so honeste [honesty] be savyd, it is venyall synne'; if done for 'delyght of dissolucyoun [dissoluteness]', it is 'dedly synne'.[6] Again, it is clearly a clever fool of minstrel status that he has in mind. In 1456/7, in the reign of Henry VI, a 'burder' of the duke of York's was rewarded with 1*s* at King's College, Cambridge; and in 1526/7 at New Romney in Kent, a wait called William Taberer was paid for his 'bourdyng'.[7]

As noted in Chapter 3, *joculator* could mean either an entertainer in general or a joker in particular. In later Latin entries, the plural *jocatores* was sometimes used of travelling players, probably comedians; but in its late fifteenth-century usage, the word invariably denoted a clever fool. One that 'joculed' before Henry VII was rewarded with 10*s* in 1494, and 'my Lorde of Oxon joculer' with half-a-mark from the same king in 1498.[8]

But the most interesting (and curiously most neglected) of these intermediate terms between the medieval *fol* and the Tudor 'jester' was *disour*, with its Middle-English equivalent *segger*, both meaning literally 'sayer'. To appreciate its significance, we have to bear in mind that the stories of the medieval *gestours* were normally sung or chanted to the accompaniment of a musical instrument, in England usually a harp.[9] The disours were those who *spoke* their stories rather than sang them. The late fourteenth-century poet John Gower makes the distinction in describing the final stage of a feast as when

> . . . every menstral hadde pleid
> And every Disour hadde seid.[10]

And if, as Chaucer tells us, the stories were 'bothe of weping and of game',[11] it will not surprise us to find that the disours inclined more to the 'game'. A joke, it is true, can take many forms and may even be put to music as a song, but is usually more succinct and effective when spoken and accompanied by appropriate gestures or actions, which a man with a harp in his hands would have difficulty in making. With the steep decline in the medieval tradition of harping in the fifteenth century, it was the disour who came to the fore as the immediate precursor of the Tudor jester.

The earliest contemporary account of a disour's performance belongs to the reign of Edward IV. It features a man called Woodhouse who is described as a 'sage dyzour', literally a 'clever sayer'.

The year was 1469. Five years earlier, Edward had secretly married Elizabeth Wydeville, the first English queen who was not of royal blood, and the marriage had given rise to deep resentment among the nobility. Elizabeth, moreover, already had two children by a previous marriage, and had not hesitated to use her new position to advance their interests and those of her relations. Her father, created a baron by Henry VI, had been promoted to an earldom and was known by his title of Rivers. The London Chronicler relates how, at

Edward IV and his court (Bodleian Library, Oxford: MS Hatton 10, f. 290, detail)

Abowth thys tyme oon Woodhows, a sage dyzour, beyng in good ffavour of the kyngys grace ffor his manerly raylyng & honest dysportys which he offtyn excercysid in the court, cam upon a daye of the hoot & drye somyr into the kyngys chambyr, clad in a short cote kut by the poyntys, and a peyer of botys upon his leggys as long as they mygth be tyed to hys peyntys of hys hosys, and in his hand a long marys pyke. When the kyng hadd beholdyn his apparayll, he ffraynyd of hym what was the cawse of his long botis & of his long staff. 'Upon my ffayth, sir', said he, 'I have passyd thorwth many cuntrees of your realm, and in placys that I have passid the Ryvers have been soo hie that I coude hardly scape thorw theym, but as I was fayn to serch the depth wyth this long staff.'

Woodhouse was here striking near to the bone, and the laughter, if any, would have been uneasy. The king, we are told, knew what was meant, but 'made thereof a dysport'. The Chronicler adds that it was 'an ill prenosticacion as ye shall shortly here afftyr', and goes on to tell of Robin of Redesdale's rebellion and the execution of Rivers and his heir, Sir John Wydeville, by the rebels.[12] Had Woodhouse been paid to give expression to the nobility's opposition to the Wydevilles' advancement, or was he warning Edward of the approaching danger? Or simply making a rude joke? His intentions and meaning remain ambiguous and doubtless were intended to be so.

Though we have no means of knowing whether Woodhouse's 'act' was typical of its time or not, its obvious satirical bite may be salutary if it causes us to question conceptions of the late medieval fool as an invariably empty-headed prattler or clown. For all his ambiguity, Woodhouse was coming as near as he dared to conveying an unpalatable truth that Edward would have been wise to have taken notice of and acted upon, but did not. The Chronicler's account of his performance also makes the point that what the disour *did*, and the costume and props with which he appeared, might be of equal or greater importance than what he *said*; something that is easily lost sight of if we rely exclusively on literary evidence, such as that of the jest-books.

An interesting comparison here is between the contemporary record of Woodhouse and the posthumous *Jests of Scoggin*, first published in 1566, though the earliest surviving complete copy dates only from 1626 and is attributed to a well-known physician of Henry VIII's time, Andrew Borde, who died in 1549. It is doubtful whether these have any historical basis other than that they may derive from earlier jest-books, which they plagiarise. The one that follows, which I give as a sample, is wittier than most, and derivative from the published exploits of Pietro Gonnella, a mid-fifteenth-century Florentine jester who served the court in Ferrara. Having been banished in turn from both England and France, Scogin is supposed to have returned to the English court, where he was soon spotted by the king. 'I did charge thee', the king says to him,

that thou shouldest never tread upon my ground of England. It is true, said Scogin, and no more I doe. What! traytor, said the king, whose ground is that thou standest on now? Scogin said: I stand upon the French king's ground, and that you shall see; and first he put off the one shooe, and it was full of earth. Then said Scogin: this earth I brought out of France. Then said the king: I charge thee never to looke me more in the face.[13]

Another episode, in which Scogin asks for and is given permission by the king to say a 'Hail Mary' secretly into his ear from time to time on public occasions and, by these means, is able to persuade the courtiers who were present to give him rich presents and cash on the pretence that he had been recommending them to the king's favour, is strongly suggestive of the dubious methods for extracting money employed by a later fool of James I, Archy Armstrong, who was contemporary with the 1626 edition of the *Jests*. Borde (or whoever its author was, which is disputed) places Scogin in the reign of Edward IV; but Shakespeare and Ben Jonson conflate him with Henry Scogan the poet, who was a friend of Chaucer's and tutor to Henry V. In reality, Scogin appears to have been no more than a mythical conglomeration of fools, some historical, some imagined, with others who were not fools at all in the professional sense from a variety of periods ranging from the fourteenth to the seventeenth century. When Shakespeare has Shallow recall how Falstaff broke 'Scoggin's head at the court gate, when a' was a crack, not thus high' (2 *Henry IV*, III.ii.28–30), he may be thought to have dealt with him in the most appropriate way.[14]

Returning to the historical record, we know that disours remained active under that description into the reign of Henry VII. The 'sheppert' that a 'disare' played before Elizabeth of York in October 1502 was not, as has been suggested, from a nativity play (not in *October*), but, more probably, a contemporary version of the popular medieval romance of 'King Edward and the Shepherd', in which a poor shepherd meets with the king in disguise and complains to him of those social abuses – the prevalence of marauding bands, harshness of the forest laws and corruptness of officials – which bore so heavily on the poor in the fourteenth and fifteenth centuries. Again (if my identification of 'the sheppert' is correct), the disare's performance was making a political point. In January of the following year, Henry's queen was to make a further payment to 'William Tyler, desare, late servaunt to Therl of Oxonford'.[15]

Later in the sixteenth century, the 'desare' becomes a 'dysarde'. An imitator of Skelton was to write of going 'gaye/With wonderfull araye,/As dysardes in a play', and in the accounts already quoted of the Christmas Revels of 1551, the Lord of Misrule's fool (John Smith) is described as a 'vice or dyssarde'.[16] The term had by then become a synonym for 'clever fool'.

It was not until the reign of Henry VIII that the jester finally emerged from among his variously named forerunners to take centre stage. And curiously, he was preceded both at court and on tour by another royal performer with the title of 'jugler'. (As 'jester' derived from *gestour* and, as the story-telling harpers fell in status, came to replace it, so 'jugler' derives from and replaces the medieval French *ioglere* or jongleur.) The particular meanings that these two ancient but newly interpreted terms were to have in the Tudor period are exemplified in the lives and travels of the men who were the first to be so described in contemporary records: Thomas Brandon and James Lockwood. To these hitherto neglected figures I devote the following chapter.

CHAPTER 11
'Jugler' and Jester

In January 1522, Henry VIII wrote to the mayor and aldermen of the City of London,

> Trusty and welbeloved we grete you well/and forasmoche as it is shewed unto us on the behalf of our welbiloved servant Thomas Brandon our pleyer how that he is greatly desyrous to bee made freman of that our Citie of london of thoccupacion of lethersellers there/We therfore disire and praye you at the contemplacion of these our letters to admitte our seyd servant with favourable expedicion freman of our seyd Citie of the seyd occupacion wherby ye shall minister unto us right thankfull pleasure/geven under our Signet at our manor of Grenewiche the xxvijth day of Ianuary.

Though Brandon had to wait until 29 March for the king's letter to be read before the City Council, he was of course duly admitted, with a marginal note in the record to the effect that the king had made no mention that he should be excused payment of a fine.[1]

Brandon was not, as we might suppose from Henry's reference to him as 'our pleyer', one of the royal interluders, but a performer of the kind that had been known as *tregetour* or *prestigiator* in the Middle Ages, and today would be billed as 'conjurer' or 'stage magician'. The contemporary term was 'jugler', which I spell in this way to distinguish it from present-day jugglers of balls and clubs.[2] And the Freedom of the City was important to Brandon because it opened a door for him on a potentially remunerative field of employment as entertainer to the City companies, over which the small and impoverished Company of Musicians and Minstrels had attempted unsuccessfully to impose a closed shop. This was circumvented by the leathersellers and others by the simple expedient of recruiting performers they wished to employ into their own crafts. Once admitted Freemen of the City, they could then be employed by any other of the City companies who wished to do so – though not without protest by the musicians. As a 'foreigner' (one not native to the City), it required this intervention by the king to secure Brandon's enfranchisement.[3]

But aside from his City engagements and court appearances (of which more later), Brandon was an inveterate tourist. A person described as 'the Kyng's Iogeler' had been rewarded at Dover in 1515/16, and at Lydd and Sandwich in 1517/18. As no one else is on record as claiming the title before him, this was almost certainly Brandon; but his first named appearance in the provinces was in 1520/1 at Shrewsbury, where his reward of 3s 4d was said to be *pro honestate ville*, 'for the honour of the town', an indication of the prestige he enjoyed as a royal retainer.[4] Occasionally in these early years, the ambiguous *joculator* was applied to him (as at Shrewsbury); thereafter he is nearly always described as *ioglere* or 'jugler'.

During the 1520s, Brandon was a regular visitor to Thetford Priory in Norfolk, and to Worcester Priory and its dependent manors. In the typically mixed vocabulary of the Thetford accounts, a visiting *Gogelyr domini Regis* had been rewarded with 1s in 1521/2, and received an increased amount of 3s 4d as 'the kyng's Iogular' in 1526/7; but it was not until 1529/30 that we get a first clear reference to *M[agistro] Brandon le Ioguler Domini Regis*, who was then accompanied by a *servus* or assistant; this was probably the 'chylde' who, in 1527, earned a tip of 8d from the prior of Worcester for his tumbling.

When, in August 1526, the ten-year-old Princess Mary visited Worcester in charge of the countess of Salisbury, her governess, to stay for a fortnight at the priory, Brandon was on hand to entertain her. As elsewhere, on his first visits to Worcester in 1519 and 1520, he appears in the prior's accounts simply as 'the Kynges Iogyller', once in company with Henry's blind harper William More, a namesake of the prior's.[5] Between 1521 and 1534, Brandon is named and rewarded on eleven occasions at Worcester and its manors, and, in 1524, by the prior when 'courting', i.e. visiting the court. His last, named visit to Thetford was in 1536/7.[6]

Though most entries by the town chamberlains and their clerks do little more than record the fees that Brandon received (normally 3s 4d), some are found to shed an incidental light on the nature and timing of his performances. There are additional charges for wine and for banquets. At Shrewsbury, there is a wine bill of 16d 'over and beyond the 2d collected from every person of the town, outsiders excepted'; on his return to the town in 1534, his fee increases to 7s 10d and the wine bill to 3s 8d. At Exeter in 1532/3, the 'Kynges Iugkelers' (presumably Brandon and assistant) perform in 'Master Mayre ys housse'. In the same year at Cambridge (where he is termed by an unrepentant Latinist *prestigiator Regis*), Brandon performs at a banquet at 'Mr Hassylles', of which the total costs were 10s 4d and, in 1535/6, receives an additional fee for a 'soper' at 'Maister Mayers'. On St Peter's Day at Barnstaple in 1542, there is a reward for the 'kynges Iuggeler' and an extra charge for 'wyne & ale for all the masters to see hem playe at Worthys hows'.[7]

It thus appears that in addition to his public performances in the guildhalls of the towns he visited, Brandon was also in demand for evening banquets in the more domestic surroundings of one of the aldermen's houses, usually the mayor's, where the flickering light of candles would have aided his illusions. In 1530/1, 'Brandon, jogelar' was rewarded by the countess of Rutland on behalf of her husband. It is not made clear whether this was at Belvoir Castle or in London; at Belvoir in 1542, a 'joggeller' was rewarded for 'hes connyng in mackyng off a lyght for the banckyt' – a self-igniting candle?[8] On the last of his Cambridge visits (in 1535/6), the entry of his fee reads 'ffor Mr Brandon and *other*'; another reference to the shadowy figure of the confederate whose services most magicians require, then as now, in bringing off their more elaborate tricks.

Thomas's court appearances are much less fully documented than his provincial travels, but this does not necessarily mean that these were infrequent; more probably the relevant records have not survived or I have failed to locate them. We have seen that the king was sufficiently interested in his 'jugler' to write to the City Council on his behalf. And we have two later accounts that fill out the sparse information provided by the records on both the content of his performances and (less reliably) his personal appearance and relations with Henry.

The first derives from Reginald Scot's *Discoverie of Witchcraft* of 1584, and gives a detailed description of one of Brandon's illusions. Though not contemporary, the reputation of its author as one of the most enlightened men of his time commands respect; especially as Scot is hard pressed to explain how the trick was done. (As his whole purpose in writing the *Discoverie* was to demystify such marvels, it would have been self-defeating on his part to invent anything so difficult of explanation.)

The chapter heading under which the passage appears is 'Of private confederacy, and of Brandons Pigeon':

> What woondering and admiration was there at *Brandon* the juggler, who painted on a wall the picture of a dove, and seeing a pigeon sitting on the top of a house, said to the king; Lo now your Grace shall see what a juggler can doo, if he be his craftes maister; and then pricked the picture with a knife so hard and so often, and with so effectuall words, as the pigeon fell downe from the top of the house starke dead. I need not write anie further circumstance to shew how the matter was taken, what woondering was thereat, how he was prohibited to use that feat anie further, least he should emploie it in anie other kind of murther; as though he, whose picture so ever he had pricked, must needs have died, and so the life of all men in the hands of a juggler: as is now supposed to be in the hands and willes of witches. This storie is, untill the daie of the writing hereof, in fresh remembrance, & of the most part beleeved as canonicall, as are all the fables of witches: but when you are taught the feate or sleight (the secrecie and sorcerie of the matter being bewraied, and discovered) you will thinke it a mockerie, and a simple illusion.

Scot then embarks on his 'discovery'. His first attempt requires a prior dosing of the bird with poison timed to take effect at a predetermined interval. Though he claims in a marginal gloss to have 'prooved' it on 'crows and pies', it is less than convincing. He may have felt this himself because, in a second marginal gloss, he gives another, quite different solution to the mystery: 'This might be done by a confederate, who standing at some window in a church steeple, or other fit place, and holding the pigeon by the leg in a string, after a signe given by his fellowe, pulleth downe the pigeon, and so the woonder is wrought.'[9] Whatever the true explanation, it is clear that Brandon and 'confederate' (the previously recorded *servus?*) kept it to themselves.

Another anecdote that possibly relates to Brandon – one that, if true, brings the jugler's career to an inglorious end – cannot be disregarded, though its source is somewhat later than Scot and far less reliable. It is told by Robert Armin in the section of his *Foole upon Foole* of 1600 devoted to Henry's innocent, William Somer, and tells how Will set out to bring a jester called Thomas into disgrace with the king. As explained in Chapter 8, some of Armin's stories of Somer are of impossible date and demonstrably fictional. This one is at least possible in that we have established that Somer began his court career in 1535, and we have seen that Brandon was still active as the king's jugler at Thetford in 1536/7, and possibly elsewhere to as late as 1542/3. Though referred to simply as Thomas and as a jester, Armin writes of his man as 'Jugling and Jesting before the King', and as one 'whose subtility heapt up wealth in rewards and giftes given him, which Wil Sommers could never abide him for'. (A 'Thomas the Jester' is recorded in Henry's Privy Purse accounts as receiving xxs in 1531 and xxiis 6d in the following year.[10]) Moreover, Thomas is described by Armin as a 'big man of a great voice, long blacke locks, and a very big round beard'; an impressive figure that would seem to fit a magician better than a joker.

In the middle of one of Thomas's sessions with the king, Somer designedly interrupts them by entering the chamber with a 'messe of milke and a manchet' (bread roll), and asks the king to lend him a spoon. 'Foole', interposes the irritated jester, 'use thy hands.' 'Will', replies the king, 'thou knowest I have none.' 'True', says Will, 'I know that, therefore I askt thee, and I wold (but for dooing thee harme) thou hadst no tongue to grant that foole' – meaning Thomas – 'his next suite, but I must eate my creame some way.' As the king and Thomas draw near, watching him, 'Wil begins thus to rime over his milke.

> This bit Harry I give to thee
> and this next bit must serve for me,
>   Both which Ile eate apace.
> This bit Madam unto you,
> And this bit I my selfe eate now,
>   And the rest upon thy face.'

At which he throws it into Thomas's face, where it sticks in his beard. As Will makes a speedy exit, the furious jester, 'forgetting himselfe, in fury drawes his dagger, and begins to protest'. 'Nay', says Henry, 'are yee so hot? Clap him fast, and though hee drawes his dagger heere, yet let him put it up in another place.' 'The poore abused Jester', we are told, 'lay in duraunce a great while'; and though Will repented of his unkindness and tried to obtain his release ('after he had broke his head, to give him a playster'), 'never after came my Jugler in the Court more, so neere the King, being such a daungerous man to drawe in the Kinges presence.'[11]

Whatever the truth of Armin's anecdote and whether or not it was indeed Thomas Brandon that he refers to as 'my Jugler', it would seem that by 1544, when a house in Bishopsgate in the City belonging to the Mercers is said to have been 'late' in his tenure,[12] Brandon had left the scene. He was followed in his

Sixteenth-century 'jugler' working at table (Christopher Collection)

office as 'royal magician' by a certain Staney or Stanway, whose earliest named appearance was at Shrewsbury in 1553/4 in the reign of Philip and Mary and who went on to serve Queen Elizabeth in the same capacity.[13]

But in the meantime another royal performer had taken to the road. This was James Lockwood. He enters the record books at Nottingham in 1540/1 simply described as 'the Kynges servante' and as receiving a reward of 3s 4d. Six years later, he was back in Nottingham as the 'Kynges bourdar'; and it was not until 1548/9 in the reign of Edward VI at Shrewsbury that he becomes 'servant and jester' (*servienti ac gestatori*) to the king. Thereafter he is always referred to as 'Kynges Jester' or, after Mary's accession and later that of Elizabeth, 'Quenes Jester'.[14]

Lockwood was named at Leicester in 1549 and 1552, and at Ipswich and New Romney in 1555/6. In 1562, he travelled as far as Newcastle upon Tyne where his named was shortened to 'Lockye'. From 1562 he was to visit Leicester almost every year (sometimes named, sometimes not) to as late as 1572 in the fourteenth year of Elizabeth's reign. As the 'kynges Iester' (unnamed) between 1542 and 1553, he was at Folkestone, Plymouth (twice, once with 'two other'), Cambridge (three times), Canterbury (three times), Dover, Barnstaple and Gloucester. Back in Gloucester and at Lydd in 1554/5, he becomes 'geister' to Queen Mary; and in the same year, the year of Mary's marriage to Philip of Spain, did a double-act with Philip's jester at Canterbury and Faversham. In Elizabeth's reign, he visited Shrewsbury in 1559/60, made three visits to Oxford between 1560 and 1567, and was at Ludlow in 1568/9.[15] This can only be the merest sampling of his actual itinerary.

Lockwood's last named performance was in 1570/1 at Leicester – perhaps home ground as he made more visits there than anywhere else. His career had extended over thirty years and he may have been little more than a boy when he began. Sadly, I have found as yet no record of his court appearances before any of the four monarchs he is said to have served, nor any clues in the bald statement of his rewards in the Chamberlains' accounts to the style or content of his fooling. One thing is clear from the sketch of his travels I have given; that his life as a performer was a good deal harder than that of Will Somer and of most of the other royal fools we have traced in previous reigns.

Though we know so little of the man or his fooling, there can be no question of Lockwood's importance as the first in a series of semi-independent, peripatetic jesters whose talents were to enliven courts, guildhalls and manors throughout the whole of the Tudor period. They were to be immortalised by Shakespeare in the character of Feste in *Twelfth Night*. Travelling long distances in the winter, as Lockwood would often have done to take advantage of the lucrative Christmas season, he could well have made Feste's song his own:

> When that I was and a little tiny boy,
>   With hey, ho, the wind and the rain,
> A foolish thing was but a toy,
>   For the rain it raineth every day.
>
> But when I came to man's estate,
>   With hey, ho, the wind and the rain,
> 'Gainst knaves and thieves men shut their gate,
>   For the rain it raineth every day.
>
> A great while ago the world began,
>   With hey, ho, the wind and the rain,
> But that's all one, our play is done,
>   And we'll strive to please you every day.[16]

CHAPTER 12

Jane: a Female Innocent

Even taking into account the occasional dwarf, female fools were rarely to be met with in European courts during the Middle Ages and seldom appear in the psalters. (The only one I have found – shown in Plate 13a – is from an English breviary of the early fifteenth century.) Jeanne, the queen of Charles I of France, had a woman fool called Artaude du Puy in 1373. Among the dwarfs was the golden-haired 'Madame d'Or' in the service of Philip the Good of Burgundy. At the wedding feast of Charles the Bold in 1468, a female dwarf named Madame de Beaugrant, dressed as a shepherdess, was presented to the bride, Margaret of York.[1] The dwarfs became more popular in the seventeenth century, not so much as fools but as court attendants generally, like those pictured by Velázquez at the Spanish court.

Though Anne Boleyn had a female fool for whom she ordered caps and gowns in the last few months of her life in 1535/6,[2] the only English woman fool of whom I have found any detailed information is that Jane who has already been mentioned, along with Will Somer, as receiving regular supplies of materials and clothing from Queen Mary (Chapter 8). But Jane goes further back than this. There are frequent references to her as one of Mary's household during the reign of Henry VIII from as early as 1537. (It is possible that Mary took her over from Anne Boleyn. There was no love lost between these two; but when Anne went to the block in May 1536 and her household was dispersed, it would have been in character for Mary to have taken pity on the abandoned innocent and given her a home – or Jane may have been placed in her care by the king or Cromwell.)

Life at this time was becoming a little easier for Mary. As a reward for her reluctant consent to the Act of Supremacy and to her own bastardisation (she had been made to sign a declaration that the marriage between her mother Katherine and the king was 'by God's law and man's law incestuous and unlawful'), she was allowed sufficient income to re-establish a modest household of her own, instead of its being attached to that of her three-year-old half-sister Elizabeth.[3] Jane is first mentioned in Mary's Privy Purse accounts in December 1537, when there was payment to a groom called Hogman for the stabling of 'Jane the fole hir horse', and another for Jane's 'housen and shoes'.[4] (Two horses had been given to Mary by Cromwell in the previous year. In thanks for the first she wrote to him, 'you have done me a great pleasure. For I had never a one to ride upon sometimes for my health.'[5] With a second mount at her disposal, Jane would have been able to accompany her.)

Portrait of Princess Mary by
Hans Eworth, 1554 (National
Portrait Gallery, London)

The thaw in Mary's relations to the king are manifest also in her increasingly lengthy visits to court, and in the visits made to her at Richmond, Greenwich and elsewhere by some of the royal minstrels. Her virginals were mended, and, in April 1537, a Mr Paston came with Philip Van Wilder ('of the Privey Chamber') to give her lessons on virginals and lute. The words, 'techyng her on the vyrginalles' and 'techyng her on the lute', are added to the manuscript page of her accounts in the princess's own hand – a touching indication of how much these lessons meant to her. Her relations with Philip were especially close. He received rewards on the occasions of his marriage in 1536 and the christening of a child, to whom she was godmother, in 1543. In an inventory of jewels, there is mention of a 'little Chayne of golde enamyled blacke' given to Mr Philip's wife.[6] On one occasion in March 1538, John Heywood brought 'his Children' (probably from the song school of St Paul's Cathedral) to perform an interlude for her. At Hampton Court, there were rewards also to William More, the blind harper, and to 'The King's iugler' (Brandon).[7] In renewing her wardrobe, the princess did not overlook the needs of her fool. In April 1538 there was an order for 'a yerde & a halfe of Damaske' and, by July of that year, this had gone into a 'gowne for Jane the Fole'.[8]

Mary's choice of attendants was not entirely free; all her appointments were vetted by Cromwell. Among those approved was a chamberer with the intriguing

Portrait of Catherine Parr by an unknown artist, 1550 (National Portrait Gallery, London)

name of Lucretia the Tumbler.[9] Perhaps, like the king's tumbler, Stephen Tosso, who had doubled as footman, Lucretia, or Lucrece as she is more often named, combined her acrobatic dancing with more domestic duties.[10] (Their names suggest an Italian origin.) Lucrece is of special interest because, in the early 1540s, she and Jane are sometimes mentioned together as receiving identical items of wardrobe. In December 1542, there is an order for a 'payr of Shoes for Jane & an other for lucrece'; and in the following month smocks are made for them both, which suggests that, for a time at least, Lucrece acted as the fool's companion or keeper.[11]

Whatever her mental status (almost certainly that of an innocent), it is clear from these and later accounts that Jane was subject to a variety of bodily ailments. From March 1543, some kind of skin infection necessitated a monthly shaving of her hair, for which a barber was paid 4*d* on each occasion. His visits continued to September of the following year; and in July 1543 a sum of 22*s* 6*d* was paid for 'Jane the foole for the tyme of hir seeknes'. In September of that year, six ells of cloth were bought 'to make Jane a pair of sheetts'. She may have helped to sew them herself; in the same month a penny was spent on needles for her.[12]

In July 1543, Henry had married the last of his six wives, Catherine Parr, and it was due in part to her that the king then decided to restore his two 'bastard' daughters to the succession; this was effected by a third Act of Succession and by a new will. Catherine was personally kind to Mary and took the ailing Jane into her care. (Her own, male fool was a man called Thomas Browne, for whom materials of grey and red were bought from a draper in 1545/6.[13]) Indeed, it is stated that Mary herself was 'retained to be with the queen', and from this time on, she and her loyal family of attendants are found to have been attached to one or other of the royal households (that of the king or the queen) as they made their customary rounds of palaces and manors.

The new queen seems to have thought that Jane had not enough to occupy her time – which may well have been so in the small world of Mary's itinerant household – and provided her with a little flock of poultry to look after in a corner of the Privy Garden. There is a strong flavour of Catherine Parr's shrewd and practical kindliness in the shopping list of 'things for the Privy Chamber' she gave to her steward in October 1544: 'viz. 3 geese for Jane Foole 16*d*, hempseed for the parrots 16*d*, cream 4*d*, wool 6*d*, mending the parrots' perch 4*d*, 3 gallons of milk 12*d*, 2 gallons of cream 8*d*, borrowing of vessel occupied for the queen at Otforde 6*d*, cream at Leeds 2*d*, and a hen for Jane Foole 6*d*.'[14] (A parrot had been sent to Mary by Lady Derby in 1538.[15])

It was precisely at this time (1544/5) that Jane makes her charming appearance in the royal family portrait now at Hampton Court (detailed overleaf), wearing a tight-fitting cap to cover her recently shorn head and a brocaded damask bodice and gown, parted at the front to show a pleated underskirt. To judge by her lively expression and arrested posture, the change of air and regime had had good effects. The Great Garden at Whitehall appears in the background.[16]

The picture as a whole (Plate 12) may be interpreted as a formal announcement of the reconciliation that took place at this time between the ageing king and his daughters, facilitated by the one person who is notably absent from it – Henry's reigning consort, Catherine Parr. It is clear that by then at least Jane was a familiar figure in the royal households, sufficiently known to be included in a peripheral role in the portrait as female equivalent and partner to the king's innocent male fool, William Somer.

In June 1546, there was a warrant to the Great Wardrobe for 'two gowns and two kirtles for Jane' in which she is described as 'the Queen's fool'.[17] Thereafter, for the remaining months of Henry's life and for the succeeding six-and-a-half-year reign of his son, the life of this least important, but none the less valued, person falls into shadow.

Jane re-emerges in a batch of Exchequer warrants for clothes from the Wardrobe for Mary and her ladies-in-waiting in the first year of her reign as queen (1553/4). Included are several orders for Dutch gowns for Jane. One is to be of 'striped purple satten, the pleites lyned with frise and buckram, the bodyes lyned with fustian'; another (similarly lined) of 'Crimson satten striped with golde', and a third of 'blew damaske chekered'. Along with the gowns, five kirtles of silk and satin (worn under the gown, showing in front), a petticoat of red cloth, and a cloak of yellow, edged with green and 'layde on with yellow whippe lace' were also requisitioned.

It is remarkable that the materials specified here and in a long series of subsequent warrants for Jane's clothes are commensurate in quality with those to

Detail from Plate 12
(The Family of Henry
VIII)

be worn by the queen's ladies, mainly wives and daughters of the nobility, and that the number of gowns and accessories ordered for Jane is greater in number than those for any other person bar the queen herself; their only distinguishing feature is that they are required to be cut in the Dutch style rather than the more fashionable French.[18]

Another indication of the equality afforded Jane is the fact of her inclusion in the St Valentine's Day lottery. On 14 February each year, lots were drawn by all the male courtiers as to who among the ladies of the court should be their partners for the evening's dancing – a ceremony of which Mary seems to have been especially fond, both before and after her marriage. In the time when she was still 'Lady Mary', there are references to one of her yeomen, George Mountejoye, and, in another year, Sir Anthony Browne, the king's Master of Horse, 'drawing my lady's grace to be his valentyne'. In 1554, there is notice of a reward of 'thre yerdes of black satten geven to Mr Herte, being Jane our Foole's Valentyne', and a Mr Barnes was rewarded in exactly the same way and for the same service in 1558 – the last year of the reign. (From the time of Mary's accession, the somewhat indefinite 'Jane the fool' becomes more specifically 'Jane *our* fool'.)[19]

Like Will Somer, for whom equally splendid outfits were warranted in the same period (often mixed confusingly with those for her), Jane was then elevated in status to an altogether grander, more prominent function in the recreations of the court. No longer was she left to feed her geese and hens, as Will had played with his monkey or gone to sleep among the greyhounds. Whether or not the change made her (or Will) any happier is, of course, impossible to say; but there can be no question of Mary's good intentions or generosity towards them both.

In an account of 1555, there is a suggestion that these two (Jane and Will) may have appeared together on some formal occasions in matching outfits: 'Item for furring of a gowne of grene figured vellat (for hym) with sixteene white hare skynnes and fourtie and six white Lambe skennes. Item for furring of a Jerkin (for hym) of the same vellat with some white hare skennes and twentie white lambe skynnes. Item for furring of a gowne of the same vellat with six white hare skynnes for Jane our foole.'[20] Furs had by then fallen out of fashion for ordinary wear in the court or Privy Chamber; they were reserved (as they are today) for the more formal ceremonies of coronations and weddings in cathedral or abbey, when the desirability of making an especially splendid show coincided with a need for bodily warmth.

In an account of 1554/5, there are several references to a 'Beden the foole', for whom a Dutch gown, kirtle and petticoat were ordered. As these orders were mixed in with others for Jane and for Will, we cannot be sure whether 'Beden' was an alternative name for Jane (perhaps her family name) or the name of a second woman fool to whom Mary briefly gave shelter.[21]

In 1555, Jane suffered another bout of illness, this time affecting one of her eyes; among Mary's New Year gifts in 1556 were a 'guilt salt with cover' to 'a woman dwellyng at Burye [Bury St Edmunds?] for healing Jane the Foole her eye', and 'two guilt saltes' to 'Maistres Ager for keping the saide Jane during the time of the healing of her eye'.[22]

On 31 October in the last year of Mary's reign, when she herself was failing in health and oppressed by a multitude of troubles, there is yet another warrant for clothes and materials for Will and Jane; for Jane, 'a gown of red fustian of Naples [a twilled fabric, resembling velvet], with a here collored furre . . . thirteen ounce and a haulfe of silk freenge to frenge a gowne and two cappes . . . thre ounce of grene silk for another gowne of grene damaske, one pece of crimson ribande and twelve pair of woollen hose', along with 'twelve peire of lether shewes'.[23]

Though Will is known to have attended Elizabeth's coronation, retiring shortly afterwards, there is no further mention of Jane. Perhaps one of Mary's ladies-in-waiting or chamber women took her into their care; one can only hope so, as it seems unlikely that Elizabeth would have bothered much about her.

In all the shifting personal loyalties and cruelties of the Tudor court, the simple facts of Mary's evident devotion to her innocent shine out like Portia's 'good deed in a naughty world' and are the more pleasant to record.

CHAPTER 13

Elizabeth's Fools

In his magisterial study of the medieval stage, Sir Edmund Chambers made an uncharacteristic bloomer when he suggested that Shakespeare took his conception of the fool less from contemporary custom than from the abundant fool-literature of the time 'for indeed we hear of no fool at Elizabeth's court'.[1] Whatever the genealogy of Shakespeare's fools (a somewhat different question), I am able to show that there was, in fact, an almost continuous succession of fools at Elizabeth's court, some known to the playwright – if not personally, by reputation. Though the queen's earlier fools pre-date him, the young Shakespeare may well have encountered Tarlton, who did not die until 1558, on one of the fool's provincial tours with the Queen's Players. As a player himself, he may even have acted with Tarlton; the Queen's Players – with a known vacancy in their ranks – were at Stratford in 1587, when Shakespeare was twenty-three.[2] Another fool (Monarcho) he mentions by name in one of his plays. From his own, later visits to court with the Chamberlain's Men, he would have gained some knowledge of Garret. Several of Elizabeth's fools came and went so quickly as to leave little trace of their presence behind them; these were probably of the peripatetic type we have already encountered in the person of Lockwood – though without his advantage of a permanent appointment. Others stayed longer and are more fully documented. Taken as a whole, they represent a wide variety of types, a cross-section of the possibilities of professional folly in the period that could hardly fail to have left its mark on contemporary drama.

As we have seen, Lockwood, first appointed by Henry VIII, continued in his office and title as jester through the short reigns of Edward VI and Mary well into that of Elizabeth; he made his last named appearance at Leicester in 1570/1. Thomas Staney, who had succeeded Brandon as the royal 'jugler' at Shrewsbury in 1553/4, also went on to serve Elizabeth. At Gloucester in 1563/4, he was described as 'shewinge pastimes and other of his Iuglinge feates to Mr mayor and other of his bretherne', and was last reported at Ludlow in 1575/6 as the 'Queenes man'.[3] But I have found no record of either Lockwood or Staney ever appearing at court, though they probably did so.

Elizabeth had come to the throne in November 1558. That Will Somer was still around in the first year of the reign is attested by a note scribbled by one of her servants, Thomas Benger, to the Master of the Revels, 'to allowe . . . William Somers man to have a red cote'; against this entry in another hand, the keeper's name is given as George Bright.[4] But Will himself remains in the shadows, and in

1560 we know that he died and was buried at St Leonard's, Shoreditch. He does not appear to have had any immediate successor.

In 1565, an intriguing encounter took place between the queen and an unnamed fool of the earl of Leicester. It is described by Guzman de Silva, the Spanish ambassador in London, in a despatch to King Philip. De Silva had accompanied the Imperial ambassador to Windsor, where the emperor's man was to take leave of the queen. On the morning after their arrival, the two ambassadors had been invited by Leicester to view Windsor Park, 'in doing which we punished three horses and saw a large quantity of game'. Arriving at the queen's apartments, 'Leicester's fool made so much noise calling her that she came undressed to the window', and, after keeping her visitors waiting for an hour and a half while she completed her toilet, came down to walk and talk with them.[5] Now according to Thomas Fuller (whose evidence I give more fully later), it was Leicester who first brought Tarlton to court. Was this the occasion of his doing so? Would anyone other than Tarlton have had the effrontery to summon the queen in the way described and to have got away with it?

However that was, the first person to be named as the 'Queen's fool' in the state records was a certain Jack Grene, for whom breeches and hose were ordered in that same year of 1565:

> a payre of Hose of russet clothe for Jacke our said foule with lyninges of lynnen . . . for making of a payre of sloppes of fryse trimmed with red frendge . . . a payre of stockinges of grene cloth stiched upon with silke of sondry colors . . . a payre of stockinges of red clothe stiched alover with yellow silke and for makinge of a payre of stockinges of grene clothe trimed with lace of silke of sondry collors with setting on of red sarceonet lyned with red kersey all of our great warderobe.[6]

At the same time, Hammond the capper was warranted for the

> lyninge of ij hattes with crimsin taphata for our said foule with one plume of feathers: for one hate conteyninge xiiij fethers of diverse colours & for making and trimming the same feathers with silver spangles . . .[7]

These specifications tell us nothing of Jack's character or fooling, though his decorated stockings suggest a dancer. (Sir Andrew Aguecheek boasts of doing 'indifferent well' in that way 'in a damned [red] coloured stock'; *Twelfth Night*, I.iii.132–3.) They do, however, feature two items of clothing we shall find to be characteristic of the wear of Elizabethan fools: 'sloppes' and feathers.

As Janet Arnold explains, citing Samuel Rowlands, slops were large voluminous breeches, first worn by fools which later, after their adoption by Tarlton, became fashionable wear among gallants:

> When *Tarlton* clown'd it in a pleasant vaine
> With conceites did good opinions gaine
> Upon the stage, his merry humours shop.
> Clownes knew the Clowne, by his great clownish slop.

But now th'are gull'd, for present fashion sayes,
Dicke Tarltons part, Gentlemens breeches plaies:
In every streete where any *Gallant* goes,
The swagg'ring Sloppe, is *Tarltons* clownish hose.[8]

But the obscure Jack Grene was, it would seem, before him in setting the fashion.

Feathers too were to become a typical decoration for fools; more common in actual use than the proverbial coxcomb, which is nowhere mentioned in the Wardrobe accounts. A plume of feathers may have been a residual token of it, and, in Shakespeare, may stand for the fool himself, as when the Princess of *Love's Labour's Lost* asks of Armado's letter, 'What plume of feathers is he that indited this letter?' (IV.i.95)

But feathers also, and from a much earlier date than slops, were fashionable wear for courtiers of both sexes; and Hammond's plume of fourteen feathers for Jack is more than matched by one that he made in the same year to decorate a hat for the queen, comprising *sixteen* feathers topped with more from an egret (white heron) and decorated with Venice gold and spangles.[9] The queen was not to be outshone by her fool. In W. Wager's *The longer thou livest, the more foole thou art* (published *c.* 1569), the foolish Moros, after he has been blessed by Fortune, is asked by an attendant vice if there is anything he still lacks. 'By my trouth', Moros replies, '. . . the thing that I desire most/Is in my cappe to have a goodly feather.' And when one is produced, naively remarks, 'This will make me a Gentleman alone,/Make it fast I pray you in my cappe.'[10] (The irony is, of course, that by wearing a feather, he is actually making himself look more like the fool that he is.) In 1608, Thomas Dekker was to recommend to the aspiring gallant 'a gilt rapier for his sides and new boots to hide his polt foot', but first and foremost 'a fether for his head'.[11]

Another set of slops and stocks with equally fanciful trimmings was made for Jack in 1567;[12] but after that we hear no more of him.

Though Elizabeth seems not to have followed her half-sister's example in retaining in her household any innocents comparable to Mary's Jane, she did include a young woman with the intriguing name of Ippolyta the Tartarian, and also a dwarf, among her female attendants.

Mystery surrounds the figure of Ippolyta who first appears in the records in 1561, when the queen was godmother at her christening and gave her a chain, two pennyweights and a tablet of gold.[13] The gift to her of a 'Baby of pewter' in 1562 suggests she was then a child; but only three years later, in a warrant of 1564, Ippolyta is described as 'oure deare and welbeloved woman', and provided with a 'Gowne & kirtle of damaske gardid withe velvett', another gown and kirtle of 'grograyne chamblett' (a fabric of mixed threads, giving a ribbed or corded effect), a 'varthingale of mockeado' (mock velvet), six smocks, six 'partelettes' (neck scarves) with ruffs, and six pairs of linen sleeves, elaborately trimmed and decorated. Ippolyta was still in Elizabeth's service in 1569 when Adam Bland, the skinner, furred a short damask cloak for her with five dozen black coney skins; but that is the last we hear of her.[14]

The queen's 'woman dwarf' – later to be variously named as Mrs Thomasen, Thomasina or Tomasin de Paris – may have taken her place in 1577. Thomasina was the recipient of a long series of attractive and elaborate gowns, petticoats and separate sleeves, some of which were adapted from dresses formerly worn by the queen. In 1579, a gown of violet cloth was provided for the dwarf's sister, Prudence de Paris, who may then have been on a visit to her.

The clothes Thomasina was given were always in the latest fashion, and included, for example, two pairs of 'verthingale sleeves of whales bone covered with fustian' to hold out her satin sleeves. As Janet Arnold suggests, she was probably a proportionate dwarf; certainly an elegant, doll-like figure about the court, and ranked among the gentlewomen of the household. That Elizabeth had a long-standing regard for her is demonstrated by the many little personal gifts she made to her (over and above the gowns that all her ladies were accustomed to receive) at regular intervals throughout the remaining twenty-five years of her reign. In 1579, she gave her two gilt rings, six pairs of Spanish gloves and a looking-glass; in the years that followed, there were silver and gold cauls (hair-nets), Holland sheets, table napkins and towels, two taffeta aprons and a green taffeta scarf, needles, knives and scissors for embroidery work, and several ivory combs. We know that Thomasina could write or was learning to write because in 1581 she was provided with a 'penner and Inkhorne'. The last of the gowns she received – a 'loose gown of tuft taffeta, trimmed with silk and silver lace, with sleeves and stomacher of white satin and a damask petticoat' – was in 1603, the year of Elizabeth's death.[15] I have found only one notice of her outside the court, and, interestingly, that was of a visit that she made in June 1580 with two others of the household, John and Mary Scudamore, to the queen's astrologer, Dr Dee, at Richmond, as noted in the doctor's diary.[16] He gives no indication of their business.

It is time to return to Elizabeth's male fools. The irreverent way in which the queen was treated by Leicester's fool in their encounter of 1565 should not lead us to suppose that she was ever careless of her dignity. Though she was not without a sense of humour, this had its limits; when the humour was turned against herself or her favourites, those who offended could find themselves in serious trouble.

It was doubtless with this in mind that her courtiers were reluctant to admit John Pace – famous in his day as 'the bitter fool' – into her presence. Pace was distinguished by his learning and his mordant wit. He had been educated at Eton, and in 1539 was elected a scholar of King's College, Cambridge. When someone told John Heywood that Pace, being a master of arts, 'had disgraced himselfe with wearing a fooles coate', Heywood had aptly replied, 'It is lesse hurtfull to the common-weale, when wisemen goe in fooles coates, than when fooles goe in wise mens gownes'. (As we have seen, Heywood himself could play the fool on occasion.) According to Thomas Nashe (writing in 1592), Pace had been jester to the duke of Norfolk. Cardinal Allen, who in his early years was a member of Norfolk's household, tells of the fool's meeting with the Protestant controversialist Bishop Jewell at a time when the circulation of Catholic books

William Cecil (Lord Burleigh) on a donkey (Bodleian Library, Oxford: Poole 73)

had been interdicted in England. Greeting the bishop with a courtly bow, Pace is said to have assured him, 'Now, my Lord, you may be at rest with these fellows [his opponents in religion] for you are quit by Proclamation' – implying, of course, that he would otherwise have had the worst of the argument.[17]

Francis Bacon reports that eventually 'some persuaded the Queen that he [Pace] should come to her; undertaking for him that he should keep compass'; but when admitted to her presence, the fool was unable to resist the challenge of Elizabeth's 'Come on, Pace; now we shall hear of our faults', in replying, 'I do not use to talk of that that all the town talks of'.[18] It was their only reported encounter.

The offence of an otherwise unknown fool called Fulsharst was not against the queen herself but Sir William Cecil, her Secretary of State, and was to land him in jail. As Cecil recorded (with a certain smugness) in his diary for June 1566, 'Fulsharst, a Foole, was suborned to speak slanderously of me at Greenwych to the Queen's Majesty; for which he was committed to Bridewell'.[19] (Bridewell was then used as a prison for vagabonds and recusant priests, and was notorious for its treadmill.)

Jack Grene was succeeded at court by Monarcho, the most eccentric of all Elizabeth's fools and the only one to have been named by Shakespeare; in answer to the Princess's question in *Love's Labour's Lost* as to 'What plume of feathers is he that indited this letter?', Boyet tells her,

> This Armado is a Spaniard, that keeps here in court;
> A phantasime, a Monarcho, and one that makes sport
> To the Prince and his book-mates.

A series of minutely detailed livery warrants issued to Thomas Ludwell, the queen's head livery tailor, and other of her artificers, extends from 1568 to 1575, and provides some clues to Monarcho's character and situation. The first, in which he is referred to simply as 'an Italian named Monarko', was for a gown of 'Red grograine chamblett', edged at the bottom with three 'gardes' (concentric bands) of richly decorated velvet; a four-quartered jerkin of the same material striped with blue velvet and decorated with copper-gold lace and buttons; and a doublet of 'striped sackecloth', 'fased' with red taffeta and padded and strengthened with fustian and cotton wool, with silk buttons.[20] The garded gown indicates a liveried status in the household; the combination of sackcloth and taffeta in the doublet reflects the ambivalent identity of a maintained nobody with delusions of grandeur. (The dutiful daughter Mildred in *Eastward Ho!* remarks that it is 'like a fool' to 'mix sackcloth with satin'.[21])

Adam Bland was commissioned to fur the gown and doublet with a dozen fox skins and 151 lamb skins for 'winter wear', and Hammond to make a hat to go with them of blue taffeta embroidered with 'Egles of golde and silke' and other devices costing 25s. Another garded gown was made for him in the following summer, along with a jerkin of tawny Spanish leather, a pair of slops, and Spanish shoes. (Thomas Nashe writes of him in 1596 as having worn 'crownes on his shooes'.[22]) At the same time, he received a velvet cap, a girdle, garters and gloves, and six shirts. Similar suits were made for him in 1574 and the following year: the last included a gown of 'olde Tyncell' (perhaps from one of the queen's discarded dresses), and another doublet of striped sackcloth trimmed with lace. 'On gallant robes', the popular poet Thomas Churchyard tells us, 'his greatest glorie stood,/ Yet garments bare could never daunt his minde.'[23]

More direct evidence of the nature of Monarcho's mental condition emerges from an account of a public debate that took place at about this time between himself and two members of the Spanish embassy in London on the question of who was 'soveraigne of the world'. Monarcho (whose real name is there said to have been Bergamasco) 'maintained himself to be he, and named their king to be but his viceroy for Spaine, the other two with great fury denying it'.[24] For the audience of Londoners the joke lay, of course, in the Spaniards' fury; but how far, if at all, Monarcho was privy to it – the extent to which he actually believed in the fantastic claims he was making – remains uncertain. Reginald Scot, in his *Discoverie of Witchcraft* of 1584, likens him to the classical madman Thrasyllus as suffering from a melancholic humour that, in the case of the Greek, led him to believe 'that all the ships, which arrived at port Pyraeus, were his', and goes on to say that 'The Italian, whom we called here in England, the Monarch, was possessed with the like spirit or conceipt'.[25]

But Churchyard, in his epitaph to 'The Phantasticall Monarke' already quoted, while admitting that his 'pride and pompe was somewhat vaine', asserts that

> The Monarcke had a deepe discoursyng braine;
> Alone with freend he could of wonders treate,
> In publicke place pronounce a sentence greate.
> No matche for fooles, if wisemen were in place,
> No mate at meale to sit with common sort:
> Both graue of looks and fatherlike of face,
> Of judgement quicke, of comely forme and port.
> Moste bent to words on hye and solempne daies,
> Of diet fine, and daintie diuerse waies:
> And well disposde, if Prince did pleasure take,
> At any mirthe that he poore man could make . . .[26]

This suggests there was an element of self-awareness in Monarcho's performance of his role, and that he was sensible to its effects. A true madman would not have been half so impressive as Monarcho clearly was to his contemporaries; nor would he, I suggest, have been tolerated for more than half a day in Elizabeth's court where we know that he remained for five or six years. Perhaps he was what has since been defined as a monomaniac: an otherwise sane person in the obsessive hold of a single fallacious idea. The warrant for Monarcho's suit of 1575 is the last reference to him in the Wardrobe accounts; as Churchyard's epitaph was published in 1580, he must have died at some time between those two dates.

Previously, he had been joined at court, if only briefly, by a certain Hoyden (a word then applied to men as well as to boisterous girls), for whom a pair of 'canyons' (thigh-fitting extensions of trunk hose, reaching to the knee) were made in 1572; and then by William Shenton, for whom Ludwell provided three complete outfits in 1574 and 1575. Both men are described in the warrants simply as 'fool' or 'the said fool', rather than with the royal possessive, 'our fool', as used of Grene. Two of the outfits ordered for Shenton included gaskins and – perhaps in imitation of Monarcho – doublets of striped sackcloth.

The second of Shenton's outfits was more elaborate and distinctive. There was a coat of wrought velvet and tufted taffeta, 'paned' in red, green and yellow, feathered hats, and two richly decorated cloth 'Cases for his Instrumentes'.

For the first time in all the Wardrobe accounts I have quoted in this and previous chapters the coat justifies in its use of panes of different coloured cloth the description of 'particoloured'. Along with this second suit, Shenton was issued with a featherbed and bolster, a pair of blankets, two pairs of sheets, six shirts, two quilted nightcaps and six pairs of shoes, which leave no doubt as to his resident status. We are not told what instruments were housed in his cases. Perhaps, like Tarlton (and Shakespeare's Feste) he played tabor and pipe.[27]

But the queen seems to have tired of Shenton rather quickly as there is no further mention of him after 1575 when, as we have seen, Monarcho also left the scene.

Some blank years follow in the sequence of fools at Elizabeth's court. The queen did, however, retain the custom first established by her grandfather Henry VII of including a fool (usually an innocent) in her riding household when she went on progress, which she did in most summers. The names of two of these are recorded. At Canterbury in 1573, 'Walter the Jester' received a tip from the City Fathers, with a long list of the queen's other attendants including her bearward, trumpeters and musicians. The musicians got 40*s* between them, the trumpeters 30*s*, the bearward 10*s* for himself, and Walter 3*s* 4*d*.[28] In the Wardrobe accounts for 1575/6, there is an item of 'one Saddle covered with motley . . . for Will our Foole', which Leslie Hotson cites in support of his thesis that motley was originally a cloth of mixed threads like homespun or tweed, predominantly 'sad' in colour. (It was not only fools who were provided with it; it was in general use at this time as padding for the backs of asses and colts, for cloak-bags, and soldiers' 'cassocks' or overcoats.)[29]

In the matter of Elizabeth's fools, the decade of the eighties belongs in a special way to Richard Tarlton; and it is time to say a little more about this favourite entertainer of hers, who was also the first court fool to achieve national celebrity for his genius as a comedian. His life as a leading member of the Queen's Players and his influence on the drama of the period will be examined in the following chapter; here we shall focus on his concurrent career as Elizabeth's jester.

There are varied accounts of Tarlton's origins. Dr Fuller, writing some fifty years after his death and mistakenly giving his first name as Thomas, states Tarlton's birthplace to have been Condover in Shropshire. 'Here', he tells us, 'he was in the field keeping his Fathers Swine, when a Servant of Robert Earl of Leicester (passing his way to his Lords Lands in his Barony of Denbighe) was so highly pleased with his *happy unhappy* answers, that he brought him to Court, where he became the most famous Jester to Queen Elizabeth.'[30] But the player and playwright Robert Wilson, a contemporary and close colleague of Tarlton's, contradicts Fuller in his play, *The three Lords and three Ladies of London*, where one of the characters (Simplicity) shows another (Will) Tarlton's portrait, and asks him, 'Didst thou never know Tarlton?' 'No', says Will, 'what was that Tarlton? I never knew him', and Simplicity replies,

> What was he? A prentice in his youth of this honourable city, God be with him. When he was young, he was leaning to the trade that my wife useth now, and I have used, *vide lice shirt* [*videlicet*] water-bearing. I-wis, he hath toss'd a tankard in Cornhill ere now: if thou knew'st not him, thou knowest nobody . . .

And a little later, Simplicity says of him,

> O it was a fine fellow, as e'er was born:
> There will never come his like, while the earth can corn.
> O passing fine Tarlton! I would thou hadst lived yet.[31]

Wilson's play was first published in 1590, only two years after Tarlton's death, and its author was in a much better position than Fuller to know the truth of the matter. In the 1570s, Wilson had been one of Leicester's Men, and it is possible

Drawing of Richard Tarlton by John Scottowe, c. 1588 (British Library: MS Harley 3885, f. 19, detail)

that his association with Tarlton began at that time. At all events, when, in 1583, the Queen's Players were brought together by Walsingham, both Wilson and Tarlton were members of it, along with several other former Leicester's Men including James Burbage, builder of the first theatre and father of Richard. Wilson's words of tribute and farewell to his former colleague are the more telling for having been given to Simplicity, a part that he himself is thought to have played.

On the strength of their membership of the new company, Tarlton and his fellows were appointed Ordinary Grooms of the Queen's Chamber – a position that Shakespeare was later to occupy. Though the office was more nominal than real (it entitled the holders to a livery but not, it would seem, to any regular wage), it did carry a certain prestige; relevant here because it put Tarlton on a different footing from any of his predecessors among Elizabeth's fools. Unlike them, he was never resident at court, never wholly dependent on jesting for his livelihood. Indeed, at one point, he is said to have been dismissed for scurrilous reflections on Leicester and Raleigh, but, if so, he was soon restored to favour; for the true source of the exceptional freedom he enjoyed, at court as elsewhere, lay in the extraordinary nature of his comedic gifts.

Though Tarlton was a talented author of ballads and plays, a Master of Fence, and, by his development of the jig and in other ways, was to have a profound effect on Elizabethan popular theatre, as a performer he was what we would now describe as a low comedian, more reliant on facial expression and gesture for his effects than on literary artifice or satirical comments. In that respect, he was at an opposite pole to Pace, and, as such, greatly preferred by the queen. As Henry Peacham was later to declare, Tarlton had only to thrust his head out of the tire-house door to

> Set all the multitude in such a laughter,
> They could not hold for scarse an houre after.[32]

Several accounts of his solo performances for Elizabeth survive. Fuller (perhaps on firmer ground for these later phases of the fool's career) tells us that when the queen 'was serious (I dare not say sullen) and out of good humour, he could un-dumpish her at his pleasure. Her highest Favourites, would in some Cases, go to Tarleton, before they would go to the Queen, and he was their Usher to prepare their advantageous access unto Her. In a word, He told the Queen more of her faults, than most of her Chaplains, and cured her Melancholy better than all of her Physicians.'[33]

Only a few of the posthumous *Tarlton's Jests* (a typical and, for the most part, disappointingly unfunny jest-book of the period) throw any light on his activities as court fool. One features Tarlton's version of that favourite and universal resort of the low comedian, the 'drunk act'. When he had called noisily for beer and some had been brought to him, the queen, entering into the spirit of the occasion, commanded that he should have no more or 'he will play the beast, and so shame himselfe'. 'Feare not you', replied Tarlton, doubtless with a large hiccup, 'for your beere is small enough.'[34]

Other evidence of his court fooling survives only on a scrap of paper found in the state archives attached to a document of August 1588, which is the more reliable for not having been subject to later revision or expansion:

> How Tarlton played the God Luz with a flitch of bacon at his back, and how the Queen bade them take away the knave for making her to laugh so excessively, as he fought against her little dog, Perrico de Faldas, with his sword and long staffe, and bade the Queen take off her mastie; and what my Lord Sussex and Tarlton said to one another. The three things that make a woman lovely.[35]

Tarlton's planned performance as the 'God Luz' remains a puzzle because, of course, he never got to it. Excited by the scent of the bacon he was carrying, the queen's lapdog provided much better material for fun as Tarlton pretended terror and allowed it to chase him round the chamber. This capacity for making use of chance circumstances, as well as his readiness to engage in impromptu badinage with Sussex, confirm his contemporary reputation as an extemporiser. Howes, for example (in his continuation of Stow's *Annales*), says that 'for a wondrous plentifull pleasant extemporall wit', Tarlton was 'the wonder of his time'.[36]

His encounter with Perrico (if the paper recording it truly belongs to the attributed date) occurred in the final month of his life. On 5 September 1588, Sir Francis Walsingham received a letter from him written on his deathbed two days earlier, informing him that

> he had been induced to put all his goods and lands into the hands of a sly fellow, one Mr Adams, fuller of law than of virtue, in trust for his child and his mother. Implores him to see that they are not defrauded; his son being six years of age, a godson of Sir Philip Sidney, whose name he carries, and his mother a silly old widow of fourscore years. Signed in three places by Tarlton, the last time evidently in the agonies of death.[37]

As Tarlton made his will, died, and was buried on the same day, 3 September, he had almost certainly been taken off by the plague. He was buried (in company with Will Somer) at St Leonard's, Shoreditch.

The fool of Elizabeth's declining years was John Garret, of whom John Chamberlain wrote to his friend Carleton in November 1602 as making as fair a show at a tilt as any of the 'young runners'. The occasion was a joust that had been held every year since 1580 in the Great Tiltyard at Whitehall to celebrate the queen's accession on 17 November. Though 'well disguised', Garret is said to have been not so well mounted, 'for his horse was no bigger than a goode bandogge [mastiff]; but he delivered his scutchion with his *impresa* himself and had goode audience of her Majestie, and made her very merry'.[38] (An *impresa* was an elaborately designed and painted insignia with appropriate motto of the kind that Shakespeare and Burbage were paid to make for the earl of Rutland at Belvoir on King James's accession day in 1613.) If Garret was proportionate to his mount, he was either a dwarf or of very small stature.

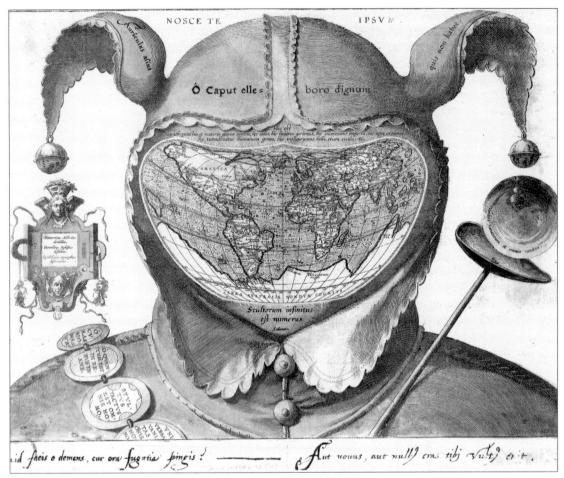

A map of the world as it was known in about 1600 is contained within the traditional symbol of folly, a fool's cap with belled ears. 'What are you doing, mad fellow', a Latin inscription reads, 'why paint fugitive shores? Tomorrow your face will be either new or nothing' (Bodleian Library, Oxford: Douce Portfolio 142.92)

And yet we hear from the contemporary 'water-poet' John Taylor, who imagines his ghost appearing and speaking to him in his *Wit and Mirth* of 1629, that, before coming to court, Garret had served under Norris in Ireland, where

> (as I could) I stood 'gainst Pope and Spaine,
> Whilst some were slaine, and some with want did starue;
> Where shot, and wounds, and knocks I gaue and tooke,
> Untill at last, halfe maimed as I was,
> A man decrepit, I those warres forsooke,
> And (with my Passe) did to my country passe . . .

According to this account, Garret followed the Monarcho fashion by clothing himself in sackcloth:

> His cloake was Sack, but not the Sacke of Spaine,
> Canara, Mallago, or sprightfull Shery,
> But made of Sack-cloth, such as beares the graine,
> Good salt, and coles, which makes the Porters weary;
> Lac'd round about with platted wheaten straw,
> For which he nothing to the Silke-man owed;
> A wearing neuer mentioned in the Law,
> And yet, far off, like good gold lace it show'd.
> Lin'd was his mantle with good Essex plush,
> Pyde Calues skins, or Veale sattin, which you will:
> It neuer was worne threedbare with a brush,
> It (naturally) sau'd the labour still.
> A hat like Grantham steeple: for the crowne
> Or Piramide was large in Altitude:
> With frugall brim, whereby he still was knowne
> From other men amongst a multitude.

'And to the Court', Garret is supposed as saying,

> I often made resort
> When Englands mighty Queene Elizabeth
> Allow'd me entertainment for disport;
> Then by the foretop did I take old time:
> Then were not halfe so many fooles as now;
> Then was my haruest, and my only prime,
> My purse receiuing what my wit did plow.[39]

After the death of the queen, in April 1604, his purse received a late harvest of '40 marks per annum, for life'.[40] In James's reign (if the same man is referred to), he joined Queen Anne's Players, and received mourning dress for her funeral in 1619. He lived on into the reign of Charles, and died – according to an epitaph of 1640 – a victim, not of sack, but claret.

> Gone is John Garret, who to all mens thinking,
> For love to claret, kill'd himselfe with drinking.[41]

But in the meantime, from December 1594, we know that Shakespeare had begun to appear at court with Lord Hunsdon's new company of players (soon to become the Lord Chamberlain's Men), along with their foremost clown William Kempe, whom Nashe was to address as 'Iestmonger and Vice-gerent generall to the Ghost of Dicke Tarlton'.[42] According to tradition, it was the queen who commanded of Shakespeare *The Merry Wives of Windsor*. If, in the final years of her reign,

Elizabeth lacked a Tarlton, she had Falstaff, Dogberry and Feste to 'undumpish' her.

The process whereby the fools moved their centre of operations from court to stage was already well advanced. But to tell the story of that – its causes and effects – requires another chapter.

Plate 9(a): A fourteenth-century, hooded fool dances with his marotte, scattering bread or stones. The king appeals for guidance to God the Father (British Library: MS Harley 2897, f. 42ᵛ, detail)

Plate 9(b): A voluminous cloak hides the nakedness of a frantic fool with marotte and wafer. His head has been tonsured. French psalter of the early fourteenth century (Bodleian Library, Oxford: MS Douce 211, f. 258ᵛ, detail)

Plate 10(a): Described as 'perhaps the most foolish-looking Fool in 13th-century English illumination' (Nigel Morgan), this 'vigorously characterised' individual from the Coldingham Breviary of 1270–80 is dressed as a monk and may actually have been one (British Library: MS Harley 4664, f. 145ᵛ, detail)

Plate 10(b): A fool (whose head and arm have been badly rubbed) is confronted by a demon with claws outstretched to seize him. Flemish, early fourteenth century (Bodleian Library, Oxford: MS Laud lat. 84, f. 130, detail)

Plate 11(a): Rare depiction of a fool bishop from an English Bible of the first half of the thirteenth century. The mitred fool, sitting cross-legged on a bishop's chair, points to his fool's club as if in excuse and is blessed by a seemingly benevolent Christ. The original is of thumbnail size (by permission of the Warden and Fellows of New College, Oxford: MS 7, f. 142b, detail)

Sed sperauit in multitudine diuitiaⱬ
suarum: & preualuit in vanitate sua.

Ego autem sicut oliua fructifera in
domo Dei speraui in misericordia Dei
in eternum, & in seculum seculi.

Confitebor tibi in seculum quia fecisti
& expectabo nomen tuum quoniam bonū est
in conspectu sanctorum tuorum Gloria
patri Sicut erat. Dixit insipiēs
in corde suo nō est Deꝰ
Corrupti sūt

Plate 11(b): a page from Henry VIII's personal psalter, written and decorated for him by a Frenchman, David Mallard, in about 1540. The miniature for Psalm 52 shows the king in the role of David, playing a Welsh harp, and Will Somer, Henry's fool, as the fool of the psalm (British Library: MS Royal 2.A.XVI, f. 63ᵛ)

Plate 12: The Family of Henry VIII *by an unknown artist of* c. *1545 (oil on canvas, 141×355cm). Will Somer stands in the archway on the extreme right; a maidservant whom I take to be Princess Mary's innocent, Jane, is in the archway to the left (The Royal Collection, © Her Majesty the Queen)*

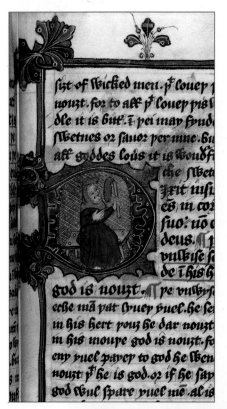

Plate 13(a): A rarely depicted female innocent with lolling tongue, wearing a feather, from a fifteenth-century English breviary (Bodleian Library, Oxford: MS Bodley 953, p. 173, detail)

Plate 13(b): The bulk of this English psalter was made in about 1260, leaving spaces for illuminated initials to be added later. The fool shown here, in his parti-coloured habit de fou *with eared hood and bells, was painted in the fifteenth century and betrays French influence (Bodleian Library, Oxford: MS Laud.lat 114, f. 71, detail)*

Plate 14(a): Portrait of Tom Skelton, domestic fool of the Penningtons of Muncaster Castle, Cumbria, c. 1659 (Muncaster Castle Collection, courtesy of the Pennington family)

Plate 14(b): The 'Haigh Hall' portrait of Tom, probably deriving from the Muncaster picture and somewhat later in date, c. 1676 (The Shakespeare Institute, Stratford-on-Avon)

Plate 14(c): John Green in the role of Nemo (Nobody), watercolour painting from a manuscript of English plays in German translation of 1608 (by friendly permission of the Stiftsarchiv Rein, Styria, Austria)

Plate 15: Anthony Van Dyck, portrait of Queen Henrietta Maria with Sir Jeffery Hudson of 1633 (oil on canvas, 219×135 cm). The knighthood attributed to Jeffery in the formal title of this portrait is apocryphal (Samuel H. Kress Collection, © Board of Trustees, National Gallery of Art, Washington, DC)

CHAPTER 14

The Player Fools

With exception perhaps of Monarcho, Elizabeth's fools were all of the clever, artificial kind; and, during her reign, one of them, Tarlton, was already spending more time on tour than he was at court. The subsequent history of the court jesters may be viewed in two ways: as a process of enfranchisement from the remaining restraints of royal and magnate patronage as more remunerative opportunities opened up to them, or as a forced accommodation to changing tastes and conditions. Both points of view are valid, and may have been complementary; for the pressure for change brought about by the shifting pattern of court patronage is likely to have prompted a perception on the part of the fools that their best interests lay in the future elsewhere. But however we look at it, the story that has still to be told can only be understood in relation to larger developments in drama and the theatre that were taking place at the same time, especially the rise in importance of the players.

Tarlton has been seen to have had a foot in both worlds: the world of the court as Elizabeth's jester and that of the popular stage as a leading member of the Queen's Players; but to discover how he came to assume this double role, we shall need to retrace our steps a little.

The origins of professional theatre in England lie much further back in time than is often supposed. Though theatres in the material sense of buildings constructed primarily, if not exclusively, for the performance of plays date, it is true, mainly from the Elizabethan period, it is now well established that groups of travelling minstrel-players had been on the road from early in the thirteenth century.

As Richard Axton has pointed out, the 'representation of the Lord's resurrection' in St John's churchyard at Beverley in about 1220 was performed outdoors in summer (out of its liturgical season) on the north, unhallowed side of the church by 'masked actors, as usual (*larvatorum, ut assolet*)' – a troupe of professional players.[1] The plays were called 'interludes' and the players 'interluders' probably because they provided amusement between the courses of formal dinners and feasts at court and in magnate households, where drama might alternate with music or displays of tumbling and other minstrel skills. (The drama was not considered to be of any greater value.) The rewards given to Griscote, Visage and Magote at the wedding feast of Elizabeth of Rhuddlan and the count of Holland at Ipswich in 1297 (cited in Chapter 5) would have been for an entertainment of this kind. In 1384/5, players (*ludentibus interludium*) were visiting King's Lynn in Norfolk and were rewarded by the mayor for their performances (again, out of their proper liturgical time) of a Corpus Christi miracle play and another on the subject of St Thomas Martyr (Thomas Becket). At Christmas 1406, Richard Mitford, bishop of Salisbury, was entertained by four *hominibus del Vise ludentibus i interludium*; and in 1428, again at Christmas, the young Henry VI had enjoyed the *Jeuues* (plays) and *Entreludes* of *Jakke Travaill & ses Compaignons*.[2] These early players travelled and performed in groups of three or four, and their use of masks (visers), enabling them to assume a variety of roles and to switch roles with ease and rapidity, is often indicated.

The first of such companies known to have been retained by magnate patrons were 'my Lord of Essex men, plaiers' and the four 'pleyers of my lord of Gloucestres' (the future Richard III) rewarded by Sir John Howard in 1482. It is not known if Richard retained his company on becoming king, but Henry VII employed four such men, described unequivocally as 'lusores regis, alias, in lingua Anglicana, les pleyars of the Kyngs enterluds' in 1494. Their leader was a man called John English; they received five marks a year, and, when not required at court, went on tour like other minstrels.[3]

It is likely that clever fools in the service of earlier kings – men such as Edward I's Tom – took part on occasion in dramatic performances of a comedic kind, but we have no firm evidence of this. The first recorded instance of a royal fool transferring in a permanent way to the profession of player relates to John Scot in the reign of Henry VII.

'Scot the fole' makes his first appearance in Henry's Privy Purse accounts on New Year's Day, 1495. The regularity of his rewards in subsequent years – receiving half-a-mark, usually twice a year at New Year and Easter as 'the Scottishe fole' – indicates payment of a regular stipend.[4] In 1494/5, the king's interluders were named as John English, Edward May, Richard Gibson and John Hamond. In 1503, these four were to accompany Henry's daughter Margaret to Edinburgh for her marriage to James IV of Scotland.[5] It may have been in the course of this visit, or shortly after their return from the north, that Scot was invited to join the company. Certainly, after March 1502 there are no further payments to him from the Privy Purse, and in 1503/4 John Scot was listed in an Exchequer account with English, Gibson and Hamond as an interluder.[6] There were other changes. May dropped out and was replaced by a William Rutter, and he in turn by Thomas Sydburgh or Sudbury. At Henry's funeral in 1509, the King's Players were named as English, Scot, Hamond, Sydburgh and Gibson.[7] Their number had thus increased to five.

John Scot continued to serve as an interluder for the first nineteen or twenty years of the reign of Henry VIII, who doubled both the size of the company and its Exchequer allowance. By introducing different scales of payment, with some individuals getting more and others less, the king was able to maintain a permanent establishment of from eight to ten players. But references in the State Papers to the 'old players' as receiving higher supplementary rewards than the others suggest that this augmented establishment continued to perform in separate units of four to five players each. (In 1509, Gibson was appointed Porter and Yeoman of the Great Wardrobe and thus became responsible for the day-today supply of costumes and props to them both.)[8] Both groups were active in touring.[9] At court they might have come together on special occasions to take part in more elaborate pageants and disguisings; but the earliest surviving court interludes – those written by the minstrel and epigrammatist John Heywood between 1519 and 1528 – contain (with one exception) no more than three or four roles and so could easily be cast from a single company, presumably the 'old players' who were the king's favourites.

Heywood, who was a skilled singer, may himself have taken some of these roles.[10] In *A Play of Love* (ll. 245ff.), 'Lover belovyd' is given a solo for which no text is supplied; it would not have been necessary if its author sang it. In *The Foure PP* (ll. 310–21), it is the Potycary who takes the lead in a duet with the Pedler, who is referred to ironically by Potycary as a 'ryght syngynge man'.

In two of the plays, *A Play of Love* and *Wether*, the fool parts are described as 'vyses'. Much scholarly ink has been expended on this term 'vice', which appears here for the first time, but evidence of other sixteenth-century usage reveals that originally it was no more than a synonym for 'clever fool' as opposed to a simple innocent.[11] In Heywood's vocabulary, the word carries no implication of 'vice' in the ethical sense. Heywood's vices are cocky, manipulative and bawdy of speech, but not malicious. Axton and Happé have said of such characters that they are 'play-makers and go-betweens, not fixed in any social "estate", but able to mimic any. They relate as easily to the audience as to the other players, taking liberties with both. Their capers and apparent improvisations add movement, dance perhaps, and song-like antics often reminiscent of children's games.'[12] In other words, they are clever fools, jesters, whose irreverent play, familiar at court, Heywood here adapts to a dramatic purpose, bringing lightness and variety to his serio-comic debates. He did not have far to go to find an exemplar; John Scot, the former court fool, was already at hand as an established member of the 'old players'.

The supposition that Scot was used in this way is supported by the fact that several of the plays' most important parts, including one of the specified vices, were written for a dwarf or man of diminutive stature. *Witty and Witless* is an Erasmian debate between characters called John and James on the question of whether it is better to be a wise man or a fool. John, when getting the worst of the argument, angrily dismisses James (who speaks for the fool) as 'Small, ah horson elfe' (l. 120), and 'elfe' was then a synonym for 'dwarf'.[13] In *The Pardoner and the Frere*, the same term is applied to the Friar (l. 630). Exceptionally, *Wether* has a cast of eleven, in which the interluders may have been joined by some of Heywood's pupils from the song school of St Paul's. The vice part, Mery Report, describes himself as 'so lyghte an elfe' (l. 121) and 'of a lyttel whelpe' (l. 300); and when a small boy ('the lest that can play') enters to complain to Jove about a scarcity of snow for making snowballs and overhears Mery Report saying to the audience, 'The greatest frende ye have in felde or towne/Standynge a typ-to shall not reche your crowne', the boy comments in an aside, 'The same is even he by al lycklyhod' (ll. 1000–3). Mery Report also performs a trick that is still in use by pantomime dwarfs. Standing with his back to the audience, he puts his head between his legs and, peering upwards, pretends to have lost it.

Alas, my necke, goddes pyty, where is my hed?
By Saynt Yve, I feare me I shall be ded!
And yf I were, me thynke yt were no wonder
Syns my hed and my body is so farre asonder. (ll. 325–8)

In the other of Heywood's interludes in which a vice (No lover nor loved) is designated, the character makes his entrance through the audience with a crown of squibs firing off from his head, and runs about the place 'tyll the fyre in the squybs be spent'.[14]

The older man, John English, the leader of the interluders and the most highly paid, is likely to have played parts such as Jove, the central character in *Wether*, and Jerome, who swings the argument back towards wisdom in *A Play of Love*. The slight but dignified figure of Heywood (as shown in his portrait) along with English and Scot, their diminutive fool, would have made an arresting stage trio.

I have suggested that the move from court to stage on the part of the fools may be seen as a first stage in their progressive liberation from the restraints imposed by their status as royal retainers, but it cannot be claimed that in switching from court fool to interluder Scot achieved very much in that way. In doing so, he may well have extended the span of his active career; but in 1528/9 he was in serious trouble for 'rebukynge of the shreffes' (Sheriffs) – perhaps a satirical skit at their expense – and was put in Newgate, where he remained for a week. He was then 'ledde betwene two of the offecers from Newgat thorrow London and soe to Newgat agayne . . . and delyverd home to hys howse'. Did his route 'thorrow London' take in St Paul's Cross, and was he there obliged to make public confession of his fault? John Heywood was to make that humiliating journey in 1544, in consequence of his alleged involvement in a political plot against Cromwell, but was later to enjoy a renaissance of his fortunes with the accession of Mary. Scot knew no such recovery for 'he toke soch a thowte [melancholy] that he dyde, for he went in hys shurte' – a probable reference to the white sheet that penitents were made to wear.[15] A sad end to thirty-five years of jesting and playing!

Richard Tarlton, as I have said, straddled the two worlds of the court and the stage, and I have already written of his role as Elizabeth's jester. As a leading 'sharer' of the Queen's Men, he was active as player, both at court and on tour, from 1583 (when the company was formed) to the time of his death in 1588. There were twelve fellows in all and, apart from Tarlton and his friend Robert Wilson (of whom more a little later), these included James Burbage and John Laneham from Leicester's Men, Laurence and John Dutton from the earl of Warwick's, and John Bentley and John Singer (another fool) from other noblemen's companies; all 'rare men' in their way and the best of their profession in the period. But no sooner had they come together, early in 1583, than they were obliged to leave London because of the plague. By June of that year they had reached Norwich, and on 9 July were in Cambridge. In the years that followed they acted at court for the queen (usually on Boxing Day or shortly afterwards)

John Heywood as pictured in the book of his allegorical poem, The Spider and the Flie, *printed 1556 (Courtauld Institute of Art, London)*

every year from 1584 to 1588, and appeared in London also at Burbage's Theatre. In the provinces, we find them visiting Canterbury, Dover, Abingdon, Southampton, Bath, Cambridge, Ipswich, Norwich, Leicester and York, Exeter and Bristol, Coventry, Worcester, Gloucester and Stratford-on-Avon, where, as we have seen, it is possible that Shakespeare was recruited.[16]

Along the way, we catch some revealing glimpses of Tarlton's stage performances. Thomas Nashe describes how, in one country town, when Tarlton 'first peept out his head' and 'the people began exceedingly to laugh', an officious Justice, seeing that with his 'beckes and nods hee could not make them cease', 'went with his staffe, and beat them vnmercifully on the bare pates, in that they, being but Farmers & poore countrey Hyndes, would presume to laugh at the Queenes men, and make no more account of her cloath in his presence'[17] – an interesting reflection of the ambivalence of Tarlton's status as both royal retainer and popular clown. Henry Peacham remembers seeing him act the part of a third son at the deathbed of his wealthy father. His elder brothers had entered in turn before him and, on being promised a rich inheritance, both had expressed the pious hope that the father would live to enjoy it himself. Then Tarlton had come in 'like a rogue in a foule shirt without a band, and in a blew coat with one sleeve, his stockings out at the heeles, and his head full of straw and feathers', whom the father rebuked as an ungracious villain to whom he had nothing to bequeath 'but the gallowes and a rope'. To this Tarlton, weeping and sobbing at the bedside as his brothers had done, protested 'Father, I doe not desire it, I trust in God you shall live to enjoy it your selfe'.[18]

But if Tarlton can truly be said to have embodied in his own person the dual roles of court jester and stage clown, he also went beyond them, and thus anticipated a further enlargement of the fools' sphere of activity from the confines of the play to that *tota joculatorum scena* – the entertainment scene as a whole – from which they had originally come and were destined to return. He was as famous in his day as a deviser and performer of jigs (a lost performance art involving story, dance and song) as he was as a player, and one of the *Jests* relates how, 'While the queenes players lay in Worcester city to get money, it was his custome for to sing extemporare of theames given him.'[19] For these solo performances, he dressed as a rustic and accompanied his singing and dancing with tabor and pipe. His costume on such occasions is described by Henry Chettle in his *Kind-Hartes Dreame* of 1592, where he claims to have recognised Tarlton's ghost by his 'sute of russet, his buttoned cap, his taber, his standing on the toe, and other tricks'.[20]

A marginal entry in Stow's *Annales* tells us that Tarlton was so beloved 'that men use his picture for their signes', and an old historian of Shoreditch confirms that as late as 1798, 'His portrait, with tabor and pipe, still serves as a sign to an alehouse in the Borough'[21] – the ultimate accolade that popular fame in England can bestow.

Tarlton, in spite of his lack of formal education, was far from being illiterate – at least in the modern sense. He was the author of published ballads, and of one of the most popular plays of his time, *The Seven Deadly Sins*, an elaborate morality

RICHARD TARLTON.

This near-contemporary drawing of Tarlton appears to be a simplified version of the Scottowe portrait shown on p. 115 (Courtauld Institute of Art, London)

in two autonomous parts. First acted by the Queen's Men, when he was a member of that company, it was revived by Henslowe for Lord Strange's Men at the Rose in 1592, and survives only in the form of a 'Plot', reminding the players at the Rose of the sequence of scenes and characters in its second part in which they were required to appear. But as an author, Tarlton was far exceeded, both in the number and quality of his writings, by another stage fool of the time, his old friend and colleague Robert Wilson – an undeservedly neglected figure of the pre-Shakespearean drama. Thomas Lodge (in his reply to Gosson's *Schoole of Abuse*) describes Wilson's lost play, *Shorte and Sweete*, as 'a peece surely worthy prayse, the practise of a good scholler'; he was one of the first of the popular dramatists to employ passages of blank verse in his plays, and Francis Meeres, whose praises of Shakespeare in his *Palladis Tamia* are so often quoted, goes so far as to commend Wilson and his collaborators of 1598 as 'the best for Comedy amongst us'.[22]

However that may have been, there occurs in Wilson's earliest extant play, *The three Ladies of London* (first published in 1584) a passage that marks a significant moment in the development of Tudor drama. In its structure and content, *The three Ladies* stands at a turning point of the change from Morality to Comedy, and its *dramatis personae* bring together old morality types such as Love, Conscience and the not-so-simple Simplicity (the fool's part, probably acted by Wilson himself) with named individuals including the benevolent Jew, Gerontus. The crucial moment occurs in the final scene, when, as in the Corpus Christi cycle plays, the characters are brought to judgement. The judge is named as Sir Nicholas Nemo (Nobody), whose real identity is explained in Wilson's sequel to *The three Ladies*, in which Nemo also appears and is described as 'the most only one/That draws no breath but of th'eternal air'.[23] But when Nemo takes his seat and orders the prisoners to be brought before him, only Love, Lucre and Conscience are still to be found. 'Where is that wretch Dissimulation?', Nemo demands.

Diligence:	He hath transformed himself after a strange fashion.
Judge:	Fraud! where is he become?
Diligence:	He was seen in the streets, walking in a citizen's gown.
Judge:	What is become of Usury?
Diligence:	He was seen at the Exchange very lately.
Judge:	Tell me, when have you heard of Simony?
Diligence:	He was seen this day walking in Paul's, having conference and very great familiarity with some of the clergy.[24]

The play ends conventionally with Nemo's judgement on the allegorical types that remain. But the vices have flown, to assume the form of individual characters in the familiar world of Elizabethan London. This may be an ingenious device of Wilson's to get round the fact that he has run out of actors (those who had previously played the missing persons being now onstage in other roles); but the point is nevertheless made that the old Morality drama was on its way out, to be replaced by the more focused comedy of Wilson's successors.

Detail from Claes Janzs Visscher's engraving of London in 1616 showing the Globe Theatre
(Folger Shakespeare Library, Washington, DC)

My procession of fools who took to the stage would be incomplete without some treatment of the two men whose playing of the fool parts in Shakespeare's plays was to bring them more lasting fame than that enjoyed by any of their predecessors: William Kempe and Robert Armin. An exploration of the roles that each of them played may also reveal how, under pressure from the practice of doubling, they were progressively absorbed into the company they joined and the ranks of the players.[25]

Like Tarlton, William Kempe pursued a double career, part in, part out of the theatre; but, unlike Tarlton who had combined his theatrical work with service at court as Elizabeth's jester and never left England, Kempe was to venture further afield and establish a European reputation as clown, musician and dancer. It was in the courts of Denmark and the Low Countries that he first attracted notice. At Dunkirk in 1585 he was known as 'Don Gulihelmo'. In the following year we find him at Utrecht and in Denmark, where he was named in an Elsinore payroll as 'Wilhelm Kempe, instrumentist'. (Like most other fools and players of the period, he was skilled as both musician and tumbler. As he was unlikely to have known any Danish or Dutch, he would often have been mainly reliant on his non-verbal skills when performing abroad.) Thomas Nashe dedicated his *Almond for a Parrat* to him in 1590, and tells how he had been embraced and made a fuss of by an Italian comedian in Bergamo merely on the strength of his acquaintance in London with 'Signor Chiarlatano Kempino'. He was the Chaplin of his day.

Our knowledge of Kempe's theatrical career dates from 1593 when he was listed as one of Lord Strange's Men, along with Shakespeare and the Burbages, James and Richard. In 1594, Strange's Men passed under the patronage of the Lord Chamberlain. That Kempe was a principal 'sharer' in the new company appears from a record of 1595 in which he is named with Shakespeare and Richard Burbage as receiving payment for plays given at court in the preceding Christmas season; his name is given first of the three. *Romeo and Juliet* was probably one of those plays, and we know that Kempe played the Capulet servant Peter in it because in the second quarto edition of 1599 the stage direction for Peter's entrance in Act IV, Scene v appears as 'Enter Will Kemp'. The part is tiny (only some forty lines) but gives a clue to Kempe's original stage persona as a country bumpkin or clown, comically out of place among the passionate young blades of Verona. The character was by then an established cliché of Tudor drama, which Kempe had taken over from Tarlton. Perhaps the excellence of Kempe's playing of Peter was felt to justify his tenth or twelfth part of the profits as sharer but, even so, is unlikely to have been his *only* contribution to the performance. There are thirty speaking parts in *Romeo and Juliet*, obviously requiring from the company a large degree of doubling. The sharers would not have stood on their dignity and refused to double minor roles, as the modern actor is inclined to do, when every hired man employed would add to the production's costs and thus reduce their personal share of the profits.

From its beginnings in the fifteenth century, doubling of parts was a characteristic and accepted feature of the native English tradition of playing; one that was to mould the structure of plays written for the professional stage by Marlowe, Shakespeare, their contemporaries and successors to as late as the Civil War and the closure of the public theatres by the Puritans.[26] And by 'doubling' here is meant that the players might often have been required to play, not just one, but two, sometimes three or more additional roles in the course of a performance. As new characters were introduced by the playwright, others were necessarily suppressed, and this might involve the player, not only in a change of role, but a switch from one acting mode to another – from 'straight' to 'character' parts, from drama to comedy, or vice versa.[27]

We know that Kempe (like Tarlton) was an accomplished dancer and inventor of jigs; four of his jigs had been entered in the Stationers' Register in the period

1591–5. He might well have been involved in staging the complex masque scene of the play (I.v) and danced in it as a masker. Marston's lines in his *Scourge of Villainy* of 1598,

> A hall, a hall!
> Room for the spheres, the orbs celestial
> Will dance Kempe's jig . . .

echo Capulet's,

> A hall, a hall, give room! And foot it, girls!
> More light, you knaves, and turn the tables up. (I.v.26–7)

Peter makes his last appearance in IV.v. Characters appearing for the first time in the final act include Romeo's fearful servant, Balthasar. That this may have been one of Kempe's doubles is indicated by another slip of Shakespeare's in the second quarto, where the stage direction for his entrance with Romeo at V.iii.21 reads, 'Enter Romeo and *Peter*'. As the two servants (Balthasar and Peter) belong to opposing houses and are clearly differentiated in both character and diction (Balthasar speaks only in blank verse in tune with the bodeful mood of Act V), this may have been Shakespeare's shorthand for saying that Kempe was to double the part, or, if the stage direction is attributed to a reporter, that he actually did so.[28]

Similar roles to Peter – all designated 'Clown' or 'clownish' – occur in other Shakespeare plays of this early period: the unnamed Clown of *Titus Andronicus*, Costard in *Love's Labour's Lost*, Launce in *The Two Gentlemen of Verona*, and Launcelot Gobbo in *The Merchant of Venice*. They were almost certainly Kempe's; but again, we cannot assume the fool's exemption from the overriding necessity for the players to double wherever possible. In a cast of over twenty, the Clown in *Titus* has no more than the same number of lines in two consecutive scenes of Act IV. When, in the opening scene of the play, Shakespeare's stage direction for the first entrance of Titus names twelve others as accompanying him 'and others as many as can be', we may be sure that Kempe was among them in one disguise or another. As Gobbo, he could easily have doubled Arragon, or the slow-moving Balthasar of III.iv: 'Madam, I go with all convenient speed' – one of the biggest laughs of the play if properly taken, very slowly.[29]

Physically, Kempe was large in build – Costard is chosen for Pompey the Great among the Worthies 'because of his great limb or joint' (V. 1. 119) – but light on his feet. That he was not limited to playing rustic clowns but went on to mine a richer vein of pompous minor officials we know, because his name was attached by Shakespeare to the part of Dogberry in his manuscript of *Much Ado About Nothing*, from which it found its way into the quarto and folio editions of the text, along with that of Richard Cowley as playing Verges. Bottom in *A Midsummer Night's Dream* is of a roughly similar type and may also have been his.

Though still in the realm of conjecture, persuasive reasons have been advanced for giving him Falstaff in early performances of the two parts of *Henry IV*. With aid of padding, the part would have been well within his physical range, but the important clue is in the Epilogue to Part Two:

> If my tongue cannot entreat you to acquit me, will you command me to use my legs? And yet that were but light payment, to dance out of your debt.

The crime the audience is here invited to pardon can only be Falstaff's, for which he has been banished by the king a few moments earlier. The speaker of the Epilogue, therefore, was the player of Falstaff, and also, it appears, a dancer. Kempe, as principal fool of the company who was famed for his jigs, fits both requirements.[30]

In his final lines, the speaker of the Epilogue reverts to his own persona as player to promise a return of Falstaff in the play's sequel.

> One word more. If you be not too much cloyed with fat meat, our humble author will continue the story, with Sir John in it, and make you merry with fair Katherine of France; where, for anything I know, Falstaff shall die of a sweat . . . My tongue is weary; when my legs are too, I will bid you good night.

And so he leads into a final jig, in which he is joined by the rest of the company and exits with them.[31]

Much discussion has revolved around the question of why Shakespeare, having thus promised a return of Falstaff in *Henry V*, should have changed his mind and kept the most popular character of the *Henry IV* plays offstage in their sequel. If, as suggested here, the part was written for, and originally played by Kempe, the reason may lie in Kempe's withdrawal from the company in February or March of 1599, when he sold his share in the newly built Globe and set out on a dancing journey to Norwich, of which he was to publish a lively account in his *Nine Daies Wonder* of 1600. (His name was included by Jonson in his actor list for *Every Man in his Humour* of 1598 but is absent from that of *Every Man out of his Humour* of 1599.)[32] Shakespeare, as a practical man of the theatre, would have been very much alive to the expectations of his public. If Kempe had made Falstaff his own in the two parts of *Henry IV* but was no longer available to play him, their author might well have balked at the need to introduce another actor in the role so soon afterwards, which might also go some way to explain why the Falstaff of *The Merry Wives* of later date is so diminished a sketch of his original self. That Falstaff was one of Kempe's parts prior to 1599 is supported by another 'rogue' stage direction from Shakespeare's 'foul papers'. For, as Dover Wilson points out, the quarto edition of *Henry IV, Part 2* has the direction, 'Enter Will', at II.iv.18, fourteen lines in advance of Falstaff's actual appearance; perhaps a cue for the prompter to check that Kempe was on his way from the tiring-house. Apart from Shakespeare himself, Kempe was the only sharer in the company of 1598 to bear the forename Will.

Though Kempe was to make some later theatre appearances in London with another company, his excursion to Norwich was followed by an extensive European tour. If he had happily failed to dance himself 'out of the world' – as

A bearded Kempe dancing on his way to Norwich from the title page of Kemps Nine Daies Wonder *of 1600 (Folger Shakespeare Library, Washington, DC)*

claimed by one of the ballad-mongers of whom he complains in *Nine Daies Wonder* – he had effectively danced himself out of the Globe.[33]

Kempe was succeeded as the specialist player of fools in Shakespeare's company by Robert Armin, a man of a wholly different stamp whom we have already encountered as a popular author and acknowledged authority on the subject of court and domestic fools. Curiously, his first known writing to be published was a preface to a work of religious controversy, *A Brief Resolution of the Right Religion* of 1590. Later, in 1609, he was to publish a verse translation from the Italian of Straparola, in which he claims to have been 'writ down an ass in his time'. (His ghost might justly complain that he has continued to be so.)

Armin had begun life as apprentice to a London goldsmith, and is said to have been a protégé of Tarlton's, who prophesied that he should 'enjoy my clownes sute after me'.[34] He had begun his theatrical career as one of Lord Chandos's Men. Though he followed Kempe into the Chamberlain's Company, he was of the same generation.

In contrast to the rustic clowns and buffoons of Kempe, Armin's Shakespearean roles (the ones written for him, rather than those he inherited) were predominantly licensed fools of the courtly type, of which Touchstone and

Feste are the outstanding examples. As such, they reverse the tendency in Shakespeare's earlier plays for the fools to assume the characteristics of people in ordinary life who, for one reason or another, are accounted foolish, to retain a separate identity as fools in the professional sense. This was an innovation in Jacobean drama, a new departure for Shakespeare that may well have owed its inspiration to his knowledge of Elizabeth's jesters. Touchstone belongs to the world of the exiled court rather than to the rustic population of the Forest of Arden, where the Duke and his courtiers have taken refuge. Feste asserts the semi-independent status of a Tarlton or a Garret. In contrast to Olivia's household servants, Fabian and Maria, and to her resident buffoons, Sir Toby and Sir Andrew, he belongs to nobody; for 'Foolery, sir, does walk about the orb like the sun, it shines everywhere' (*Twelfth Night*, III.i.39–40). Like the earlier vice of the interludes, if Feste belongs to anybody or anything, it is to the world of the play. The clown Lavache of *All's Well that Ends Well* of later date exhibits a similar restlessness. Lavache is a man without a master who 'runs where he will' (IV.v.64), but has nowhere to go. How much, if at all, the personality or expertise of Armin contributed to this changing conception of the fool's dramatic function is impossible, of course, to say.

The role of the unnamed Fool in *King Lear* (*c.* 1605) was another departure for Shakespeare, and unique in his plays as an expression of that special relationship we have found to have existed between certain historical monarchs and their 'wise naturals', notably Henry VIII and Will Somer. And here, as I have already suggested, a possible source is discernible in Armin's study of such innocents, including Somer, in his *Foole upon Foole* of 1600, which went through three editions in eight years. There is no doubt as to whom this fool belongs; he belongs to Lear, and, when dismissed from the play in Act III, sinks into that limbo of uncertain existence where so many of Shakespeare's suppressed characters go. (In his famous last line, 'And I'll go to bed at noon' – a riddling response to Lear's 'We'll go to supper i' th' morning' (III.vi.82–3) – there may be a glancing reference to Somer's habit of falling asleep at unusual times and in unusual places; a characteristic deriving solely from Armin's account of him.) By 1605, Armin would have been too mature a man to play the 'pretty knave', 'lad' or 'boy' addressed by the king, and the part was probably taken by a boy apprentice under Armin's instruction as a double with Cordelia.[35] Armin himself is more likely to have been cast as Edgar – a more demanding role in which, for the greater part of the play, he is required to disguise himself as the madman Tom. 'Edgar', he tells us (in II.iii), 'I nothing am.' Nor is that the only one of the character's transformations. In IV.vi, he enters 'dressed like a peasant', and, in V.ii, becomes the avenging knight of the play's denouement. Vocally, he begins IV.vi as the peasant, changes to a stranger when he pretends to find his father Gloucester at the foot of the cliff, affects a West Country dialect in his altercation with Oswald, and finishes the scene as Edgar and his father's son.

Armin seems to have delighted in these rapid changes of appearance and diction. As Feste, he fools Malvolio by becoming Sir Topas; and in his own play, *The History of the two Maids of More-clacke* (published 1609), he not only played Blue John (an adult innocent resident in Christ's Hospital of whom he had

THE

Hiſtory of the two Maids of More-clacke

VVith the life and ſimple maner of Ioнн
in the Hoſpitall.

Played by the Children of the Kings
Maieſties Reuels.

Sam

VVritten by Roвеrт Arміn, ſeruant to the Kings
moſt excellent Maieſtie. *K*

LONDON,
Printed by *N.O.* for *Thomas Archer*, and is to be ſold at his
ſhop in Popes-head Pallace; 1 6 0 9.

The title page of Armin's play, History of the two Maids of More-clacke *of 1609, with
portrait of Armin in the character of Blue John (British Library)*

written in *Foole upon Foole*) but also the clever fool Tutch, who in turn impersonates both John and a Welsh knight; a *tour de force* of doubling and quick changes in which he alternated four roles.[36]

Further evidence of Armin's versatility is provided by his inclusion in the actor lists of Jonson's comedies: *Every Man out of his Humour* of 1599 (as Carlo Buffone?) and *The Alchemist* of 1610, in which we can safely assume that he played Abel Drugger. When Face proposes to the little tobacconist that he should disguise himself as a Spaniard, he tells him,

> Thou must borrow
> A Spanish suit. Hast thou no credit with the players?

To which Abel replies (an 'in-joke' if ever there was one),

> Yes, sir, did you never see me play the fool? (IV.vii.67–9)

His listing by Jonson in *The Alchemist* in his last recorded appearance; he must have retired from the stage between 1610 and 1613. Shakespeare's omission of the 'fellow/In a long motley coat guarded with yellow' (unmistakably Will Somer) from *Henry VIII* may, as Hotson proposed, be taken as confirmation that by 1613 Armin was no longer of the company. As in the analogous circumstances of Kempe's unavailability to play Falstaff in 1599, better perhaps no Will at all than a Will played by anyone other than his biographer and the outstanding player of fools in his time. Armin died in 1615; the register of St Botolph's Aldgate records his burial there on 30 November of that year.[37]

The Chamberlain's or King's Men (as they became in 1603) were only one of several companies alternating seasons in London and at court with extensive provincial tours; each would have had at least one player specialising in fool parts but able to double others when required. The Admiral's Men had John Singer, praised by Thomas Heywood in his *Apology for Actors* in 1612, with other dead actors whose 'deserts yet live in the remembrance of many'.[38] Queen Anne's company had Garret, a former jester of Elizabeth's. If I have focused here on the Queen's and Chamberlain's Companies, it is because the fuller records that survive of them enable us to discern, in the succession of Tarlton by Kempe and Kempe by Armin, an indication of the way in which the fools were progressively integrated into the companies they served. Tarlton, the court fool, making the move from court to stage, but keeping a foot in each; Kempe, the popular clown and dancer, extending his range to play major comedy roles but torn between the disciplined world of the theatre and an itch to travel and exploit his talents in a wider scene; and Armin, the fully committed player, who was to remain with the same company, exhibiting a chameleon-like versatility, to the end of his career.

But by then popular tastes were already changing. Among the vices and virtues of the old interludes, the morally ambiguous figure of Simplicity/Folly had survived longer than any others in the plays of the English dramatic renaissance; but for him too the end was in sight. Of Shakespeare's later comedies and romances only one, *The Tempest*, includes a declared jester among its characters. (It was given at court in 1611, and, as this was unlikely to have been its first performance, Armin might still have been there to play him.)

In the best tradition of his predecessors, Trinculo sees through the self-deceit of Stephano and Caliban to tell the unvarnished truth about their situation in the strange new world in which they have found themselves. 'Servant-monster!', he declares, echoing Stephano. 'The folly of this island! They say there's but five upon this isle: we are three of them; if th'other two be brain'd like us, the state totters.' (III.ii.4–6)

CHAPTER 15
The Last of the Jesters

It was, as we have seen, in the Elizabethan period that court fools made the decisive break away from the restrictions of personal patronage in the service of royal and other great lords to the larger freedom of the stage. Tarlton had managed to function in both worlds with equal success, but he was the last fool of any note to do so. The player-fools who came after him – Kempe, Armin and their successors – had no lasting connections with the court; and though as players they still depended on noble, in some instances royal, patrons for protection against vagrancy laws and Puritan critics, their relations with them appear to have been no closer than those of other members of their companies. It was no longer a personal allegiance they owed to them but one that was shared on an equal basis with the rest of their fellows.

As court fool, however, Tarlton was not the last of his kind; he was succeeded, not only by Garret, but in the reign of James I by the notorious Archy Armstrong, by several innocents, and, in the following reign of Charles I, by a remarkable dwarf, Jeffery Hudson. They are the subject of this and the following chapter.

But first, I should mention one or two survivors from the reign of Elizabeth who probably were most active in that time but of whom the records that survive date mainly from the Jacobean period. Charles Chester was a buffoon plain and simple, who is chiefly remembered as the model for Carlo Buffone in Ben Jonson's *Every Man out his Humour* of 1599: 'an impudent common jester, a violent rayler, and an incomprehensible *Epicure*; one, whose company is desir'd of all men, but belov'd of none; hee will sooner lose his soule then a jest, and prophane even the most holy things, to excite laughter . . .'[1]

John Aubrey and Sir Nicholas Lestrange tell anecdotes of rough treatment of Chester by Sir Walter Raleigh in his 'youthfull time'. According to the first, the man was a 'bold impertenent fellowe, and they could never be at quiet for him; a perpetuall talker, and made a noyse like a drumme in a roome. So one time at a taverne Sir W.R. beates him and seales up his mouth (i.e. his upper and neather beard) with hard wax.'[2] In Lestrange's account, Raleigh went so far as to brick him up in the corner of a room and 'threat'ned to cover him in, but that he begg'd hard and swore he would abuse them no more; so they lett him stand till night'.[3] But the classic description of the type, if not the man himself, is given by Thomas Lodge in his *Wits Miserie* of 1596; as a person who is

comely, in apparell courtly, but in behaviour a very ape, and no man: his studie
is to coine bitter jeasts, or to show antique motions, or to sing baudie sonnets
and ballads: give him a little wine in his head, he is continually flearing and
making of mouthes: he laughs intemperately at every little occasion, and dances
about the house, leaps over tables, out-skips mens heads, trips up his
companions heeles, burns Sacke with a candle, and hath all the feats of a Lord
of misrule in the countrie; feed him in his humor, you shall have his heart, in
meere kindness he will hug you in his armes, kisse you on the cheeke, and
rapping out an horrible oth, crie Gods Soule Tum, I love you, you know my
poore heart, come to my chamber for a pipe of Tabacco, there lives not a man in
this world that I more honor; In these ceremonies you shall know his courting,
and it is a speciall marke of him at the table, he sits and makes faces: keep not
this fellow company, for in jugling with him, your Wardropes shall be wasted,
your credits crackt, your crownes consumed, and time (the most precious
riches of the world) utterly lost.[4]

'Stone the Fool' is more difficult to place. An anecdote in Selden's *Table Talk* in
illustration of the moral precept that 'A gallant man is above ill words', citing 'ye
old Lord Salisbury' as a model, tells of Stone calling some lord about court a
fool, of the lord complaining, and Stone being whipped for it. 'Stone crys I
might have cald my Lord of Salisbury foole ofteen enough before he would have
had me whipt.'[5] As Salisbury (Robert Cecil) died in 1612, this appeal to his
example puts Stone in the early years of the century. If the same man is referred
to, the record of a reward of three shillings to 'Stone, a jester' by the earl of
Rutland, visiting London in 1586, puts him further back still.[6] In 1604, Stone
was in trouble again, and for the same fault as before – if, indeed, the occasion
was not identical to the one recalled by Selden in more general terms. Sir
Dudley Carleton, reporting to Secretary Winwood on the earl of Nottingham's
preparations for his peace mission to Spain that was to take place in the
following year, tells how 'There was great Execution done lately upon *Stone the
Fool*, who was well whipt in *Bridewell* for a blasphemous Speech, *That there went
sixty Fools into Spaine, besides my Lord Admiral* [Nottingham] *and his two Sons.*'[7]
Though he is said to have been soon released, poor Stone may never have
recovered from his whipping because the next we hear of him is in Jonson's
Volpone (first acted in 1605), where the news of his death causes surprise and
consternation to Sir Politic Would-Be.

Peregrine:	. . . Stone, the fool, is dead
	And they do lack a tavern fool, extremely.
Politic:	Is Mas' Stone dead!
Peregrine:	He's dead, sir, why? I hope
	You thought him not immortal? . . .
Politic:	Stone dead!
Peregrine:	Dead. Lord! How deeply, sir, you apprehend it!
	He was no kinsman to you?
Politic:	That I know of.[8]

James I by Daniel Mytens, 1621
(National Portrait Gallery, London)

For all his foolishness, we can sympathise with the expatriate knight. The passing of a favourite clown can still seem, to those who enjoyed him in earlier years, severance of a precious link with the past.

I said in my introductory chapter that the nature of the exchanges between king and fool were invariably determined by the king. In his choice of fool and the kind of humour the fool supplied, we may therefore see a reflection of the character of the king himself; perhaps, in some instances, a side of his character that was not the one he normally presented to the world of his time, or presents to ours. Nowhere is this general tendency better exemplified than in the choice by James I of Archibald Armstrong as his jester. For James – as even recent, revisionist historians of his reign would admit – was a man of contradictory tendencies. On the one hand, he was certainly one of the most literate and learned individuals ever to have occupied the English throne, a respected Latinist, theologian and author whose love of peace and dislike of religious persecution were in advance of his age; but conversely, there was a coarser side to his nature that revealed itself in a predilection for crude jokes and late-night horseplay with his male buffoons. For after supper, the king 'would come forth to see pastimes and fooleries', hear bawdy songs composed by Edward Souch and sung by Sir John Finett; when

Sir George Goring ('Master of the game') would present 'David Droman and Archer [*sic*] Armstrong, the Kings Foole, on the back of the other fools, to tilt at one another, till they fell together by the eares'.[9] If Will Somer had reflected a humane streak in the otherwise ruthlessly egoistical character of Henry VIII and was universally loved for it, Archy Armstrong mirrored the less admirable side of James, his favouritism, self-indulgence and conceit, and was generally resented. The pawky humour they both possessed was a redeeming factor and, if a 'traditional' account of Archy's beginnings is to be believed, was the quality in Archy that first attracted the king to employ him.

'A border sheep-stealer', we are told,

> with the *corpus delicti* upon his shoulders, was tracked by the minions of justice to a moorland cottage, where they found no one but an apparently 'half-witted' lad vacantly rocking the cradle of some younger relative. The baffled officers were on the point of retiring, when a sudden thought instigated them to turn over the infantile couch, and to their amazement the sleeping innocent turned out to be the missing sheep. The astute but discomfited delinquent was at once seized upon and carried to Jedburgh, where James the Sixth was holding a Justice-aire.

The story so far is suspicious in that the stolen sheep disguised as a baby is clearly borrowed from folklore. (It had earlier been used in the Second Shepherds Play of the Wakefield cycle of mystery plays.) The ensuing dialogue between king and fool has a more interesting, idiosyncratic flavour:

> Condemned to die for his crime, Archie Armstrong – for it was he – pleaded with the King that he was a poor ignorant man, who had but recently heard of the Bible, and who was desirous, for his soul's sake, of reading through the precious volume: would his Majesty's grace be pleased to respite him until he had done this? The good-natured monarch easily acceded to the petition, on which Archie immediately rejoined, with a sly look, 'Then de'il tak' me an' I ever read a word o't as lang as my een are open!' [In other words, never.] The King was so pleased with the fellow's ready wit, that he forthwith employed him in his service.[10]

It makes a good story and, whatever the truth of the rest, we know that Archy was indeed a native of the Border country, who later settled at Arthuret in Cumberland, and was already in James's service when the Scots king set out on his journey south in 1603 to assume the English throne.[11]

The earliest, near-contemporary notice of him is at Newmarket races before 1612, when he is said to have created friction between the king and his eldest son, Prince Henry, by pointing out to James that when he and the prince parted company, a greater number of courtiers accompanied the prince than stayed with him. His reward was to be 'tossed like a dog in a blancket' by the prince's friends whenever they met him.[12]

The first mention of Archy in the State Papers relates to 1611, when he was favoured by the king with a 'pension' (wage) of 'two shillings per diem during pleasure', which, a month later, was re-granted 'for life'.[13] In October of the same year, his coat (no details are given) was to be the object of a prank on the part of the Danish ambassador, whose 'care for Archy's coat' was reported to the king as 'like to make sport'.[14] (They may have sewn up the sleeves or some such trick.) In 1612/13, he was provided from the Great Wardrobe with 'so many yardes of Crimson Velvett, and so many ounces of gold lace to lace the same, as shalbe thought fitt by you, and a suite of Apparrell agreable to it'.[15] This was for Archy to wear at the wedding of James's only daughter, Elizabeth, to Frederick, the Elector Palatine, in 1613. Surviving portraits show that (for such special occasions at least) he was accustomed to wear clothes of a style more appropriate to courtiers than servants, and took pride in showing them off.

In the same year, Archy is found to have followed Garret in contributing a mock combat to the celebration of Accession Day: in James's reign on 24 March. A letter of Sir Henry Wotton, the learned Provost of Eton, to Sir Edmund Bacon reports that,

> Towards the evening a challenge passed between Archy and a famous knight, called Sir Thomas Parsons, the one a fool by election, and the other by necessity, which was accordingly performed some two or three days after at tilt, tourney, and on foot, both completely armed, and solemnly brought in before their Majesties, and almost as many other meaner eyes as were at the former; which bred much sport for the present, and afterwards, upon cooler consideration, much censure and discourse, as the manner is.[16]

The occasion was enjoyed, but with that undertow of guilt, surfacing later, that perhaps it ought not to have been enjoyed so much as it was.

Precedent was also followed in that Archy was normally one of the riding household that accompanied the king on his progresses around the country, and was well rewarded in doing so. He was at Coventry in 1617, where he collected 'apparrell' and £5 in cash from the town chamberlains.[17] In the same year, we also find him at Aberdeen. The king had been expected there in person, but, for some reason (perhaps an attack of the gout), had remained behind in Angus and sent a party of courtiers with Archy to represent him. On this occasion, 'his Majesties plesant' (as Archy is described in the town records) was admitted a burgess, and presented with a gold Portuguese ducat.[18]

In February of the following year (1618), he had passed a petition from Sir Thomas Lake to the king in favour of a recusant – doubtless in return for a sizeable fee. Six months later, and notwithstanding James's well-known aversion to smoking, he was granted a monopoly to grant licences for the making of 'Tobacco-pipes', which, 'though yt seeme a small matter, yet they say yt concerns a number of poore men'.[19]

It is evident that Archy was making full use of his privileged position to line his own pocket, and that a pattern was being set whereby those wishing to curry favour with the king were well advised to be generous to his fool; a belief, not without foundation, that Archy was to exploit to the utmost.

In 1621, John Taylor, the popular poet, dedicated a poem on the subject of beggars and begging 'To the Bright, Eye-Dazeling Mirrour of Mirth, Adelantado

Portrait of Archy Armstrong from the 1636 edition of A Banquet of Jests
(British Museum)

of Alacrity, the Pump of pastime, spout of sport, and Regent of ridiculous Confabulations, Archibald Armestrong, *alias* the Court Archy'; but in his dedicatory letter (omitted from the collected edition of his poems that appeared in 1630) he also refers to Archy's 'nimble tongue, to make other mens money runne into your purse'.[20]

In the spring of 1623, Archy travelled to Spain as one of those appointed to attend Prince Charles in his wooing of the Spanish Infanta, and, as often happens when people travel abroad and are obliged to put their observation of events into writing, it is in the form of the many letters and memoirs recording this mission that the best and fullest information about Archy's character and 'licence to rail' survives.

It was at his own request, and in despite of his previously expressed opposition to the Spanish match, that Archy was made one of the party.[21] He had wanted to take a servant with him, but this was denied. The 'Privy Chamber Gentlemen' had, it would seem, already had cause to complain about him, and would 'complain still more, if the fool is allowed the same attendance as they'.[22] An inventory in the State Papers suggests that Archy went to considerable trouble to furnish himself with a suitable wardrobe, 'including apparel of the Spanish fashion which he had from Gondomar' – the Spanish ambassador in London.[23] This may have paid off at the Spanish court, where, according to James Howell who was present in Madrid on another mission, 'Our Cousin Archy' was allowed 'more privilege than any, for he often goes with his Fool's-coat where the Infanta is with her Menina's and Ladies of Honour' (more than Prince Charles ever managed to do) 'and keeps a-blowing and blustering among them, and flurts out what he lists'. 'One day,' Howell continues,

> they were discoursing what a marvellous thing it was that the D[uke] of Bavaria with less than 15,000 Men, after a long toilsome March, should dare to encounter the Palsgrave's Army, consisting above 25,000, and to give them an utter discomfiture, and to take Prague presently after: Whereunto Archy answer'd, that he would tell them a stranger thing than that: Was it not a strange thing, quoth he, that in the Year 88 there should come a Fleet of 140 Sail from Spain to invade England, and that ten of these could not go back to tell what became of the rest?[24]

Sir William Brereton, in his Journal of 1635, recalls another eruption of Archy's subversive humour in conversation with the count of Olivares, Philip IV's principal minister. The occasion was a solemn procession of the Blessed Sacrament through the streets of Madrid (perhaps at Corpus Christi), when Olivares had demanded of Archy 'whether hee did nott beleeve that Christ was there really and personally present'. Archy answered,

> Noe: for hee had heard itt said: that when hee was uppon the earth: that the whoresome theeves crucified him, therefore hee will come noe more amongst them: Herewith Olivaries much taken asked him another question: 'Dost nott

thou beeleeve that the Popes Holliness is guided with such an infallible spiritt, as that hee cannott erre: soe as if he say your red coate be black, you are bound to beeleeve him.'

Archy throws the question back at him, 'What saith your Excellence?', and when the count pauses and is unable to reply, Archy tells him, 'If the Pope say soe, hee is ill of eyesight.' 'These answers', Brereton adds, 'were reported to the King and Queen of Spaine, who were much affected therewith and then was there conferred, and is still continued, a pension of 100*l* per annum.'[25]

One wonders who reported these conversations and in what language they were conducted – presumably through an interpreter. (See Archy's letter to King James below.) But the pension seems to have been real enough,[26] and of an 'extraordinarie rich suit' given him by Olivares, we are to hear later. What the Spanish really made of him we may never know; but they were clearly impressed.

Relations between Archy and the prince's other attendants in Spain had begun badly, and deteriorated. Sir Tobie Matthew – a known Catholic with the reputation of a wit – was so 'distasted' by their verbal encounters that 'once at a dinner he was faine to forsake the table'.[27] Below the level of royalty, Archy was no respecter of persons, and, according to a Spanish source, was even prepared to take on James's beloved 'Steenie' (Buckingham), whom he criticised for the way the whole marriage negotiation had been handled – not, it should be said, without justification. When the newly created duke, unable to silence him, threatened to have him hanged, Archy is reported to have replied 'in a way worthy of one of better sense: No one has ever heard of a fool being hanged for talking, but many Dukes in England have been beheaded for their insolence'.[28]

If this is true, Archy must have been very sure of his royal protector. The confidence he had in James, and the intimacy of their relations, are apparent in a letter that he wrote to him from Spain. It was dictated, and ends with his mark. 'My great and gracious King', he begins, 'To lett your Majestie know never a foole was better accepted on by the King of Spaine, except his own foole and to tell your Majestie secretly I am better accepted on then hee is.'[29] In a unique blend of flattery, boastfulness and religiosity, Archy prattles on,

I is sent for by this King when none of your owne Men nor your sons men can come near him to the glorie of God and prayer of you I shall think myself better and more fewle then all the fewles here for ought that I see yet I thank God and Christ my saviour and you for it; whoe did think that your Majestie kept a Gull and an Ass of me he is a Gull and an As himself; To let your Majestie know yt I cannot tell you the thought of Kings hearts, but this King is of the bravest colour that ever I saw yourself except, this King will not let me have a Trunchman [interpreter], I desyre your Majesties help with all speed, for I cannot understand him, but I think myself as wyse as hee or any in his Court as grave as you think the Spaniard is, you will wryte to your son and Buckingham, and charge them to provyde me a Trunchman and then you shall know from your foole with Gods help Christe help and the virgin Mary's, more secrett Buisines than from all your wyse men here . . .

Then, after a request to the king to 'give thanks' to Lord Aston, the English ambassador, for providing him with hospitality and a pair of white boots 'when my own trunk was not come up', he ends his letter with a further muddled dose of flattery and professed affection:

> I think every day l year tyll I see your Majesties gracious face, for you will never be mist tyll you are gone, and the chylde thats unborne will say a lese for, but I hope in god for my owne part never to see it, the farther I goe the more I see, for all that I see here are fooles to you . . . with grief in my eyes and tears in my heart, and praying for your Majesties happy and gracious continuance among us.
>   Your Majesties servant Archibold Armstrong X your best foole of State both here and there.
>   Court of Spain, 28th April, 1623.[30]

'Whoe did think that your Majestie kept a Gull and an Ass of me he is a Gull and an As himself.' There is no doubting Archy's shrewdness or (despite illiteracy) his way with words.

Negotiations for the Spanish match having failed (to the delight of Protestant opinion), Charles and his party of advisers returned to London in September 1623. In November of that year, a Requiem was said in Ely House for the repose of the souls of the ninety English Catholics who had perished shortly before in the collapse of a secret chapel in the Blackfriars Gatehouse. John Chamberlain tells how Sir Tobie Matthew was a principal mourner and had much to do in 'audiences at court, where his frend Archie was in his highest bravery an extraordinarie rich suit geven him by the Conde de Olivares'.[31]

If, in the Spanish fashion and to fit the occasion, the suit was black, it may be the one referred to by Ben Jonson in his play of 1625/6, *The Staple of News*, where he writes of a cabal of Puritans in Amsterdam, that was

> Found out but lately, and set out by Archie,
> Or some such head, of whose long coat they have heard,
> And being black, desire it.[32]

Surprisingly perhaps, Jonson, that mighty scourge of folly, seems to have regarded Archy with indulgent amusement. In the masque he wrote to celebrate Charles's return from Spain, *Neptunes Triumph* of 1624, he speaks of 'tales and stories told of the Sea-Monster Archy' (we have listened to some of them); and later, as an example of 'Heare-say newes', imagines him conferring with the Spanish keeper of an elephant presented to Charles by the Great Mogul in 1630 with a view to stealing Windsor Castle and carrying it away on the elephant's back.[33]

But if Jonson liked him, he was in a minority among contemporary authors. To Bishop Corbett, he was 'salt Archy', to Francis Osborne a 'foul-mouthed Scot'. Unless there is a touch of Archy in Lavache or the drunken Porter of *Macbeth*,

Shakespeare had ignored him. At court, his propensity for extorting bribes made more enemies than friends. It was among the mass of ordinary Londoners, whose prejudices he shared, that he became a popular figure. Like them, he was disapproving of bishops, suspicious of foreigners, and resentful of the tyranny of over-mighty ministers. At a time when any expression of what we would now describe as 'public opinion' was ruthlessly suppressed, reports of his taunts against such establishment figures as Northampton, Buckingham and Laud were greeted with delight in the City taverns, and endlessly repeated. Northampton came under fire when the newly created earl had provided what was thought to be substandard hospitality to the king on a progress in 1619. Archy, 'upon an old grudge told the king that now the Earle had obtained what he sought for [the earldom], he might see what account he made of him and his followers'.[34]

The bishops were a favourite target, and he was not afraid to express his opinion of them to the king, who believed that kingship and episcopacy were mutually dependent ('No bishop, no king'). When James was complaining one day of the leanness of a hunting horse in spite of good feeding, Archy told him, 'If that be all, take no care: I'll teach your Majestie a way to raise his fleshe presently; and if he be not as fat as ever he wallow, you shall ride me.' How? asked the king. 'Why, doe but make him a Bishoppe, and I'l warrant you, sayes Archee.'[35] It was his later hostility to Archbishop Laud in particular that was finally to bring him down.

In view of all this, it is surprising that Archy survived so long as he did – for twelve years – the death of James in 1625. Perhaps Charles I (who could not have been more different in character to his father, but remained remarkably loyal to his memory) continued to protect him for sentimental reasons. Indeed, Archy was to claim that the new king had given such 'special direction for his payment' that he was better off than he had been before.[36] Charles even granted him 1,000 acres of land in Ireland; if intended as a retirement grant, Archy was in no mood to take the hint.[37]

A letter he dictated in November 1628 to James Hay, earl of Carlisle (one of James's former Scottish favourites, then on a diplomatic mission to The Hague), shows him in high spirits, as full of conceit and ready as ever to meddle in politics. He rejoices in the recent assassination of Buckingham ('the greatest enemy of Three Kings'), and tells Carlisle of the birth of a son. 'Refusing the King and the Lord Steward' (Pembroke) as godfathers, he says he had chosen the Lord Chamberlain (Philip Herbert) 'only for the King of Spaines sake' (for whom the child was named) '& plainely tolde wherefore I did it'.[38] But for all his brave words, Archy's influence was not what it was, and he was riding for a fall.

An anecdote in a later edition of *A Banquet of Jests* (a popular jest-book of the period, first published in 1630) may derive from this time. Entitled 'Arche over-reached', it tells how, on New Year's Day, the fool received a 'gracious reward' from a nobleman at court: 'twenty good pieces of gold in his hand':

But the covetous foole expecting (it seems) a greater, shooke them in his fist, and said they were too light. The nobleman tooke it ill from him, but dissembling his anger he said, I prethee Arche, let mee see them againe, for

Another portrait of Archy from a later edition of A Banquet of Jests *(Courtauld Institute of Art, London)*

amongst them there is one peece I would be loath to part with. Arche supposing hee would have added more unto them, delivered them backe to my lord, who putting 'em up in his pocket, said well, 'I once gave money into a *foole*'s hand, who had not the *wit* to keepe it'.[39]

It was, however, in playing to the gallery of his popular following that Archy triggered the sequence of events that led to his disgrace.

His enmity to Laud, Charles's archbishop of Canterbury, was well known. Like himself, Laud was a man of small stature, and on one occasion at a dinner in Whitehall, when Archy had obtained permission to say grace, he is said to have blurted out, 'Great praise be given to God and little Laud to the devil.'[40] In March 1637 (as reported in a letter from a Mr Garrard to Wentworth), 'being in a Tavern in Westminster, drunk . . . speaking of the Scotish Business, he fell a railing on my Lord of Canterbury; said, he was a Monk, a Rogue, and a Traitor'.[41] The 'Scotish Business' was the attempt by Charles, at Laud's prompting, to impose the English liturgy on the church in Scotland. When news reached London of the fracas in St Giles's Cathedral, where the dean in first attempting to read from the Book of Common Prayer had had a stool thrown at his head, Archy was exultant, tagging the offending stool 'the stool of repentance'.

Encountering Laud on his way to a meeting of the Privy Council, he added aggravation to insult by dogging the archbishop's steps, calling out as he did so, 'Whea's feule now? doth not your Grace hear the News from Striveling about the Liturgy? with other words of reflection.'[42] This was too much for Laud. He complained to the king in council, and it was there and then ordered that Archy 'should be carried to the Porter's Lodge, his Coat pulled over his Ears, and kicked out of the Court, never to enter within the Gates, and to be called into the Star-Chamber'. Garrard adds that 'The first Part is done, but my Lord of Canterbury hath interceded to the King, that there it should end'.[43]

No further action was taken; but Archy could never forgive the injury that Laud had done him, and was to take every opportunity that came his way in the years ahead to complain of it.

He lingered for a while in London, calling in loans he had formerly made to impecunious courtiers and clergy (at interest, of course), including £200 claimed from the dean of York.[44] About a week after his dismissal, he was spotted wandering disconsolately in Westminster Abbey, dressed 'all in black'. When asked what had happened to his usual coat, he explained that 'my Lord of Canterbury hath taken it from me, because either he or some of the Scots Bishops may have use for it themselves: but he hath given me a black coat for it to colour my knavery with; and now I may speak what I please (so it be not against the Prelates) for this Coat hath a farre greater priviledge then the other had.'[45] It was of a kind worn by the clergy.

Francis Osborne, in the second part of his *Advice to a Son* of 1658, criticises Laud in retrospect that by endeavouring to 'explode Archy the court', he unwittingly provided a rallying point to his enemies, and enabled Archy to 'belch' in his face injustices that he was really guilty of that otherwise might have been forgotten. James Welwood in his *Memoirs* is also critical of Laud's action, describing it as a 'piece of Weakness in so great a Man'.[46]

In 1641, when Laud lay in prison and Archy was enjoying a comfortable retirement in Cumberland, a pamphlet was issued entitled *Archy's Dream, sometimes Iester to his Majestie, but exiled the Court by Canterburies malice*, in which the fool vented his spleen on his fallen enemy by consigning him to hell to join 'blind Bonner, and Woolsey dancing a galliard, whipt forward by a company of Hellish haggs'.[47] As we know Archy to have been illiterate, this unpleasant piece of work was probably ghosted for him as a propaganda exercise by one of the Presbyterian party.

Archy had been married some years before, and (as previously mentioned) had fathered a son called Philip in 1628. We know that he had also several daughters because he refers to them in his *Dream*. Arthuret in Cumberland is said to have been his birthplace, and there, having 'jested himself into a fair estate', he retired. His wife may already have died. According to the parish register, Archy, who would then have been in his late fifties or early sixties, fathered an illegitimate son in 1643 and, eighteen months later, married again.[48]

Archy's place at court as the king's jester was rapidly filled by a man called Muckle John, whose principal recommendation for the job appears to have been

This early seventeenth-century painting by an unknown artist features two smiling innocents with a wooden marotte under the title of Wee Three Loggerheads. *They have been identified as Tom Derry (for whom see below) and Archy Armstrong; but we have only to compare the figure on the right with the contemporary portraits of Archy given above to see that the latter identification is mistaken. The painting is more likely to belong to Charles' reign than to that of James (as was previously thought) and to feature Tom Derry and Muckle John. To judge by his more fanciful costume (though I suspect some later over-painting), I take the man on the right to be John (courtesy of the Shakespeare Birthplace Trust, Stratford-on-Avon)*

the belief that 'he will ne'er be so rich, for he cannot abide Money'.[49] Only some Wardrobe entries survive of him, and these suggest that 'Big John' may have compensated for his aversion to money by a taste for expensive clothes:

> One pair of crimson silk hose, and one pair of gaiters and roses for Muckle John, 61*s*. For a pair of silk and silver garters, and roses and gloves suitable for Muckle John, 110*s*. For a hat covered with scarlet, and a band suitable; and for two rich feathers, one red, the other white, 50*s*. Stags-leather gloves, fringed with gold and silver. One pair of perfumed gloves, lined with sables, 5*s*.[50]

Tom Derry, though sometimes described as a jester, was an innocent in the keeping of James's consort, Anne of Denmark. The few surviving records of him couple his name with that of his keeper, John Mawe. In 1612 there is a warrant for six months' 'diet' for the two of them at the rate of 7*s* a week.[51] And in September 1620 (after the death of the queen in March of the previous year) Mawe was granted a pension of '4*s* per diem during the life of the said Derry, and of 2*s* should he survive him'. In the same year, Tom's diet and lodging was assessed by the Treasurer of the Chamber at 9*s* 6*d* per week.[52] One of the queen's former Danish servants, William Belou, who had been less generously treated, was to complain bitterly to Secretary Conway that he had been 'worse used than a natural fool, witness Tom Duri' and 'than a counterfeit, witness Archie Armstrong'.[53] Nothing is recorded of Tom himself, but the naming of a gallery in Somerset House after him – perhaps one where he had been accustomed to walk with his keeper – attests that he was memorable to those who had known him.

  If the Archibald Armstrong named in the Arthuret parish register was Archy the fool, he must have lived through the Civil War to a very advanced age in the reign of Charles II; he was buried, aptly enough, on 1 April 1672.

Portrait engraving by John Droeshout of Jeffery Hudson from the frontispiece of the miniature
New Yeeres Gift *of 1636 (Courtauld Institute of Art, London)*

CHAPTER 16

Jeffery Hudson: Court Dwarf

To say that the court of Charles I was a different place from that of his father would be an understatement. Though occupying many of the same chambers and halls in the same palaces and manors, it was another world; one in which a foppishly dressed innocent such as Muckle John might be patronised and indulged, but in which there could be no lasting retreat for the turbulent humour of an Archy Armstrong.

It was into this more ordered and sophisticated court that the last of our dwarfs, Jeffery Hudson, made his appearance; actually from under the crust of a cold pie served to King Charles and Queen Henrietta Maria when they were on a visit to Burleigh on the Hill, home of the duke of Buckingham.[1]

Jeffery had been born at Oakham, Rutland, in 1619, the son of John Hudson, Buckingham's bearward. Both his father and mother were of normal stature, as were their other children; but between the ages of seven and thirty Jeffery is reported to have grown to little more than a metre in height.[2] Described as 'without any deformity, wholly proportionable', he was one of those rare characters I wrote about in Chapter 2: a *hypopituitaristic* or proportionate dwarf of the kind we have since encountered in the persons of Eleanor of Provence's Jean and Elizabeth's Thomasina. At an early age, Jeffery had been taken into Buckingham's household as a 'rarity of nature', and, on stepping out of the pie, was presented to Henrietta Maria, who there and then took him into her service.[3] One has only to look at Van Dyck's superb portrait of the two of them together (Plate 15, painted a little later, in 1633) to appreciate the appeal that young Jeffery would have had to the nineteen- or twenty-year-old queen, still childless, in the early, difficult years of her marriage to Charles.[4]

With Buckingham out of the way, the royal couple were to discover a deep and lasting affection for each other; and, as the queen's own children were born at regular intervals – Charles in 1630, Mary in 1631, James, Elizabeth and Anne within the same decade – Jeffery would have grown to manhood in a court which, however formal, even rigid, in its etiquette, had at its centre a web of loving family relationships, untouched thus far by the gathering political storms that eventually were to tear it apart.

It is apparent from his later displays of courtly accomplishments that Jeffery was educated as a gentleman of the household and, unlike other of the queen's dwarfs who were transported from place to place in a cart with her monkeys and dogs and the 'billiard board',[5] belonged to the 'upstairs' world of the privy apartments and the audience chamber. As the queen's especial favourite, he would certainly have learned to converse with her in French. He was taught to handle a sword and a pistol, to ride and to hunt.[6] Naturally, under Henrietta's influence and that of her chaplains, who would have concerned themselves in his education, he became a Catholic; and later (in 1636) when Father George Con came from Rome as delegate of the Pope and had distributed rosaries to the queen's converts among her ladies-in-waiting, Jeffery's voice was heard calling out, 'Madam, show the father that I also am a Catholic'.[7]

The sprightly boy had already given Henrietta a fright when he had tumbled out of a window at Denmark House (harmlessly, as it transpired), but in 1630 he was to be the cause of greater anxiety to her. The queen being then pregnant, having suffered a previous miscarriage, Jeffery was allowed to accompany her dancing master to France to fetch a midwife recommended by Marie de Medici (Henrietta's mother) and to escort her across the Channel. On the way back, the vessel in which they were embarked along with several of the midwife's assistants was intercepted by Flemish pirates and the whole party taken captive to Gravelines. Jeffery had been given charge by Queen Marie of jewels for her daughter to the value of £2,500, and a wagonload of other presents worth even more. But when the news reached England, it was the loss of Jeffery that was of most concern to Henrietta. She was so distraught that a courtier complained that his abduction had caused more upset 'than if they had lost a fleet'.[8] The captives owed their release to the Governor of Calais who, 'hearing they were taken, attached all the persons, and seized upon all the goods of the Archduchess's [Flemish] subjects there'.[9] The money and jewels were not recovered, but the queen safely gave birth to her first child (the future Charles II) on 29 May, so the expedition may still have been judged a success. It became the subject of a long, tiresomely facetious poem in mock heroic style by Sir William Davenant, entitled *Jeffereidos, Or the Captivitie of Jeffery*, written shortly after the event, which has the dwarf fighting for his life with a farmyard turkey and the midwife coming to his aid.[10] To those involved, especially the eleven-year-old Jeffery, the experience cannot have been much of a joke. It was the first of a series of strange adventures he was to undergo in the course of his life.

One of the courtly arts that Jeffery had acquired was dancing, and he was able to show off his talent for this in the court masques of the period, for which Inigo Jones designed spectacular sets and costumes. These were something more than pleasurable diversions in which the whole of the royal household joined with enthusiasm; they were also an aesthetic expression of Charles's deeply held beliefs about kingship, reflecting Neoplatonic ideals of Love, Virtue and Order. However, Jeffery's parts were in the antimasques – contrasting interludes of grotesque dancing and comic byplay – that Ben Jonson had introduced to precede the entry of the principal masquers. He was to play the part of Tom Thumb in Jonson's *Fortunate Isles* of 1625; and, in the same

A costume design by Inigo Jones for a dwarf in an unidentified masque. The proportionate stature and lively pose of the dwarf strongly suggest it was intended for one of Jeffery's roles – perhaps Tom Thumb or the 'little Swiss' (Devonshire Collection, Chatsworth; by kind permission of the Chatsworth Settlement Trustees. Photograph: Courtauld Institute of Art, London)

William Evans, Jeffery Hudson and Thomas Parr: the tallest, smallest and oldest men of their time. Broadside print by George Glover, 1636 (British Museum)

author's *Chloridia* of 1631, presented by Henrietta and her ladies, the stage direction for the third entry of the antimasque reads, 'The Queenes Dwarfe, richly apparel'd, as a Prince of Hell, attended by six infernall Spirits; He first danceth alone, and then the Spirits: all expressing their joy, for Cupids comming among them.'[11]

According to Thomas Fuller, he performed in another antimasque with the king's giant porter, William Evans, seven and a half feet tall, who created a sensation by producing a loaf of bread out of one of his pockets, and Jeffery from the other.[12] They appear together (at left and centre), along with Thomas Parr who is said to have attained the age of 152 years 'and upwards', in a broadside print of 1636, reproduced above.[13] Davenant also made use of Jeffery's comedic talents in an antimasque to his *Salmacida Spolia* of 1640, in which he was cast as a 'little Swiss who played the wag' with two other Swiss 'as they slept'.[14] This was the last of the court masques to be staged before the Civil War.

In these years, Jeffery was at the apogee of his fortunes and, in 1636, was paid the singular compliment of a miniature book published in his honour, with his portrait as frontispiece (as shown on p. 152). It was entitled *The New-Yeeres Gift: Presented at Court, from the Lady Parvula to the Lord Minimus (commonly called Little Jefferie), Her Majesties servant, with a Letter as it was penned in short-hand wherein is proved Little Things are better then Great. Written by Microphilus*. Under the portrait, an inscription reads,

> Gaze on with wonder, and discerne in me,
> The abstract of the worlds Epitome.[15]

Jeffery would have been proud to have become the object of such flattering notice. Perhaps too proud. Fuller writes that, from the moment of his adoption by the royal family, he 'ever after lived (whilst the court lived) in great plenty therein, wanting nothing but humility (high mind in a low body), which made him that he did not know himself, and would not know his father, and which by the king's command caused justly his sound correction'.[16]

But by the late 1630s, the time of plenty was coming to an end, and Jeffery was then to demonstrate that there was more to him than a charming exterior, the polished manners of a courtier, and a talent to amuse. In 1637 we find him a volunteer along with the earls of Warwick and Northampton at the retaking of Breda by the Dutch, where he was characterised in an eye-witness account of the fighting as 'Strenuous Jeffry, that Cyclopian creature, whose Gygantisme body made the Bulwarkes of Breda to tremble'.[17] It was at Breda that he would first have come into contact with the young Prince Rupert, who was there with his brother Maurice, gaining useful experience for the battles ahead.

Back in England in May 1641, Jeffery was present at the marriage of William, fifteen-year-old son of the Prince of Orange, to Princess Mary, then only ten. At the formal bedding ceremony that followed, he raised a laugh with a pair of shears, pretending to cut the princess's nightdress which had been sewn up as a precaution.[18] (In the want of anyone else and when occasion required it, as here, he seems to have been ready enough to take on the function of a court jester.) But the wedding was only a brief distraction from political crisis as relations between the king and his Parliament went from bad to worse.

In January 1642, in fear for the safety of his wife and children in London, Charles took them to Hampton Court, then to Windsor; and in February, accompanied Henrietta and Princess Mary to Dover, from where they sailed to Holland. We know that Jeffery went with them because of a *faux pas* committed at The Hague by the newly accredited Dutch ambassador. In taking leave of Henrietta on his departure for London, the ambassador had mistaken the 23-year-old dwarf for Prince Charles, then aged twelve and with his father in England, and had kissed his hands.[19]

Jeffery was still in attendance on the queen when, a year later, she returned from Holland with much-needed money and supplies for the Royalist army. Landing at Bridlington in Yorkshire after a stormy crossing, Henrietta and her terrified ladies had to take shelter in a ditch on being bombarded from the sea by a squadron of Parliamentary ships.

We know little of Jeffery's involvement in the Civil War. He had probably remained with the queen during the early part of 1643, which she spent in rallying the north to Charles's cause, leading the troops she raised towards Oxford, where the king had made his headquarters. At Stratford-on-Avon (where she lodged with Mistress Judith Hall, Shakespeare's only surviving child), Henrietta was met by Prince Rupert, who escorted her to a reunion with Charles at Kineton, near Edgehill. Rupert would have remembered Hudson from their service together at Breda. Knowing of his soldierly capabilities, it may have been he who recommended his commissioning as a Captain of Horse. In that capacity, he may have served under Rupert. That he could be effective on horseback we know from a later episode, but no details have survived of his part in the fighting that followed. The next we hear of him is in a woodman's hut in Devon, waiting with Jermyn and a few others for a distressed and fugitive queen to accompany her into exile.[20] Sailing from Falmouth, again under fire, they arrived at Brest on 16 July, where Henrietta was said to be more dead than alive. She was sent by her doctors to take the waters at Bourbon. It was at Nevers, three months later on a journey to Paris, that the event occurred that was to bring Jeffery's court career to an end.

He was, as we have seen, a proud man, and his recent experiences in the Civil War would not have tended to make him any more tolerant of the jokes and taunts that his small size occasioned from insensitive strangers. Angered by one such insult from a certain Crofts, brother of the Lord Crofts who was captain of the queen's guard and her Master of Horse, Jeffery challenged him to a duel. When Crofts arrived at the rendezvous armed only with a toy 'squirt', the dwarf was provoked into issuing a more deadly challenge to meet him on horseback with pistols, in which the difference between them in stature would have been of little account. As a newsletter of the time bluntly reported, 'Jeffry, running his horse in full career, shot his antagonist in the head, and left him dead on the spot'.[21]

This must have been a further blow to the queen in the midst of all her greater griefs and worries; and placed her in the dilemma of having to adjudicate between her sympathy and affection for Jeffery and the need to satisfy calls for retribution from the dead man's brother, equally high in her favour. She wrote first to her sister-in-law, the French queen, and to Cardinal Mazarin, asking to dispose of the matter herself, 'dispensing either justice or favour' as the combatants were 'both English, and my servants'.[22] Having obtained the necessary *carte blanche* – thus shielding Jeffery from the severer penalties of the French law – she imposed on him the least punishment available to her: banishment. We do not know how long his exile was intended to last because, almost immediately, Jeffery was caught up in another misadventure.

Having made his way to a Mediterranean port – aiming, perhaps, for Italy or the Holy Land – the ship on which he embarked was attacked by a Turkish rover, and he was carried to the Barbary coast and sold into slavery, where doubtless he fetched a good price. (This may read more like romance than sober history, but the danger from such Mediterranean pirates was all too real, and well recognised at the time.[23])

It took Jeffery many years to regain his freedom. We have no information as to how he achieved it, or what efforts, if any, had been made to redeem him. Of the sufferings and humiliations to which he was subject during the time of his captivity, we know only that on his eventual return to England, he was found to have gained a foot in height (to three feet, nine inches), which he ascribed to the 'hardship, much labour, and beating, which he endured when a slave to the Turks'.[24] He was to remain at this height for the rest of his life.

The year of his return has not been recorded.[25] That in itself may be significant. Not only was he returning to a land irrevocably transformed by years of civil war, but he was also changed. To his former fellows and patrons – those that remained – the middle-aged man, aged still more by his years of captivity and taller in height, would have been hardly recognisable as the fresh-faced manikin of Henrietta's household or the dashing young cavalry officer they remembered. It would have been a sad homecoming.

We are told that he remained quietly in the country for some years, living on a pension subscribed by the son of his first patron, the duke of Buckingham, and other royalists; so he was not entirely forgotten. He may have gone to Rutland and renewed contact with his surviving relatives there. But his misfortunes were not yet over.

The lure of the court of the restored Charles II brought him back to London; and there, in 1679, as a self-confessed Catholic, he was arrested on suspicion of involvement in the Popish Plot, and incarcerated in the Gatehouse. That Charles did something to help him appears from a record of payments from the king's 'secret service' fund to 'Capt. Jeffery Hudson' of £50 in June 1680 and £20 in April 1681.[26] He died shortly after his release from prison in 1682 at the age of sixty-three; morally, if not formally, a Confessor for the Old Faith he had adopted so many years before.

Jeffery Hudson was not the only small person to have served in royal or other magnate households during the reign of Charles I; nor was he the only proportionate dwarf among them. Paintings by Rubens of the Arundel family, and by Johan Priwitzer of William Russell, 1st duke of Bedford, include portraits of equally small and well-proportioned attendants.[27] At court, a dwarf called Richard Gibson was employed as 'page of the back stairs', but became better known as a painter, having studied under Sir Peter Lely. Gibson married a dwarf of the queen's, Anne Shepherd. Charles and Henrietta were present at their wedding, which was celebrated by Sir Edmund Waller in some charming verses.[28] When the twelve-year-old Prince James was brought to London as a prisoner of Parliament in 1646, he was separated from his servants, 'not so much as excepting a dwarfe whom his Royall Highness was desirous to have retain'd with him'.[29] But none of these was ever to attain the degree of royal affection or status at court enjoyed by Jeffery Hudson.

He had no successors. Nor were there any replacements for such innocents as Muckle John or the far from innocent Archy. If the information given to Pepys was true – that 'Tom Killigrew hath a fee out of the wardrobe for cap and bells, under the title of the King's foole or Jester, and may with privilege revile or jeere

Preliminary drawing by Rubens of the earl of Arundel's dwarf, Robin, for his portrait of the Arundel family, 1620 (courtesy of the Nationalmuseum, Stockholm)

anybody, the greatest person, without offence, by the privilege of his place' – the appointment was more facetious than real, and similar freedom was allowed to other royal buffoons.[30] The fatal shot fired by Jeffery Hudson at Nevers in 1644 may truly be said to have brought the story of English court fools and dwarfs to a close.

In my two concluding chapters, I take an overall view; in the first, of the many detailed entries from Wardrobe accounts I have quoted in the preceding pages, and attempt some resolution of the much-disputed question of the fools' 'motley'. When banished from court, the fools whose history I have traced so far did not altogether disappear from the scene or cease to exist. In a final chapter, I give a brief account of what happened to them – both innocent and clever – in the years that immediately followed, and return to one of the themes of my introduction: the court fool's ambiguous status as 'Mr Nobody'.

Portrait of Will Somer by Francis Delaram, c. 1615–24 (British Museum)

CHAPTER 17

The Fools' Motley

The Jacobean engraving reproduced opposite, which purports to be a portrait of Will Somer, exposes several of the difficulties that stand in the way of our obtaining a clear view of fools' costuming in any given period. Though properly belonging to the reigns of Henry VIII and his children, Will is pictured in contemporary fools' wear of the Jacobean period. He is dressed in an 'idiot's robe' of speckled motley with hanging sleeves; he has a feather in his hat, a 'muckender' (wipe) at his belt, and carries the bugle-horn of a Tom o' Bedlam. None of this bears any relation to Will's actual wardrobe as detailed in the records I have previously cited (pp. 70–8), or his appearance as shown in the contemporary portraits I have reproduced (Plates 11b and 12); it tells us only of how he might have appeared in plays such as Rowley's *When you see me, you know me* of 1605.

To the Jacobeans, of course, the whole idea of historical costuming remained as foreign as it had been to their medieval and Tudor forebears. If Shakespeare's audience was accustomed to a Julius Caesar or a King Lear in doublet and hose, they are unlikely to have blinked at a Will Somer in speckled motley. (Theatre-goers had to wait until the nineteenth century to see historical plays dressed throughout in something approaching authentic period costumes.) But it is not just that Will's appearance as portrayed by Delaram was anachronistic; he had also mistaken the nature of Will's position at the court of Henry VIII. For though Will was an innocent in the sense that he was wholly maintained by the king and was not in receipt of either wages or rewards, he was one of that rare category of 'wise naturals' who, in the performance of the admittedly limited functions required of them, were mentally bright as a button. For such as Will, an 'idiot's robe' would have been inappropriate and insulting to the fool's sense of his own identity. The confusion between clever and innocent fools on the one hand, and between 'idiots' and wise naturals on the other, has bedevilled most writing on the subject of fools and their costuming ever since.

Leslie Hotson, in his study of the wear of Elizabethan and Jacobean fools, claimed that the term 'motley' referred to a utilitarian material of mixed threads, subdued in colour, that corresponded in appearance to our present-day tweed; and furthermore, that the characteristic costume worn by fools in the period (including those in Shakespeare's plays) was long, descending to the ankles, and all-enveloping; sometimes gathered at the waist with a belt.[1] His intention in making these claims, which are supported by a brilliant display of apt quotation, was to overturn the simplistic notion that Shakespeare's fools should properly wear some variant of the supposedly traditional *habit de fou* of short tunic, belled hood and particoloured hose, in which they were commonly dressed on stage until fairly recent times. In this he succeeded. If his arguments failed to win complete agreement from his fellow scholars (then or later), it is because the choice of texts on which they were based was selective; they do not take account of statements from the same period that defy interpretation in the limited terms he proposed.

For 'motley', though certainly used in a technical sense of a cloth of mixed *threads*, was also applied (especially in literary and dramatic contexts) to garments comprising a combination of variously coloured *cloths* – whether paned, chequered or striped.[2] And the long 'idiot's robe' he describes was worn (as the name indicates) mainly by innocents or 'naturals', and much less by the jesters of the period.[3] Unfortunately for Dr Hotson's thesis, Shakespeare's fools (with one notable exception) were jesters rather than innocents.

Innocents wore the material called 'motley' for practical reasons which are easily understandable. It was inexpensive, warm, hard-wearing, and did not show marks or stains so readily as single-coloured cloths. Robert Armin in his *Foole upon Foole* of 1600 says of Jack Oates, an exceedingly simple domestic fool in the keeping of Sir William Holles,

> Motley his wearing, yellow or else greene,
> A collored coate on him was seldome seene.[4]

Motley (the material) might be predominantly yellow, green or russet in ground, but was described at the time as 'sad' in appearance rather than coloured. We know that Jack's coat was long because in the later, expanded version of Armin's book (retitled *A Nest of Ninnies*), he tells us that Jack was

> Writh'd in th' knees, yet who sees
> Faults that hidden be? . . .
> In Motly cotes, goes Jacke Oates,
> Of whom I sing this song.[5]

Another of the household innocents featured in *Nest of Ninnies* is described as going 'motly warme'.[6] Armin's authority as the foremost observer and performer of fools in Shakespeare's time can hardly be disputed.

Royal and gentry households were not the only refuge for these innocents; they were also kept – perhaps more from charitable motives than for any amusement or simple wisdom they provided – in monasteries and towns. In Worcester Priory, a fool called Roger Knight was sheltered by Prior William More. Roger is first mentioned in 1519. In April of that year he was supplied with a 'coote of moteley' at a cost, including the making, of 11*s* 6*d*. Elsewhere it is described as a 'pety coote', a coat with long, pleated skirts like those worn by women and children. At various times in the months and years that followed, shirts, socks and shoes were provided and renewed as necessary. By December 1520 the original robe was

Carving of a fool from the chantry chapel of Bishop Thomas Bekynton in Wells Cathedral. As chapel and tomb were built in 1450, fifteen years in advance of the bishop's death in 1465, this touching memorial of his innocent fool may well have been modelled from life. Note the monastic-type hood (by kind permission of the Dean and Chapter of Wells)

beyond repair and a replacement was made for it with the purchase of six and a
half 'styckes' of motley at 20*d* a 'stycke' (piece). Thereafter, it was replaced
annually till 1524, when Roger apparently died or retired.[7]

Motley, however, was not the only material from which such coats were made.
That supplied to Elizabeth of York's innocent, William, in 1502 was of Kendal, a
coarse woollen cloth, usually green in colour, which had similar utilitarian uses.
We can deduce that it was long and enveloping because of the quantity of material
supplied: no less than ten yards, with the addition of 5½ ells (about seven yards) of
canvas for interfacing and lining.[8] A succession of 'official' fools of varying
simplicity (but none of any evident cleverness) was retained by the Corporation of
Newcastle upon Tyne between 1561 and 1635 for whom various types of garment
were made, utilising a mixed bag of materials. In 1594, one Allon was provided
with a 'longe cote', and Thomas Dodds with a 'peticote'. In the following year,
seven yards of white cotton were purchased for a 'petycote' for Allon and as
'lyninge for the vpper bodie [bodice] of his coate'. In 1599, six yards of rug (a
shaggy material of wool) was required to make another 'petticoate' for Dodds, and
in 1607, eight yards of broad grey frieze (another coarse woollen cloth) were
bought for him. Of these fools, only a man named Marshall was consistently
clothed in motley; that was in the period 1601–16.[9] 'Leane Leonard', who in
Armin's *Nest of Ninnies* goes 'motly warme', is clothed in a 'long coate of Frieze
both hot and colde' in *Foole upon Foole*.[10]

A gown similar to that supplied to these innocents was also worn by young
boys in the Tudor period, including pupils of Christ's Hospital. The portrait of
Blue John (as played by Armin, reproduced on p. 135) shows him wearing such a
gown, which of course would have been blue in colour. Among the clothes
supplied to Archy Armstrong's innocent successor, Muckle John (the last of the
court innocents), was a 'long coat and suit of scarlet-colour serge'.[11]

Apart from their length and the homespun materials from which they were
made, another common feature of innocents' gowns was their 'garding': the
addition of sewn-on strips of cloth of contrasting colour near to the lower hem as
a sign of the wearer's liveried status. The use of such gards was not limited to
fools; they decorated the uniform dress of many other royal servants (especially of
the Privy Chamber); but their presence is a useful aid in distinguishing the
innocents among the fools from their counterfeit colleagues the jesters, who, as we
have seen, generally enjoyed a more independent lifestyle.

Along with the Kendal and canvas for his gown, Elizabeth of York's William
was supplied with a yard of Kersey, a lightweight woollen cloth, narrow in width,
to 'bordre' or gard it. (His shoes were 'clouted' – reinforced with a thick piece of
leather to the soles, a 'clump', to give extra wear.) The only one of the Newcastle
fools specifically described as a 'naturall' is also distinctive in that his coats and
caps were consistently garded throughout the fifteen years of his service; usually
by red Kersey over broadcloth of various colours. The three-quarter length tunic
worn by Will Somer in the contemporary portrait shown in Plate 11b is seen to be
garded with a single band of black. Most of the more elaborate coats and gowns
ordered later for Will by Queen Mary were garded with velvet, several with
yellow velvet (see above, pp. 77–8). Shakespeare may have been mistaken when he

wrote of the non-appearing Will of *Henry VIII* as a 'fellow/In a long motley coat'
but uncannily right in distinguishing the coat as 'guarded with yellow' (Prologue,
ll. 15–16). Bassanio in *The Merchant of Venice* (II.ii.147–8) instructs his followers
to give the newly employed Launcelot Gobbo 'a livery/More guarded than his
fellows' – that is, with more concentric bands around the hem than were worn by
his other servants; usually, a single gard was thought sufficient.[12]

The dubiousness of the honour bestowed by such garding is well brought out
in John Marston's *The Malcontent* – or rather, in one of the additions made to the
play when the King's Men took it over from a company of 'little eyases' and
performed it at the Blackfriars in about 1603; the part of Passarello, a bitter fool,
was probably written for Armin. Malevole, the disguised duke of Genoa, greets
Passarello's entrance by exclaiming at the garded gown he is wearing.

> You are in good case since you came to court, fool. What,
> guarded, guarded!
>
> *Passarello*   Yes, faith, even as footmen and bawds wear velvet, not for an
> ornament of honour, but for a badge of drudgery; for, now the
> Duke is discontented, I am fain to fool him asleep every night.

And at the end of the scene, as he exits, the fool's garding is remarked on again.

> *Passarello*   You'll know me again, Malevole.
> *Malevole*   O, ay, by that velvet.
> *Passarello*   Ay, as a pettifogger by his buckram bag. I am as common in the
> court as an hostess's lips in the country; knights, and clowns, and
> knaves, and all share me: the court cannot possibly be without
> me.[13]

To a clever fool such as Passarello, garding was a badge of the drudgery implicit
in his newly acquired, liveried status: to Gobbo, the rustic clown, coming from
Shylock's house to be the fool of so fine, if poor, a gentleman as Bassanio, it was a
mark of preferment.

We have only to glance again at the detailed specifications for the wear of
Elizabeth's fools to see that clever fools of the period wore a costume entirely
different from the innocents' robe or 'petycote'. Of the clothes warranted by the
queen for her fools, only those intended for the half-deranged Monarcho and
Ippolyta the Tartarian (another dependant) were garded, and the only mention of
motley is in an order of 1575–6 for a 'Saddle covered with motley . . . for Will our
Foole' – not Will Somer, who by then was long since dead, but another innocent
required to accompany the queen on a progress. The garments ordered for her
jesters conform to the normal, contemporary dress for men of doublet and hose,
stockings and hats. In their design, they reflect the changing fashions of the day,
but in one instance – that of Grene's 'slop', later adopted by Tarlton – anticipate
them and set a new fashion. They are distinguished from courtiers' wear only by
the idiosyncrasy of their decorations and combination of contrasting colours and

materials. When *seen*, they would certainly have been *known*, but not in the way that either Rowley or Hotson envisaged. They were motley in the broader, non-technical application of the word.

I shall return to these in a moment; let us remind ourselves first of earlier fashions, and test the assumption common to both Hotson and his opponents in the 'motley' debate that, whatever they may have worn in the Elizabethan and Jacobean periods, their predecessors of the jesting kind wore some variant of the continental *habit de fou*. If we ignore for the present the pictorial evidence of the psalters and other ecclesiastical sources and fix our attention on English documentary records, we find in fact that medieval fools of the clever kind were issued with clothes similar, if not identical, to those supplied to other royal servants of equivalent rank.

In 1241, the knighted buffoon, Sir Fortunatus de Lucca, was given liveries by Henry III 'just as for one of the king's knights'. The indications are that Tom le Fol was supplied by Edward I with the same lengths and materials of varying colours ('with a lamb's fur for trimming') issued twice yearly to the royal minstrels. Even Jean, *fol* to the French king Jean le Bon during his captivity in England in 1359–60 (who of all the individuals cited might have been expected to wear something different) was provided with furs and furred garments comparable in style and value with those for the king and his son. No mention is made in the detailed accounts that survive of any distinguishing features.

In the fourteenth century, 'ray' and other striped materials came into use. Some time after 1328, Robert IV, the clever fool of Edward III's consort, Philippa of Hainault, received an outfit of 'striped cloth of Ypres' and of furs. In the early years of Richard II, his fool William was given a long tunic, tabard and hood 'parted' (i.e. particoloured in two halves joined together vertically) of 'short camlet and rayed caynet . . . faced with red, and two pairs of breeches'; but (as Hotson points out) Richard and two of his earls were clothed in similarly 'parted' hunting suits at about the same time, and whereas theirs included, among the materials used, 'green motley', William's did not. The Black Prince is also on record as supplying a long list of his retainers, including minstrels, with 'cloth of ray'.[14] A fifteenth-century source cited in the new *Oxford English Dictionary* (under *motley*, B.1) equates 'ray' with 'motle' or 'medlee'. Here, perhaps, is the origin of the association of folly with 'motley' in its broader meaning of particoloured. But we should also take note that in the fourteenth and early fifteenth centuries, ray was in general use for royal servants, great and small, and that 'parted' gowns and hoods were fashionable wear for all classes from the king downwards.

In 1469, Woodhouse, the 'sage dyzour', came before Edward IV 'clad in a short coat cut by the points [laces], and a pair of boots upon his legs as long as they might be tied to the points of his hose' – in other words, in waders up to his thighs. The implication is that (like Tarlton a century later) he wore different costumes to suit different occasions, and, in a dramatic, semi-theatrical context, dressed for the role he was playing.

Returning with these earlier precedents in mind to the wear of Elizabeth's jesters, and to the wardrobe supplied to William Shenton in particular, we find our first detailed descriptions of that elusive article of clothing, a jester's 'coat'.

Shenton's outfit of 1574/5 comprised a coat of wrought velvet and tufted taffeta, 'paned red, grene and yellowe', striped with decorative buttons and loops of braid; a cassock (three-quarter-length coat) of 'chaungeable mockeado', lined with buckram for stiffening and decorated with silk buttons; and a doublet of striped sackcloth with silk buttons and a taffeta girdle. The chequered jacket of red, green and yellow panes, with its buttons and braid, reminds us of the costume worn by Harlequin in some versions of the Italian *commedia dell'arte*, then becoming popular throughout the whole of Europe; the 'chaungeable mockeado' of the cassock is explained by Janet Arnold as a type of mock velvet of which warp and weft were of different colours, giving an iridescent effect; and the plainness of his sackcloth doublet (inherited, perhaps, from Monarcho) would have been well set off by its silk buttons and taffeta belt.[15] The dull material known to the queen's tailors as 'motley' would have been out of place here, and is nowhere mentioned; but in their combination of materials and colours, all three garments would qualify as 'motley' in Shakespeare's use of the word and that of his contemporaries. When Archy Armstrong was admitted to the presence of the Spanish Infanta and her ladies on the strength of his 'fool's coat', or when 'his Coat was pulled over his ears' on his being ignominiously expelled from the court of Charles I, the coats in question, though Jacobean in style, would doubtless have been equally colourful, not to say gaudy.

Patient readers of these and earlier accounts of the fools' wardrobe will have been struck by some notable omissions from the items of clothing and props specified in them. There has been no mention whatever of eared or belled hoods, nor of the coxcombs, baubles or marottes (sticks with a miniature fool's head at the top) so frequently pictured in continental illustrations of fools, such as those reproduced by Francis Douce in his *Illustrations of Shakespeare*, and in other, more recent, manuals of historic costume. After telling us of the motley coat of sad appearance worn by the innocent Jack Oates, Armin goes on to say that he wore 'No fooles cap with a bable and a bell', preferring 'a Hat of straw . . . in colours red and blew'.[16] Most other English fools of the Tudor period appear to have made similarly personal choices. The juxtaposition of sackcloth and taffeta in Monarcho's doublet (though prescribed by his keepers) has been seen to reflect the peculiarity of his mental condition. Garret's adoption of a cloak made entirely of sackcloth, interwoven with straw, with a high hat may derive in part from folk tradition, but, for a court fool, is unique in the records. Nor should it be assumed that clever fools like Garret and Tarlton wore always the same outfit. We know that Tarlton appeared as a simple rustic for his solo performances; on stage or at court, he would have dressed for the part or role he was playing – whether dishevelled rogue, drunken sot, or 'the God Luz'; abroad in the City taverns and streets, he affected the gallant in modish 'slop', with a rapier to hand.

The eared hoods of some fourteen and fifteenth-century psalter fools, along with their bells, baubles and marottes, can be dismissed altogether from

Roman terracotta of a mimic fool (from F. Ficoroni,
Dissertatio de larvis scenicis et figuris comicis antiquorum
romanorum, *Rome, 1754, as reproduced by A. Nicoll,* Masks,
Mimes and Miracles, *1931)*

consideration here as belonging to a disparate tradition; one that originated in the
Feast of Fools and, more particularly, in the secular *Sociétés Joyeuses* of France,
Germany and the Low Countries that had come into being under the Feast's
influence and were to survive into the seventeenth century. In their adoption of
the eared hood, they appear to have been in touch with a surviving tradition of
the *centunculus*: the costume worn by Roman mimic fools which (as illustrated
above) featured asses' ears and a curiously shaped hood with falling peak that may
have suggested a coxcomb. Though (as noted in Chapter 6) attempts had been
made to introduce such fool societies to England, they had been quickly
suppressed, and the English Bibles and Psalters that feature fools of that kind are
known to have been influenced by the Parisian school of illumination – both in
their choice of subjects to illustrate particular psalms and the way these were
depicted. (For a fifteenth-century example, see Plate 13b.) As Chambers
suggested in his cautious way, the *habit de fou* may never have crossed the Channel
so far as the actual wear of English court or domestic fools was concerned.[17] We
can now go a little further than that and state that if any English fool of the kind
(innocent or clever) was accustomed to wear such an outfit, there is no trace of his
having done so in any surviving record or authenticated portrait.

In so far as the imported image of the eared fool with bells and bauble
infiltrated popular culture in England in the Tudor period – the annual round of
country festivals, summer games and Christmas Lords, the Maypole and the
Morris – it came, not by way of imitation of court fools with whom (until
Tarlton) the mass of the population had little contact, but through the extensive
fool literature of the later Middle Ages and Renaissance, and ecclesiastical
iconography.[18] More specifically, it was from images in stained glass and carved
wood in their parish churches, and illustrations in printed books as these began to
circulate more widely in the sixteenth century, that people took their ideas of
what a fool should look like – or *had* looked like in some vaguely situated former
age. It thus became part of the language of emblems, entered into proverbial

Wood carving of a reclining jester playing bagpipes from All Saints church, Elm, Cambridgeshire (courtesy of the Churchwardens; photograph by Birkin Haward)

speech, and remains current today. We see it (above) in compellingly realistic detail among the roof rafters of a fifteenth-century Cambridgeshire church, and (overleaf) in the Betley window of about 1621, which, with its Maid Marian, Friar and other folk heroes, has been recently interpreted as an 'historical recreation of a *supposed* pre-Reformation morris'.[19]

It is significant that the only actual coxcomb I have been able to find in all my reading of the records occurs in an inventory of 'play clothes' kept in a chest at St John's College, Cambridge, in 1548/9, 'to be preserved & kept from yere to yere of him which shalbe Lord in Christmas': 'A silk gold capp with a cockes hed in ye crown'.[20] It relates to that sole-surviving legacy of the Feast of Fools in England, a Lord of Misrule. It was important for 'him which shalbe Lord in Christmas' – the occasional, amateur fool – to *look* the part he was to play precisely because it was only a part: a once-in-the-year opportunity for him and his fellow students to let off steam before returning to the academic grindstone. By assuming the conventional symbol of the coxcomb, he becomes the role for so long, and only so long, as he wears it. The professional fool had no such need to suit his appearance to the expectations of his audience; for him it was more than a 'part' he was playing; he was wholly what he purported to be, a fool. Indeed, the more authentic the fool (then as now), the more idiosyncratic his choice of costume is likely to be, and the less inclined he will be to conform to generalities or expectation.

Fool of the Betley Window, said to have come from Betley Hall, Staffordshire, c. 1621 (Victoria & Albert Museum)

I have said that the stereotyped image of the fool in 'cap and bells' entered into proverbial speech, and both medieval and Tudor poets did not hesitate to give some features of it concreteness in their imaginative fiction and drama. Baubles (inflated bags on sticks) are most often featured. John Gower, in his tale of 'The Courtier and the Fool' in *Confessio Amantis* (*c.* 1390), tells how a king's fool

> Sat be the fyr upon a stol,
> As he that with his babil pleide.

And in Skelton's play *Magnyfycence* (*c.* 1515), Folly enters 'shaking his bauble'.[21]

But coxcombs make few, if any, appearances in English literature until the Elizabethan period, and the earliest use of the French *marotte* was in 1611, when it was applied derisively to people.[22] Though the Tudor interludes and moralities commonly featured vices and fools, the surviving texts have little to tell us of their costume or props. And when, in the school or university play *Misogonus* (*c.* 1564–77), the double-dealing Cacurgus pretends to be a fool and is dressed by his master in 'foolish weed', an eared hood and 'scogginly feet', the prodigal son Misogonus fails to recognise either him or his costume. 'Body of God', he exclaims,

	Stand back! What monster have we here?
	An antic or a monk? A goblin or find?
	Some hobbyhorse, I think, or some tumbling bear.
	If thou canst, speak and declare me the kind.
Cacurgus	My young master. Ho! Ho! Ho!
Misogonus	Passion of me! It is Robin Hood I think, verily.[23]

But Misogonus is meant to be very stupid.

Though also writing for the stage where the advantage of an easily recognisable if emblematic costume may be excused as taking priority over historical fidelity or contemporary naturalism, Shakespeare, with his fool consultant and performer Armin at his side, knew better. His court fools, whether contemporary or historical, innocent or clever, are authentically clothed and equipped. His use of coxcomb and bauble is figurative rather than literal. 'Coxcomb' usually denotes a foolish, vain person, as in Emilia's rebuke to Othello, 'O murderous coxcomb! what should such a fool/Do with so good a woman?' (V.ii.234–5); or merely the fool's head, as in Aguecheek's complaint to Viola in *Twelfth Night*, 'If a bloody coxcomb be a hurt, you have hurt me' (V.i.188). When the Fool in *Lear* offers his coxcomb to Kent (I.iv.93), we need not suppose that his cap was decorated with the head of a cock when a feather or plume of feathers would have carried the same meaning to a Jacobean audience.[24] In *All's Well that Ends Well* (IV.v.27), when the clown Lavache proposes to give his bauble to the wife he wishes to seduce ('do her service'), it is clearly not of any theatrical prop he is speaking.[25]

Feste wears gaskins (large, wide breeches) as Elizabeth's Shenton had done, and, in one scene (III.i) enters playing a tabor and pipe in the manner of Tarlton. Touchstone wears a sword at his side and is dressed in courtly style. The rustics call him 'Master' and tip their hats to him; yet to Jaques he is a 'motley fool', or simply a 'motley'; one that gives him so much joy by the quality of his wit that he is 'ambitious for a motley coat' and claims that 'Motley's the only wear'. Like Feste, Touchstone wears a motley combination of colours: 'When you see me, you know me.' Jaques knows him for what he is (a fool) because he is familiar with the fashions of the court; the rustics fail to do so because his dress is not sufficiently different to their uninstructed eyes from that worn by the other courtiers they meet.[26] All this is in perfect conformity with what we have learnt from the records.

The Fool in *King Lear* is alone among Shakespeare's fool characters in being an innocent of the Will Somer type. Though, as we have seen, there is no record of Somer ever having worn a long motley robe, we know that Shakespeare thought that he did, and so it would not be inappropriate for Lear's fool to wear one. There is no doubt that this costuming would (as Hotson suggests) add to the pictorial effect of the scene (III.vi) in which the blanketed Edgar in his impersonation of Tom o' Bedlam ('Thou robed man of justice', as Lear describes him) would be paired by a similarly robed Fool as his 'yoke-fellow of equity' to sit in judgement upon Goneril.[27]

There is one traditional fool prop that, unlike the coxcomb and bauble, we do find in actual use by English fools and players of fools. This is the painted wooden dagger or sword. In Tudor interludes – especially those of the *psychomachia* type in which the soul of a representative figure of humanity is fought over by alternately good and evil allegorical characters – we find it in the hands of a 'vice'. Feste recalls this vice's dagger in the song with which he exits after Malvolio's dismissal.

> I am gone, sir, and anon, sir,
>   I'll be with you again,
> In a trice, like to the old Vice,
>   Your need to sustain;
> Who, with dagger of lath, in his rage and his wrath
>   Cries, 'Ah ha!' to the devil:
> Like a mad lad, 'Pare thy nails, dad.
>   Adieu, goodman devil!'[28]

The 'play' dagger or sword wielded by fools in their mock combats belongs to an older tradition of which we found a possible, early trace in the *targe* supplied to Robert III by Edward I in 1312, and, as suggested in Chapter 1, may be a relic of still earlier times when the Celtic *riogdruth* and Norman *joculator* carried real weapons and were expected to use them in defence of their lords. It was for a mock combat that Will Somer was provided with cardboard armour in the Christmas revels of Edward VI, when 'vyces daggers' and 'squertes' were also given to the numerous amateur fools attendant on the Lord of Misrule. Along with the coxcomb kept at Cambridge in the 1540s for use of their Christmas Lord, there were also fools' coats and a 'dagger of wodd'.[29] On stage, the court fool Rafe Simnel remarks to the prince in Robert Greene's *Friar Bacon and Friar Bungay* of about 1590, 'Marry, sirrah Ned, thou shalt put on my cap and my coat and my dagger, and I will put on thy clothes and thy sword, and so thou shalt be my fool'; and in *The Devill is an Asse* of 1616, Jonson has the Devil recall that fifty years earlier, 'every great man had his Vice [meaning his domestic fool] stand by him/In his long coat, shaking his wooden dagger'.[30]

Whether the Fool in *Lear* was equipped in this way, we do not know. There is no reference to a dagger in the text, though it might be useful to the actor. Like the 'idiot's robe', it would be a telling visual symbol of that quality in the Fool aptly defined by one editor as his 'destructive energy of innocence'.[31]

CHAPTER 18

Mr Nobody

I said in my introductory chapter that the fools owed whatever freedom of action they enjoyed at court to their nebulous status; as nobodies they had no competitors. Though Tom Derry and Muckle John were the last of their innocent kind to be maintained at court, others lingered on in noble and gentry households for very much longer. And though they had much to contribute to those who kept them in their capacity to amuse and return with interest whatever affection they received, they could also require a lot of indulgence.

Tom Skelton, a family fool of the Penningtons of Muncaster Castle in Cumbria, was one of these. Though shrewd enough to keep on the right side of his patrons, he was far from being wholly sane and seems to have taken a perverse pleasure in making himself objectionable to everyone else with whom he came into contact. One of his wittier and least offensive tricks was to daub the banisters of the great stairs at Muncaster with grease; when questioned as to whether he was responsible, he replied that 'everyone had had a hand in it'.

Two full-length portraits of Tom survive and are reproduced in Plate 14. The first (still at Muncaster) has been dated to about 1659; the second (now in the Shakespeare Institute) appears to derive from the first. In both, Tom wears a long, pleated robe of a chequered material in white, blue and yellow. He holds a broad-brimmed hat in one hand and, in the other, a white stave – a symbol of office relating to the fictitious claim he makes in his will (inscribed in full on the first of the portraits) to be Bailiff of Wigan and Under-sheriff of Lancashire. The basin with handles he is holding under his arm is also explained in the will:

> The Dish with Luggs wch I do Carry here
> Shews all my living is in good strong beer.

In 1659, Tom moved with the young heir of the family, William Pennington, to Haigh Hall in Lancashire, where he was to remain till his death in 1668.[1]

To judge by the lines inscribed on the headstone of another nobody's grave in Berkeley churchyard, Gloucestershire, Dicky Pearce was an innocent of the more agreeable kind.

> Here lies the Earl of SUFFOLK'S Fool,
> Men call'd him DICKY PEARCE;
> His Folly serv'd to make Folks laugh,
> When Wit and Mirth were scarce.
>
> Poor Dick, alas! is dead and gone,
> What signifies to cry?
> DICKYS enough are still behind,
> To laugh at by and by.
>
> Buried June 18, 1728, aged 63.[2]

Francis Douce gives the names of a few others. Lord Chancellor Talbot (1685–1737) is said to have kept a Welsh jester named Rees Pengelding, and Lord Bussy Mansel of Margam a certain Robin Rush, described as 'an idiot by nature, but who often said very witty things'. Of Robin, Douce (writing in 1806/7) adds, 'There are people now alive in Wales, or lately were, who well remembered him.'[3]

A namesake of the learned doctor, Samuel Johnson, born in 1691, was perhaps the last of his kind. He had begun his career as a dancing master in Manchester, and went on to achieve celebrity in London as author of the nonsense play *Hurlothrumbo* in which he played the part of Lord Flame – 'sometimes in one key, sometimes in another, sometimes fiddling, sometimes dancing, and sometimes walking on high stilts'. The notoriety of this success (which he was never able to repeat) appears quite literally to have gone to his head because for the last thirty years of his life he half-believed that he *was* Lord Flame and a peer of the realm, and was maintained in that delusion in a hall belonging to Lord Harrington in the village of Gawsworth in Cheshire; to the villagers, however, whom he condescended to entertain with his fiddling, he was known as 'Maggoty' or 'Fiddler Johnson'. Though perhaps more eccentric than naturally foolish, he is worth recalling for the epitaph of his own composition that he instructed to be inscribed in stone over his isolated grave in a copse outside the village, where he was buried in 1773.

> Stay thou whom Chance directs or ease persuades,
> To seek the Quiet of these Sylvan shades,
> Here, undisturb'd, and hid from Vulgar Eyes,
> A Wit, Musician, Poet, Player lies;
> A Dancing Master, too, in Grace he shone,
> And all the arts of Opera were his own:
> In Comedy well skill'd he drew Lord Flame,
> Acted the Part and gain'd himself the Name.
> Averse to strife, how oft he'd gravely say,
> These peaceful Groves should shade his breathless Clay
> That, when he rose again, laid here alone,
> No friend and he should quarrel for a Bone,
> Thinking that were some old lame Gossip nigh
> She possibly might take his Leg or Thigh.[4]

Samuel Johnson in one of his later, disastrous productions, The Blazing
Comet, or The Mad Lovers *of 1732, in which he is seen – still fiddling on stilts
– as Lord Wildfire paying court to Lady Flame. Both are quite mad. The scene
ends with Wildfire climbing in through the window to taste the 'Joys of
Immortality' (Burney Collection in the British Museum)*

In Elizabeth's reign, as we have seen, a process was already under way whereby the clever fools – or at least the more talented and adaptable of them – were already finding an alternative means of livelihood among the players, and Archy Armstrong was the last of the jesters to hold a permanent position at court. The creation of the stage Clown – the simple rustic grotesquely out of place in city and court – has been attributed to Tarlton, though the type can be traced in embryo to the interludes of the pre-Shakespearean drama.[5] Though not limited to such parts, William Kempe specialised in them. When, in 1599, Robert Armin succeeded Kempe as the principal fool of the Chamberlain's Men, he may have taken over some of his clown parts; but his unique contribution to the concept of the fool in the drama of his time lay in his performance of the more courtly fools of Shakespeare's middle comedies. Trinculo in *The Tempest* may well have been Armin's swan-song as well as that of the stage jester. But if this was the close of a chapter, it was far from being the end of the story; for the period that followed – from James's accession to the closure of the public theatres in 1642 – was a time of harvest for the stage fools in which they were to play a prominent, sometimes even dominant, role in the companies to which they belonged and the plays in which they appeared.

No-body and Some-body has the subtitle, *With the true Chronicle of Elydure*. As R.A. Foakes points out, it may have been a revision of an earlier play of the 1580s or early 1590s when plays about mythical English kings were in vogue. It contains allusions to the reign of James I and was entered in the Stationers' Register in March, 1606.[6] The leading comedy role is that of Nobody, who is dressed exclusively in an enormous pair of breeches. When asked, 'Why doe you goe thus out of fashion? You are even a very hoddy doddy, all breech', Nobody adds, 'And no body', and goes on to complain,

> But if my breeches had as much cloth in them as ever was drawne
> betwixt Kendall and Canning street, they were scarce great enough
> to hold all the wrongs that I must pocket.
> Fie fie, how I am slaunderd through the world.
> *Nobody* keepes tall fellowes at his heeles,
> Yet if you meete a crew of rogues and beggars,
> Aske who they serve, theile aunswere, *Nobody*.
> Your Cavaliers and swaggerers bout the towne
> That dominere in Taverns, sweare and stare,
> Urge them upon some termes: theile turne their malice
> To me, and say theile fight with *Nobody*:
> Or if they fight, and *Nobody* by chaunce
> Come in to part them, I am sure to pay for it,
> And *Nobody* be hurt when they scape scotfree:
> And not the dastardst coward in the world
> But dares a bout with me. What shall I doe?[7]

In the course of the action that follows, Somebody, the villain of the piece who in opposition to Nobody is dressed in a costume that is all doublet and no breeches, sets a braggart to attack Nobody. He is rescued by a Clown, who acts throughout as Nobody's servant. The play is an uneasy mix of old-fashioned mythical history in which a tyrant king is displaced by his virtuous brother and satirical comedy, targeting the social abuses of contemporary society; and it is clear from the title page of the published text (overleaf), which is dominated by the names of Nobody and Somebody and an engraving of Nobody in his enveloping breeches, 'printed for John Trundle . . . to be sold at his shop in Barbican, at the figure of No-body', that of the two the comedy was by far the more popular with Jacobean audiences.

Here then is that 'picture of Nobody' to whom Trinculo attributes Ariel's mysterious accompaniment to his and Stephano's catch in *The Tempest* (III.ii.125).[8] The conceit was not new. It had featured in the story of Odysseus' escape from the Cyclops as told by Homer in his *Odyssey*. When the drunken Polyphemos asks his name, Odysseus tells him it is 'Nobody'. So later, when Polyphemos is blinded and his friends come running to his aid and ask him who is killing him and the giant replies 'nobody', they attribute his afflictions to Zeus and leave him alone. It had been employed to similar ironical effect by the poet Hoccleve in his *Regement of Princes* of about 1412; and, more recently as we have seen, Nemo had made a dramatic appearance as Judge in Robert Wilson's play, *The three Ladies of London*.[9]

In 1607/8, *Nobody and Somebody* was one of the plays taken to Germany by the player-manager, John Green. The *Englische Komödianten*, of whom Green was a leading figure in the Jacobean period, were to have considerable and beneficent influence on German drama; and the clown names with which the fools among them became associated – Thomas Sackville with 'John Bosuet' or 'Posset', George Vincent and others with 'Pickleherring' were to enter into German folklore.[10]

Green himself is believed to have played Nobody, and it is probably a portrait of him that is given as frontispiece to a manuscript translation of the *Nobody and Somebody* play into German (Plate 14c). It was seen at Graz in Austria by the Archduchess Maria Magdalena in 1608. In a letter to her brother Ferdinand, who was away from Graz at the time, she tells him that it was '*gewaltig artlich*', vastly agreeable.[11]

In his portrait, Green looks out at us with his arms wide, a rosary in one hand and a Mass-book in the other. (His continental career was pursued mainly in the courts of the Catholic Hapsburg princes.) The plume of feathers he wears in his hat mark him out as a fool. He gives us a quizzical look as though appealing to our understanding and sympathetic judgement. '*Neminis Virtus ubiq[ue] laudabilis*', he is saying. 'The virtue of Nobody is everywhere worthy of praise.' Did he ever reflect on the pertinence of his role as Nobody to his own nebulous status as player and fool?

Back in England, *Greene's Tu Quoque* provides a classic example of how a popular fool could hijack a play from its author in the estimation of the play-going public. It was written as *The City Gallant* by an otherwise unknown dramatist, John Cook. The central character, Bubble, is a servant who has recently come into a fortune and tries to pass himself off as a gallant – a variation on the Moros/Tarlton theme of the rustic clown. Whenever at a loss for words, and because he has been told that 'a gentleman should speak Latin sometimes', Bubble replies to all and sundry with the Latin phrase, *Tu quoque* – and the same to you! Bubble was played by Thomas Greene (who may have been a brother of John

NO-BODY,
AND
SOME-BODY.

With the true Chronicle Historie of Elydure,
*who was fortunately three seuerall times
crowned King of England.*

*The true Coppy thereof, as it hath beene acted by the
Queens Maiesties Seruants.*

Printed for Iohn Trundle and are to be sold at his shop in
Barbican, at the signe of No-body.

Title page of the anonymous No-body and Some-body *of c. 1606 (courtesy of the
Henry E. Huntington Library, San Marino, California)*

Detail from the title page of Thomas Heywood's A Mayden-head Well Lost *showing William Robbins as Clown (British Library)*

Green, the German Nobody), and his success in the role was so great that the play became known as *Greene's Tu Quoque* and was published under that title in 1614. This was at the Red Bull Theatre, which was occupied until about 1617 by Queen Anne's Men.[12] Again, a relatively minor character in the comic subplot that William Rowley contributed to Middleton's powerful tragedy, *The Changeling* of 1622, was to attract disproportionate attention. This was Antonio, the Changeling of the title, who pretends to be an idiot to gain access to his beloved Isabella, whose jealous husband keeps a madhouse and has confined her within it. At the Red Bull, it was played by the comedian William Robbins, seen above (extreme right) in typical wear of the period as the Clown in Heywood's *A Maidenhead Well Lost*. When the play was licensed for its first publication in 1653, it was described by the official censor as a 'Comedie . . . written by Rowley'.[13]

In the decades of the thirties and forties, though retaining much of their popularity with the public, the fools were to come under increasing economic and political pressure along with the rest of the players. In 1641, Andrew Cane of Prince Charles's Company and Timothy Reade of Queen Henrietta's Men ('the most incomparable mimicke upon the face of the Earth') were featured together in a pamphlet entitled *The Stage-Players Complaint*, 'A pleasant Dialogue between Cane of the Fortune, and Reed of the Friers', in which they are represented as 'Deploring their sad and solitary conditions for want of Imployment/In this heavie and Contagious time of the Plague in London'.[14] But the effects of the plague were soon eclipsed by a greater disaster for in the following year the public theatres were closed altogether, and, though occasional performances continued to be given in some private indoor playhouses, they were under continuous threat of being interrupted and the players arrested. In one such raid, poor Robbins was shot in the head and killed 'as he was turning and acting like a Player'.

Ultimately, however, it was neither the Puritans nor the exigencies of the Civil War that brought the long-standing popularity of the player-fools to an end, but the change of taste that had been taking place in the nineteen years of restricted theatrical activity coincident with the Interregnum. At the Restoration, a new conception of drama more in tune with classical ideals, a more 'select' audience, and a different style of theatre architecture succeeded the old in which the fool was to have no place. His exclusion was not without protest or expressions of nostalgic regret.

In a *Praeludium* written in about 1638 to a much older play, *The Careless Shepherdess*, Landlord, a country gentleman, when told that fools were out of fashion and were not to feature in the performance to follow, reminisces fondly of the former time with particular reference to Timothy Reade's performance as the pretended madman of *The Changeling*.

> Why I would have the Fool in every Act,
> Be't Comedy, or Tragedy, I 'ave laugh'd
> Untill I cry'd again, to see what Faces
> The Rogue will make: O it does me good
> To see him hold out's Chin, hang down his hands,
> And twirle his Bawble. There is nere a part
> About him but breaks jests. I heard a fellow
> Once on this Stage cry, *Doodle, Doodle, Dooe*,
> Beyond compare; I'de give the other shilling
> To see him act the Changling once again.

To which the London citizen Thrift replies,

> And so would I, his part has all the wit,
> For none speaks Craps and Quibbles besides him:
> I'd rather see him leap, laugh, or cry,
> Then hear the gravest Speech in all the *Play*.
> I never saw Rheade peeping through the Curtain,
> But ravishing joy enter'd into my heart.[15]

In Thomas Shadwell's *The Woman Captive* of 1679, the Fool was to receive explicit dismissal, and for a reason specifically linked with his earlier banishment from court and from gentry households. The play opens with Sir Humphrey Scattergood, who has recently come into an estate, dismissing all his father's old retainers. 'How now, why stays that Fool?' he asks of his Steward. 'Because that Fool has more wit than to go away', interposes the Fool.

Sir Humphrey:	Sirrah! begon! I will not keep you. –
Fool:	Some body I see has us'd wicked Court Policy to supplant me in my employment.
Sir Humphrey:	I'll keep no Fool, 'tis out of fashion for great Men to keep Fools.
Fool:	Because now adays they are their own Fools, and so save Charges: But for all that they delight in Fools out of Livery. When do you see any of 'em favour a Wit?
Sir Humphrey:	I'll have none, 'tis exploded ev'n upon the Stage.
Fool:	But for all that *Shakespear*'s Fools had more wit than any of the Wits and Criticks now adays: Well, if the History of Fools were written, the whole Kingdom would not contain the Library; yet a vast number of Fools have been in Print, and written their own Histories.
Sir Humphrey:	You are a Satyrical Fool, and will give offence.
Fool:	Indeed this Age is not able to bear Satyr; and yet 'tis a very laughing jeering age: all Fools laugh at one another, and scarce any one is such a Fool, but he has a sub-Fool that he can laugh at –
Sir Humphrey:	Begon Sirrah! I'll have no fooling.
Fool:	Good Sir *Humphrey*, I will be a fashionable Fool, and learn to lisp, speak French, and be very much affected. I will be a well-bred Fool, a Flatterer, or a Pimp, if you please, you may turn away a Knave or a Chaplain for me.
Sir Humphrey:	Who waits there! take away the Fool!

And a stage direction adds with brutal directness, '*They thrust*'.[16] He never returns.

The play remained in the eighteenth-century repertoire; though by 1744 when it was produced at the Haymarket in an adaptation by Thomas Odell under the title of *The Prodigal*, the part of the Fool was performed by Charlotte Charke, Colley Cibber's daughter, who specialised in breeches roles.[17]

From the time of the Restoration, fools in general were in such disfavour that their parts were even cut from revivals of Shakespeare's plays. In Nahum Tate's notorious rewriting of *King Lear* in 1681, in which Cordelia survives to marry Edgar, Lear was wholly deprived of his 'friendly knave', and Garrick's Lear (as is apparent from contemporary portraits) endured the 'pitiless storm' in heroic solitude. Lear's Fool had to wait until Macready's production of 1828 to be restored to the play, and even then the part was savagely cut and played by a girl for pathos.

In the meantime, the player fools were to follow Kempe's early precedent in finding larger scope for their anarchic humour in more proletarian forms of amusement and, in so doing, return to their origins among the peripatetic *mimi et histriones* of early medieval England. We find them in the drolls of Bartholomew Fair and in many an obscure booth theatre, where some of their former roles such as Falstaff, Bubble and the Changeling were briefly revived in truncated and caricatured versions of the plays in which they had originally featured. As Jack Puddings and Merry Andrews, they were reduced to the functions of barkers, fiddlers or contortionists in country fairs. The gradual process whereby they were able to rise again to something approaching their former popularity and renown belongs to another story.[18] Though they have yet to find a significant role in contemporary drama or to make more than an occasional return to the parts in Shakespeare's plays that were once their own, their peeping through the curtain of make-believe can still produce that lift of joy to the heart of which Citizen Thrift had spoken in 1638.

Abbreviations

The following abbreviations are used in the notes. Other works and sources are cited in full on the first reference to them in each set of notes; thereafter by abbreviated title. Place of publication is London except where otherwise stated.

BL British Library	
Bullock-Davies, *Minstrels*	Constance Bullock-Davies, *Menestrellorum Multitudo, Minstrels at a Royal Feast*, Cardiff, 1978
Bullock-Davies, *Register*	Constance Bullock-Davies, *Register of Royal and Baronial Domestic Minstrels, 1272–1327*, Woodbridge, 1986
CCR	Calendar of Close Rolls
CCW	Calendar of Chancery Warrants
CLR	Calendar of Liberate Rolls
CSPD	Calendar of State Papers, Domestic
Chambers, ES	E.K. Chambers, *The Elizabethan Stage*, 4 vols, Oxford, 1923
Chambers, MS	E.K. Chambers, *The Mediaeval Stage*, 2 vols, Oxford, 1903
DNB	*Dictionary of National Biography*
Doran	John Doran, *The History of Court Fools*, 1858
EETS	Early English Text Society
EMM	John Southworth, *The English Medieval Minstrel*, Woodbridge, 1989
Hazlitt's 'Dodsley'	*Dodsley's Old English Plays*, first issued 1744, ed. W.C. Hazlitt, 15 vols, 1874–6
HMC	Historical Manuscripts Commission
Hotson	Leslie Hotson, *Shakespeare's Motley*, 1952, reprinted New York, 1971
Jonson	Ben Jonson, *Works*, ed. C.H. Herford, P. and E. Simpson, 11 vols, Oxford, 1925–52
L & P	*Letters and Papers, Foreign and Domestic, of the Reign of Henry VIII*, ed. J.S. Brewer, J. Gairdner and R.H. Brodie, 21 vols, 1862–1918. Vol. 1, revised R.H. Brodie, 1920. *Addenda*, 2 vols, 1929–32
MSC	Malone Society Collections
II, Part 3	(includes 'Players at Ipswich' and 'Dramatic Records of the City of London'), ed. E.K. Chambers, A.J. Mill and W.W. Gregg, Oxford 1931
VII	*Records of Plays and Players in Kent, 1450–1642*, ed. G.E. Dawson, Oxford, 1965
XI	*Records of Plays and Players in Norfolk and Suffolk, 1330–1642*, ed. J. Wasson, Oxford, 1981
Nichols's 'Progresses'	John Nichols, *The Progresses and Public Processions of Queen Elizabeth*, 3 vols, 1823
OED	*The Oxford English Dictionary*, ed. J.A. Simpson and E.S.C. Weiner, Oxford, 1989

PRO	Public Records Office
REED	*Records of Early English Drama*. General Editor, A.F. Johnston, Toronto, 1979–
Cambridge	Ed. A. Nelson, 2 vols, 1988
Chester	Ed. L.M. Clopper, 1979
Coventry	Ed. R.W. Ingram, 1981
Cumb., West., and Glos.	*Cumberland, Westmorland and Gloucestershire*, ed. A. Douglas and P. Greenfield, 1986
Devon	Ed. J.M. Wasson, 1986
Hereford and Worcester	*Herefordshire and Worcestershire*, ed. D.N. Klausner, 1990
Lancs.	*Lancashire*, ed. D. George, 1991
Newcastle	*Newcastle upon Tyne*, ed. J.J. Anderson, 1982
Norwich	*1540–1642*, ed. D. Galloway, 1984
Salop	*Shropshire*, ed. J.A.B. Somerset, 2 vols, 1994
York	Ed. A.F. Johnston and M. Rogerson, 2 vols, 1979
RS	Rolls Series
TFT	*Tudor Facsimile Texts*, issued by J.S. Farmer, 143 vols, 1907–14
Welsford	Enid Welsford, *The Fool, His Social and Literary History*, 1935

Shakespeare quotations are from the Arden editions of the plays, and abbreviations of play titles as given in C.T. Onions, *A Shakespeare Glossary*, 1953 edition.

The English translation of Psalm 52 (53 in the Authorised Version) I have used is that of the Jerusalem Bible of 1966.

Notes

Chapter 1: King and Fool

1. Thomas Fuller, *The Holy State and the Profane State* (Cambridge, 1642), pp. 182–3.
2. See Paul Radin, *The Trickster* (1956).
3. Enid Welsford, *The Fool, His Social and Literary History* (1935).
4. *The Chronographia of Michael Psellus*, tr. E.R.A. Sewter (1953), pp. 170–8.
5. See D.J. Gifford, 'Iconographical Notes towards a Definition of the Medieval Fool', in *Journal of the Warburg and Courtauld Institutes*, XXXVII (1974), p. 338. It was not until the fourteenth century that more playful and amusing depictions of the fool began to appear in the psalters.
6. K.H. Jackson, *The Oldest Irish Tradition: A Window on the Iron Age* (Cambridge, 1964).
7. Welsford, pp. 148–9 and note.
8. *The Miscellaneous Remains of Cardinal Perron* (1707), p. 77.
9. See Kenneth Muir's introduction to his Arden edition of *King Lear* (9th edn, 1972), pp. lvi–vii.
10. Perron (n. 8), p. 14.
11. Sima Qian, *War-Lords*, tr. W. Dolby and J. Scott (Edinburgh, 1974), p. 168. This same megalomaniac ruler was responsible for the recently excavated mausoleum at Mount Li with its pottery army.
12. *Chronicon Angliae*, ed. E.M. Thompson (RS, 1874), pp. 11–12; Doran, p. 243.
13. *Moriae Encomium* (*Praise of Folly*), tr. Betty Radice (Harmondsworth, 1971), p. 119.
14. *The Holy State and the Profane State* (n. 1), p. 181.

Chapter 2: The Elusive Dwarfs

1. Véronique Dasen, *Dwarfs in Ancient Egypt and Greece* (Oxford, 1993), pp. 25–9.
2. Ibid., p. 133. Cf. Welsford, pp. 56–7; G. Maspero, *The Dawn of Civilization* (4th edn, 1901), pp. 397–8, 433–4.
3. J.H. Breasted, *Ancient Records of Egypt* (Chicago, 1906), I, pp. 160–1.
4. R.O. Faulkner, *The Ancient Egyptian Pyramid Texts* (Oxford, 1969), p. 191.
5. *Lucian*, tr. A.M. Harmon (Loeb edn, 1979), I, 430–3.
6. 'On the Sublime', in *Classical Literary Criticism*, tr. T.S. Dorsch (Penguin Classics, 1965), p. 157.
7. *Martial: Epigrams*, XII, 93; tr. W.C.A. Ker (Loeb, revd edn, 1978), p. 383.
8. *Cath Maige Mucrama*, ed. Máirín O'Daly (Irish Texts Society, Dublin, 1975), p. 41. A similar story is told of the legendary hero Cuchulainn and a dwarf called Senbecc, for which see Vernon J. Harward Jr, *The Dwarfs of Arthurian Romance and Celtic Tradition* (Leiden, 1958), p. 8.
9. *Silva Gadelica*, ed. S.H. O'Grady (1892), II, pp. 115–17; *Duanaire Finn* (Irish Texts Society), I (1908), ed. Eoin MacNeill, p. 196; II (1933), ed. G. Murphy, pp. 207, 227.
10. *Silva Gadelica*, II, pp. 269–85.
11. Welsford, p. 93 and note.
12. *The Mabinogion*, tr. G. Jones and T. Jones (Everyman's Library, revd edn, 1989), p. 187.
13. Medically speaking, there are many different causes of dwarfism, and as many types of dwarf, but only two broad categories need concern us here: the *pituitary* or 'proportionate' dwarfs, who have normal proportions of limbs and trunk and are without obvious deformity, and those who are subject to *achondroplasia* (the commonest form), in whom arms and legs are abnormally short and the head somewhat large in relation to the rest of the body. In the proportionate dwarfs, their condition

may be hereditary (as with the African pygmies) or, more rarely, 'spasmodic', i.e. occurring in families of European and other descent where there is no previous history of dwarfism. It is important to note that in both categories those affected are of normal, often exceptional, intelligence, which enables them to make the best of society's varying attitudes towards them and, as frequently in the past, to turn these to their advantage. Among present-day dwarfs – or 'persons of diminutive stature' as many now prefer to be called – there are those who would strongly deny that their small size is a form of 'disablement' in the usual meaning of the term, and have no wish to be treated as if it was.

14. For these, see Christine E. Fell, *Edward King and Martyr* (Leeds, 1971), pp. iii–xxviii.

15. *Lestorie des Engles*, ed. T.D. Hardy and C.T. Martin (RS, 1888–9), I (text), pp. 168–71; II (translation), pp. 126–9.

16. The name 'Turold' is usually applied by recent commentators to the messenger on the dwarf's immediate right; but, with one exception (a depiction of the Conqueror), the names embroidered in the Bayeux Tapestry appear *above* the persons they are intended to identify; and whereas the second of the two messengers is of no particular interest or importance in the pictorial record, the figure of the dwarf is unique and would therefore seem more likely to justify naming. In an attempt to prove a Kentish origin for the tapestry and a connection with Bishop Odo who became earl of Kent, the 'messenger Turold' has been identified with a 'Turold of Rochester', who was one of the bishop's tenants in the period prior to 1086. But, as Sir Frank Stenton has pointed out, the name was quite common at the time. It was shared, among others, by the poet or transcriber of the famous *Song of Roland*, where it appears in the final line '*Ci faut la geste ke Turoldus declinet*' ('Here ends the story that Turold wrote'). The earliest surviving manuscript of the *Song* was written in England, and is usually dated to the final decade of the eleventh century; we know that a '*cantilena Rollandi*' was sung before the Battle of Hastings. In view of the association of dwarfs with the composition of poetry and music recorded in Ireland in the twelfth century, it is not impossible that the dwarf of the tapestry and the author or redactor of the *Song of Roland* (probably a minstrel) were one and the same person, and that he was given a retrospective 'walk-on' role in the tapestry in recognition of his share in the composition of the *Song*. (For the '*cantilena Rollandi*', see following chapter, pp. 26–7 and note 25.)

17. See Harward, *Dwarfs of Arthurian Romance* (n. 8), *passim*.

18. Johannis de Oxenedes, *Chronica*, ed. H. Ellis (RS, 1859), p. 163; *The Illustrated Chronicles of Matthew Paris*, tr. Richard Vaughan (1993), p. 113.

19. Similar association of dwarfs with the numina is found in Indian and Scandinavian mythologies, and in South-east Asia. In the Vāyu Purāna, Vishnu in the third of his avatars takes the form of a dwarf whose three diminutive strides encompass the world. In a Norse creation myth recounted in the *Prose Edda of Snorri Sturluson*, the four corners of the sky are supported by dwarfs with the names of East, West, North and South. In Java, a law that continued in force to 1950 required all dwarfs born throughout the kingdom to be delivered to the royal palace (J.R. Brandon, *Theatre in South East Asia*, Cambridge, MA, 1967, p. 15).

Chapter 3: Warrior Fools

1. *The Greek Alexander Romance*, tr. Richard Stoneman (Penguin Classics, 1991), pp. 60–1. Diogenes was to find his way into the jest-books. See, for example, *Pasquils Jests* of 1604 in *Shakespeare Jest-Books*, ed. W.C. Hazlitt (1864), III, pp. 55–7.

2. Sima Qian, *War-Lords*, tr. W. Dolby and J. Scott (Edinburgh, 1974), p. 32.

3. Ibid., pp. 159–68.

4. *Martial*, *Epigrams*, VIII, 13; tr. W.C.A. Ker (Loeb, revd edn, 1978), p. 13.

5. J.D.A. Ogilvy, '*Mimi, Scurrae, Histriones*: Entertainers of the Early Middle Ages' in *Speculum*, XXXVIII (1973), p. 605.

6. In medieval Latin, *joculator* – deriving from a rare Latin verb, 'to joke' – was the usual term for a professional court fool, excluding 'naturals'; but confusingly the same word was also applied to popular entertainers in general as an undiscriminating alternative to *mimus* and

histrio, both meaning literally, 'actor'. *Joculator* is usually translated as 'jester', and, where this occurs in quotations, I have let it stand; though, as previously noted, 'jester' in its present meaning dates only from the Tudor period, and has associations with Tudor and Jacobean stage fools that are inappropriate here; the medieval *gestour* was a teller or singer of *gestes* or stories. To avoid confusion in what follows, I stay as near as possible to the original Latin, using 'fool' or 'joker' when the context suggests that a court fool is referred to, 'performer' or 'entertainer' where it seems that a broader meaning is intended. For the *scurrae*, see following chapter.

7. For these quotations, with citation of sources, see Ogilvy (n. 5), pp. 607–9.

8. Ibid., p. 608.

9. *De Gestis Regum Anglorum*, ed. W. Stubbs (RS, 1887–9), I, p. 177; tr. J. Sharpe, ed. J.A. Giles as *William of Malmesbury's Chronicle of the Kings of England* (1889), pp. 158–9.

10. It is true that those who first put the Irish sagas into writing were probably monks; but their situation was different from that of the English clerics in that they had been able to reach a fruitful compromise with an older, but still flourishing, secular tradition of learning. See Alan Harrison, *The Irish Trickster* (Folklore Society, Sheffield, 1989), pp. 13–20.

11. From 'The Destruction of Da Derga's Hostel' in *Early Irish Myths and Sagas*, tr. J. Gantz (Penguin Classics, 1981), pp. 94–5, 101–2.

12. I have made use of an edition with English translation of the 'Brussels' text of *Cath Almaine* (thought to best reflect the original form of the story as composed in the tenth century) by Joan Newlon Radner in *Fragmentary Annals of Ireland* (Dublin, 1978), pp. 67–80. For Úa Maigléine and other Irish fools, see also Alan Harrison's *The Irish Trickster* (n. 10).

13. *Cath Maige Mucrama*, ed. and tr. M. O'Daly (Irish Texts Society, Dublin, 1975), pp. 40–3.

14. Ibid., pp. 92–3. For a similar story featuring Ailill, Cú Chulainn and a fool called Tamon, see *Táin Bó Cúalnge* ('The Cattle-raid of Cooley'), ed. and tr. C. O'Rahilly (Irish Texts Society, Dublin, 1967), p. 207.

15. In thirteenth- and fourteenth-century England, some senior minstrels and heralds were given the title *Le Roy* before their names, and the *reges haraldorum* wore crowns on State occasions (EMM, pp. 64–5). Do Déra wears his in battle. The 'shameful haircut' was a distinctive form of tonsure.

16. P.H. Sawyer, *Anglo-Saxon Charters* (Royal Historical Society, 1968), no. 1647, p. 452; HMC, *Fifth Report* (1876), I, p. 448, where the name is given as 'Hitard'.

17. I draw in the following pages on my earlier account of Taillefer in EMM, pp. 30–5.

18. *The Carmen de Hastingae Proelio of Guy, Bishop of Amiens*, ed. and tr. C. Morton and H. Muntz (Oxford, 1972), pp. 26–7.

19. Ibid., pp. 81–2.

20. *Lestorie des Engles*, ll. 5271–5305; ed. T.D. Hardy and C.T. Martin (RS, 1888–9), I (text), pp. 223–4; II (translation), pp. 167–8.

21. *Henrici Archidiaconi Huntendunensis Historia Anglorum*, ed. T. Arnold (RS, 1879), pp. 202–3.

22. *Roman de Rou*, ll. 8035–64; (text) ed. H. Andresen (Heilbron, 1879), II, pp. 348–9; tr. E. Taylor as *Master Wace, His Chronicle of the Norman Conquest from the Roman de Rou* (1837), pp. 189–90.

23. *De Gestis Regum Anglorum* (n. 9); for text, II, p. 302; for Sharpe's translation, p. 277.

24. *The Song of Roland* (laisse 172), tr. R. Harrison (New York, Mentor edn, 1970), p. 122.

25. See David Douglas, '*The Song of Roland* and the Norman Conquest of England' in *French Studies*, XIV, April 1960, no. 2, pp. 99–101. M.T. Clanchy in *From Memory to Written Record* (Oxford, 2nd edn, 1993, pp. 215–16) conjectures that 'as a consequence of their victory, the Normans came into contact with the only culture in Roman Christendom which possessed heroic vernacular verse in writing, sustained over the centuries from *Beowulf* to *The Battle of Maldon*. This confrontation with Anglo-Saxon literature may have inspired the Norman conquerors to have the *Chanson de Roland* written down, in order to commemorate their victory at Hastings and show that the French (as *The Anglo-Saxon Chronicle* called the Normans) had something as good in their language.'

26. Domesday Book, ed. J. Morris (Chichester, 1982), 15, p. 162a.

Chapter 4: Norman Buffoons

1. *From Domesday Book to Magna Carta* (Oxford, 2nd edn, 1955), p. 97.
2. *History of Recent Events in England* (*Historia Novorum in Anglia*), tr. G. Bosanquet (1964), p. 206.
3. *The Ecclesiastical History of Orderic Vitalis*, ed. and tr. M. Chibnall (1969–81), III, p. 319.
4. The identification was first suggested by Charles Stothard; see 'Some Observations on the Bayeux Tapestry' in *Archaeologia*, XIX (1819), p. 189.
5. *Roman de Rou* (ll. 3671–5), ed. H. Andresen (Heilbron, 1879), II, p. 177.
6. Quoted by Frank Barlow in *William Rufus* (1983), p. 99.
7. *Ecclesiastical History* (n. 3), IV, pp. 186–9.
8. Ibid., III, pp. 102–3.
9. Ibid., VI, pp. 62–3.
10. *The Book of the Foundation of St Bartholomew's Church in London*, ed. N. Moore (EETS, 1923), pp. 2–3.
11. Thomas de Chabham, writing about 1220. Quoted from Allardyce Nicoll in *Masks, Mimes and Miracles* (1931), p. 152. For Latin text, see 'Chabham's *Penitential* and Its Influence in the Thirteenth Century' in *Publications of the Modern Language Association of America*, XL (1925), pp. 232–3.
12. For the biographical data given here, see Sir Norman Moore's article in DNB, under 'Rahere'.
13. Helen Waddell, *The Wandering Scholars* (Pelican edn, 1954), p. 200n.
14. *Book of the Foundation*, op. cit., pp. 12–13. The smear laid on Rayer's character by a nineteenth-century historian of the Fair (Henry Morley in *Memoirs of Bartholomew Fair*, 1859, pp. 10–15) implying that he used his 'juggler's skills' to counterfeit cures and miracles with a view to attracting donations for the building, and later for the upkeep of the hospital, rests on nothing more than Protestant prejudice and a misunderstanding of the nature of his former profession. Rayer was never a 'juggler' or 'conjurer' in the modern sense as Morley wrongly supposed.
15. See Hugo Rahner, *Man at Play* (New York, 1972), pp. 91–105.
16. *Book of the Foundation*, p. 3. The scale of Rayer's achievement is reflected in the permanence of the institutions he left behind him. Having survived the Reformation, the Great Fire, the London Blitz and terrorist bombs, the choir of the priory church that he built is now the oldest parish church in the City of London. There his body still lies under its fifteenth-century canopy. It is the only known resting place of a medieval joker – albeit one who became a monastic founder and, in all but formal title, a saint. The Fair, as well as raising funds for the upkeep of the hospital, provided Londoners with an annual feast of popular entertainment to as late as 1855. The hospital still stands, though in new and larger buildings, on its original site; only very recently (in 1996) – after 800 years of continuous service to the sick – was it threatened with closure by a 'Conservative' government. As this goes to press, its fate remains uncertain.

Chapter 5: Minstrel Fools

1. *De Nugis Curialium*, ed. M.R. James (Oxford, 1983), pp. 438–9. I have used here the English translation of F. Tupper and M.B. Ogle (1924), p. 274.
2. *Patrologiae Latina*, ed. J.P. Migne (Paris, 1855), CCVII, Letter 14, col. 49; tr. L. Wright, 'The Role of Musicians at Court in Twelfth-century Britain' in *Art and Patronage in the English Romanesque*, Society of Antiquaries Occ. Paper (New Series), VIII (1986), pp. 98–9. Mr Wright takes *candidatrices* to be a mistake for *cantatrices* and translates as 'female singers'.
3. Edmond Faral, *Les Jongleurs en France au moyen âge* (Paris, 1910), pp. 103–6. For a contrary view and further references, see L.M. Wright, 'Misconceptions Concerning the Troubadours, Trouvères and Minstrels' in *Music and Letters*, 48 (1967), pp. 35ff.
4. For a full account of the waferers, see Bullock-Davies, *Minstrels*, pp. 44–50.
5. See W.L. Warren, *Henry II* (1973), pp. 306ff.
6. Chrétien de Troyes, *Erec and Enide*, tr. W.W. Comfort in *Arthurian Romances* (Everyman's Library, paperback edn, reprinted 1984), p. 28.
7. Verse 4 of the Jerusalem translation of the psalm which, as in the Authorised Version, is numbered 53.
8. The normality of the fool's dress depicted in Plates 2 and 3 is in striking contrast to the naked or semi-naked madmen of some contemporary and later psalters referred to

in the following chapter. If these clothed fools may reasonably be taken as representative of the minstrel-fools, the disapproving attitude of the clerics towards them is revealed, not only in their consumption of the 'bread of the poor', but also in the fixed grin and cloven feet of the 'Trinity' fool. The devil in disguise? For a basis to this demonic association in contemporary theology, see Sandra Billington, *A Social History of the Fool* (1984), pp. 20ff.

9. Ll. 10553–6; ed. I. Arnold (Paris, 1940), II, p. 553; tr. R.A. Baltzer, 'Music in the Life and Times of Eleanor of Aquitaine' in *Eleanor of Aquitaine, Patron and Politician*, ed. W.W. Kibler (1976), p. 68.

10. *Erec and Enide*, vv. 2036ff., tr. L. Wright, 'The Role of Musicians', *op. cit.* (n. 2), pp. 100–1. Similar passages occur in other early medieval romances; see, for example, the thirteenth-century *Flamenca* of Bernadet the Troubadour, tr. H.F.M. Prescott (1930), p. 13.

11. As at this period the term 'minstrel' implied association with a particular patron or place, an 'itinerant minstrel' (in the sense of one who was unattached) would be a contradiction in terms; which is not to deny that minstrels were often highly mobile and undertook lengthy tours apart from their patrons. See EMM, pp. 1–4.

12. Domesday Book, ed. J. Morris, 4 (Chichester, 1982), l. 25.

13. *Charters of the Honour of Mowbray, 1107–1191*, ed. D.E. Greenway (British Academy Records, Oxford, 1972), p. xl and no. 308. See also no. 200, p. 142.

14. 'Earldom of Hereford Charters', ed. D. Walker in *Camden Miscellany*, 4th Series XXII (1964), p. 15, no. 7; tr. M.T. Clanchy in *From Memory to Written Record* (Oxford, 2nd edn, 1993), p. 89.

15. *Rotuli de Dominabus et Pueris et Puellis de XII Comitatibus*, XXX (for 1185), (Pipe Roll Society, 1913), p. 72; Bullock-Davies, *Minstrels*, pp. 46–7.

16. It has been suggested that the name 'Follus' may have been inherited, and that Roger was merely an otter-hunter (*lutrarius*) and not a fool, though possibly descended from one. But not only were inherited surnames rare at this date (see Gustav Fransson, *Middle English Surnames of Occupation 1100–1350*, Lund, 1935, pp. 39–40); but,

alone among his colleagues and successors, Roger is described in contemporary records as *Follus Lutrarius* or *Folutrarius*, indicating that he was both otter-hunter and fool (for references, see following note).

17. The text of the grant is preserved in an 'Inspeximus' of 1378, for which see CPR, *Richard II, 1377–81*, p. 176, and J.H. Round, *The King's Serjeants* (1911), p. 299. Some earlier references are as follows: for 1178 to 1188, *Great Roll of the Pipe* (Pipe Roll Society) XXVIII, p. 73, and succeeding volumes in the series to XXXVIII, p. 120; for 1189, *Calendar of the Pipe Rolls of Richard I for Bucks. and Beds.* (Beds. Hist. Rec. Soc. VII), p. 36. If, like Godfrey's manor, Roger's office of otter-hunter was a retirement grant, it was no sinecure. Apart from the sport they doubtless provided for the king on the occasions of his anticipated visits, the otter-hounds were required to protect the royal fish-stews, on which the court depended for its supplies of fresh-water fish during Lent and on days of abstinence. For the otter-hounds and subsequent history of the office, see J.H. Round, *King's Serjeants*, pp. 298–303.

18. For references to this 'Hemingstone serjeanty', as it came to be called, see (for 1185) *Rotuli de Dominabus* (n. 15) XXXV, p. 62; (for 1212–50) *The Book of Fees* (*Testa de Nevill*), I, pp. 136, 386; II, p. 1174; (for 1331) Bullock-Davies, *Register*, p. 174.

19. *City of God*, Book XIV, 24; tr. H. Bettenson (Penguin Classics, 1972), p. 588. 'Farting in tune' is referred to by Langland in the fourteenth century; see quotation on p. 44 below. The skill (or trick) survives to the present.

20. *Rotuli Normanniae in Turri Londinensi*, ed. T.D. Hardy (1835), I, pp. 20–1; tr. Welsford, p. 115. The name 'Picol' may have been traditional. In the twelfth century anonymous tale of 'Tristan's Madness' (tr. in Beroul's *Romance of Tristan* by A.S. Fedrick, Penguin Classics, 1970, pp. 154–5), the hero, disguising himself as a madman ('frantic fool'), takes the name 'Picous', and is later addressed by its diminutive, 'Picolet'.

21. *Rotuli de Liberate ac de Misis et Praestitis Regnante Johanne*, ed. T.D. Hardy (1844), pp. 148, 153.

22. CLR, *Henry III, 1245–51*, p. 125.

23. *Close Rolls of Henry III, 1227–31*, p. 557.

24. CLR, *Henry III, 1226–40*, pp. 60, 299; *1245–51*, p. 1.
25. *Nichil in his letum nisi letiferum*; *De Nugis Curialium*, ed. James (n. 1), pp. 10–11.
26. *The Antiquarian Repertory*, II (1779), pp. 58–9.
27. Enid Welsford (p. 115 and note) cites two similar, though later, examples from France and Burgundy, where payments were made to '*Jehan le Heraut foul*' and '*le trompette de l'arcevesque de Coulongue le quel fait le sot*'.
28. CLR, *Henry III, 1226–40*, p. 480; *Issues of the Exchequer* (Pell Records, 1837), ed. F. Devon, p. 27.
29. *Close Rolls of Henry III, 1247–51*, p. 468; *1256–59*, p. 83; *1253–54*, p. 256.
30. 'Some Notes on the Court and Chancery of Henry III', in *Historical Essays in Honour of James Tait*, ed. J.G. Edwards *et al.* (Manchester, 1933), pp. 310–11.
31. *Close Rolls of Henry III, 1259–61*, p. 321; Bullock-Davies, *Register*, p. 74. The date was 25 December.
32. See EMM, pp. 10–19.
33. Ibid., pp. 87–93.
34. Welsford, p. 120 and note.
35. Bullock-Davies, *Register*, pp. 167, 171. The final entry on p. 167 refers to another, later Robert in the service of Edward II.
36. *Records of the Wardrobe and Household, 1286–89*, ed. B.F. and C.R. Byerly (1986), p. 232; CCR, *Edward I, 1288–96*, p. 253; CCW, *1244–1326*, pp. 47, 56; BL Add. ms 7965, ff. 29v., 52r, 127r; Bullock-Davies, *Register*, p. 205. The term 'yeoman' (*valletus*) was of wide application at this period, and covered a great variety of rank and function from the royal cook, baker and tailor at one extreme, to youths of good family awaiting knighthood at the other; see *Letters of Edward Prince of Wales, 1304–5*, ed. H. Johnstone (Roxburghe Club, 1931), pp. xv–xvi.
37. For further information about these, see EMM, pp. 61–83. The earliest secular interlude of which a partial text survives, *Interludium de Clerico et Puella*, is contemporary (*c.* 1300). It is of a bawdy, satirical kind and, like the Ipswich interlude, features three characters. The original Middle English text (only the title is in Latin) has been printed with a modern translation by Glynne Wickham in *English Moral Interludes* (1976), pp. 195–203.
38. Bullock-Davies, *Minstrels*, pp. 17–18.
39. Ibid., p. 79.
40. *The Vision of Piers Plowman*, B-text, *passus* xiii, ll. 226–234; modernised by Terence Tiller (1981), p. 153.
41. Bullock-Davies, *Register*, p. 53.
42. I base this conjecture on the fact that some later French fools such as Jehan le Fol, fool to Jean le Bon, who visited England in 1359 (see pp. 83–4 below) are known to have been dwarfs though not specifically described as such. The title 'le Fol' may itself have carried that meaning.

Chapter 6: The Innocents

1. Welsford, p. 78.
2. Ibid., pp. 80–1.
3. ll. 260–6 in *Hoccleve's Works*, ed. F.J. Furnivall (EETS, 1897), III, p. 3.
4. ll. 3395–6, ed. J.R. Reinhard (Paris, 1926), p. 146. See Edith A. Wright, 'Medieval Attitudes towards Mental Illness', in *Bulletin of the History of Medicine*, XI, Part 3 (March 1939), pp. 352–6.
5. For the Celtic tradition, see Welsford, pp. 97–105.
6. *Middle English Metrical Romances*, ed. W.H. French and C.B. Hale (2 vols, 1930; reissued in one volume New York, 1964), p. 938, ll. 170–3.
7. *Madness and Civilization*, tr. R. Howard (1967), chapter 2, pp. 38ff.
8. 'Tristan's Madness' in Beroul, *The Romance of Tristan*, tr. A.S. Fedrick (Penguin Books, 1970), pp. 153–5.
9. R.W. Southern, *Saint Anselm, a Portrait in a Landscape* (Cambridge, 1990), pp. 129–34.
10. For Paul, *1 Corinthians* 3:18; for Gregory and Francis, see Barbara Swain, *Fools and Folly during the Middle Ages and Renaissance* (New York, 1932), pp. 36–40 and notes. The Langland quotation is from B-text, *Prologus*, ll. 123–7 in the prose translation by J.F. Goodridge (Penguin Classics, revd edn, 1966), p. 28.
11. *Summa Theologiae* of 1265–74, tr. concisely by T. McDermott (1989), p. 371. For baptism of the congenitally insane, see ibid., p. 565.
12. Matthew 19:30.
13. The basic facts from which this general summary has been drawn are in Chambers, MS, I, pp. 274–335; though Chambers, by including his account of the Feast in the section of his work devoted to 'Folk Drama', and, more explicitly, in describing it as

'largely an ebullition of the natural lout beneath the cassock' (p. 325), takes a very different line towards it than the one adopted here. For full text of the 'prose of the Ass', see ibid., II, appendix L, pp. 279–82.

14. Ibid., I, pp. 321–3. For surviving traces of the Feast in Devon, 1333–60, see REED: *Devon* (texts) pp. 6–14; (translations) pp. 319–27.

15. For the *Sociétés*, see Chambers, MS, I, pp. 372–84.

16. *The Household Book of Queen Isabella of England*, ed. F.D. Blackley and G. Hermansen (Edmonton, 1971), p. 103.

17. See Hilda Johnstone, 'The Eccentricities of Edward II', in *English Historical Review* XLVIII (1933), pp. 264–7. The list of companions is from Higden's *Polychronicon*, and includes 'buffoons'.

18. *Calendar of Documents Relating to Scotland*, ed. J. Bain (Edinburgh, 1884), II, p. 369.

19. Hilda Johnstone, *Edward of Carnarvon, 1284–1307* (Manchester, 1946), p. 130. Edward's love of boating was sufficiently notorious for the Scots to have mocked the English after Bannockburn with a popular song drawing on the oarsman's traditional chant of 'Heavalow, Rumbalow'. The maidens of England are invited to mourn their men to the tune of 'Heavalow' and to query whether the king could ever have conquered Scotland with 'Rumbalow'. Michael Prestwich, *The Three Edwards* (1980), p. 81, citing *The Brut*, ed. F.W.D. Brie (EETS, Oxford, 1906), p. 208.

20. One hundred and thirty years later, the then abbot complained to Henry VI that 'a certain idiot named Robert Fole' had been sent to them by Edward I as the first in a long series of royal pensioners without prior agreement of abbot or convent. See CPR, *Henry VI, 1436–41*, p. 90.

21. For whom, see above, p. 43. He had left the country on Eleanor's death in 1290.

22. Bullock-Davies, *Register*, p. 168, citing BL ms. Cott. Nero. C. viii, ff. 83v., 85r. Dr Bullock-Davies interprets the targe as for a 'sword and buckler dance'. For the mother, *Archaeologia* XXVI (1836), p. 344.

23. Bullock-Davies, *Register*, p. 9, citing PRO ms. E101/375/8, f. 32r.

24. Bullock-Davies, *Register*, p. 53, citing BL ms. Cott. Galba. Eiii, f. 188v.

25. *Register of Edward the Black Prince*, IV (England, 1351–65), pp. 472, 509–10.

26. CCR, *Edward III, 1360–64*, p. 280; *1364–68*, pp. 48–9.

27. For Jakeman, *Issues of the Exchequer*, ed. Devon, p. 197. For the terms of the statute, see *Halsbury's Laws of England*, ed. Hailsham (reissue of 4th edn, 1992), 30, p. 576. These ensured that insane people were cared for during the remainder of their lives; on death, their property was to pass to their legal heirs. But the system was open to grave abuse; for instances, see the case of Roger Stanlake in *Calendar of Inquisitions Post Mortem* XIII (Edward III), pp. 264–5, and CPR, *Henry IV, 1408–13*, p. 145; and that of Joan Jordan (certified 1397) in *Anglo-Norman Letters and Petitions*, ed. M.D. Legge (Anglo-Norman Text Society, Oxford, 1941), pp. 16–17.

28. Leslie Hotson, *Shakespeare's Motley* (1952), p. 34, citing PRO, ms. E101/400/4. 'Camlet' is thought to have been a fabric of mohair or mixed threads; 'caynet' I have failed to identify.

29. Servants, however, could be 'great' as well as 'little'. In a list of liveries supplied by the Black Prince to members of his household in 1357, six minstrels are provided with 18 ells (22½ yds) of 'cloth of ray', and three justices with 21 cloths of the same material, with furs of 'bys' (a dark fur used for trimming) and miniver for robes and hats. Ray is also included in the liveries for esquires, yeomen, yeomen of the chamber and grooms. *Register of the Black Prince*, IV, pp. 228–9.

30. *Foedera, Conventiones, Literae* etc., ed. T. Rymer (1707–17), IX, p. 335. In the Middle Ages, such furs were mainly used for lining coats and gowns. As many as 800 squirrel skins might be needed for lining a single gown. 'Pured' miniver was the most costly form of squirrel, made from the winter coats of northern animals from which the grey markings had been cut away, leaving only the white fur. Calabrian squirrel (*calabre*) was cheaper. The smaller quantities of ermine and budge were probably for trimming those parts of William's clothes that were turned back at neck and wrist to show the fur. See Elspeth M. Veale, *The English Fur Trade in the Later Middle Ages* (Oxford, 1966), pp. 24–5, 29, and glossary, 215–29.

31. *Archaeologia*, LXII (1911), Part 2, pp. 503, 511.

32. Doran, pp. 240–1; Welsford, p. 119.
33. REED: *Devon*, pp. 92–3.
34. *The Household Books of John Howard, Duke of Norfolk* (reprinted from Roxburghe Club edns of 1841 and 1844, Richard III and Yorkist History Trust, 1992), Part 2, as indexed. For Edward IV's 'jesters' and other clever fools of the period, see Chapter 10 below.
35. For Martyn, *British Library Harleian MS. 433*, ed. R. Horrox and P.W. Hammond (Richard III Society, 1980), II, p. 25; for Mr John, *Privy Purse Expenses of Elizabeth of York*, ed. N.H. Nicolas (1830), p. 196n.

Chapter 7: Tudor Innocents

1. For these and following references to Henry VII's fools, see (except where otherwise noted) Sydney Anglo, 'The Court Festivals of Henry VII, Payments Relating to Court Entertainments, December 1491–April 1509', in *Bulletin of the John Rylands Library, Manchester*, 43 (1960–1), pp. 12–45. I have also made use of Craven Orde's transcript (BL ms. Add. 7099) from the original records (some of which are now missing), and of S. Bentley's extracts from it with useful notes in *Excerpta Historica* (1833), pp. 85ff. As all these sets of accounts are printed chronologically, I refer to them by date only.
2. *Privy Purse Expenses of Elizabeth of York*, ed. N.H. Nicolas (1830), pp. 74, 93.
3. Ibid., pp. 5–6, 24, 26, 61, 80–1. For the coat, and 'petycotes' in general, see below, pp. 164–6.
4. Though there are many earlier references in the English records to 'bringing in the may' and to 'somer rodes', the first 'maypole' to be so called was erected by Henry at Westminster on 22 May 1506 (Anglo, 'Court Festivals', n. 1 above, p. 41). The earliest recorded performance of a Morris ('mourice daunce') in England was that rewarded by him on 2 January 1494 (Anglo, p. 28); see also Barbara Lowe, 'Early Records of the Morris in England' in *Journal of the English Folk Dance and Song Society*, 8 (1957), pp. 61ff.
5. Anglo (n. 1), p. 16.
6. John Evelyn, the diarist, adds in the margin of his copy of Browne, 'Of Charles I, and one Osborn, an hedger, whom I often employ'd'.

See *The Works of Sir Thomas Browne*, ed. G. Keynes (1964 edn), III, p. 113.
7. I follow here Craven Orde's transcription of extracts from Heron's Privy Purse Expenses (BL Additional ms. 7099, f. 48); but Dr Anglo (pp. 15–16, 33) reads 'hooses' (breeches) as 'hoofes', and supposes that natural fools were made to wear them in imitation of horses 'to make sport for their noble masters'. I find no supporting evidence for this interpretation. Saddles, bridles, etc., were supplied to fools for the equipment of the horses they required to accompany the king on his progresses, not to wear themselves!
8. L & P, I, Part 1, p. 15.
9. Anglo (n. 1), pp. 37–8. *Privy Purse Expenses of Elizabeth of York* (n. 2), p. 2.
10. L & P, II, Part 2, p. 1463; III, Part 1, pp. 171, 408; *A Collection of Ordinances and Regulations for the Government of the Royal Household* (Society of Antiquaries, 1790), p. 201.
11. I date the epitaph to the period 1509–25 by reason of its references to 'the kyng and the quene thou madyst so merye', and to Erasmus and Luther (st. 4).
12. *Nugae Poeticae*, ed. J.O. Halliwell (1844), pp. 44–6. The style is suggestive of Skelton. It is possible that later use of the word 'lob' as meaning a 'country bumpkin: clown, lout' (OED, 2) derives from the name of this fool. OED gives its earliest use as 1533. Shakespeare's 'Farewell, thou Lob of 'spirits', as addressed to Puck (MND, II.i.16), and Dekker's 'The sight of a flat-cap was dreadfull to a Lob' (*Wonderfull Yeare*, D.iij), point to 'clown' as the primary meaning.
13. *The Privy Purse Expenses of Henry VIII, 1529–1532*, ed. N.H. Nicolas (1827), p. 5. Subsequent references are by date only.
14. *The Proverbs and Epigrams of John Heywood* (Spenser Society, 1867), p. 106.
15. *The Life and Death of Cardinal Wolsey by George Cavendish* in *Two Early Tudor Lives*, ed. R.S. Sylvester and D.P. Harding (New Haven and London, 1962), pp. 105–7.
16. *Chronicle of King Henry VIII of England*, tr. M.A.S. Hume (1889), p. 29. The tomb was real enough, but seems never to have been finished. Wolsey was buried in Leicester Abbey where he died.
17. In a way analogous to 'Lob', the use of 'Patch' as a synonym for 'fool' may derive

from Sexton's nickname. Thomas Wilson in his *Arte of Rhetorique* of 1553 (I quote from the 1560 edn, ed. G.H. Mair, Oxford, 1909, pp. 173–4) gives as an example of a particular rhetorical device: 'to call one Patche or Coulson, whom we see to doe a thing foolishly, because these twoo in their tyme were notable fooles.' (I have found no trace of Coulson.) Shakespeare uses it in this way, applying it to the jester Trinculo in *The Tempest* ('Thou scurvy patch', III.ii.62), Launcelot in *The Merchant of Venice* ('The patch is kind enough but a huge feeder', II.v.45), to one of the Dromios by the other in *The Comedy of Errors* ('What patch is made our porter', III.i.36), to Dull in *Love's Labour's Lost* ('a patch set on learning', IV.ii.30), and the mechanicals in *A Midsummer Night's Dream* ('a crew of patches', III.ii.9). I know of no evidence to support the common view among Shakespeare's editors that the word derives from what they suppose to have been the 'patched dress' worn by fools of the time.

18. *The Chronicle of Calais*, ed. J.G. Nichols (Camden Society, 1846), pp. 10–11.

19. *Calendar of Letters, Despatches and State Papers . . . at Simancas*, V, Part I, p. 520.

Chapter 8: William Somer

1. L & P, X, p. 64.

2. *Archaeologia*, IX (1789), p. 249; calendared in L & P, VIII, pp. 366–7.

3. The anonymous, so-called *Pleasant History of the Life and Death of Will Summers* (1676). A similar origin is attributed, on equally poor authority, to Elizabeth's Tarlton. It is inherently improbable that Somer (or anyone else) would have gone straight from the situation of a village idiot or rural wag to court service as a royal fool, as the jest-book suggests.

4. Revd J. Granger, *A Biographical History of England*, quoted from 5th edn of 1824, I, pp. 149–50.

5. *Hall's Chronicle* (1809 edn), p. 838; *Collin's Peerage of England*, augmented E. Brydges (1812), IV, pp. 198–200. See also DNB under 'Fermor'.

6. L & P, XIV, Part 2, p. 333.

7. L & P, *Addenda*, I, Part 2, p. 618; *Literary Remains of King Edward the Sixth*, ed. J.G. Nichols (Roxburgh Club, 1857), I, pp. xliv–v, n.(c).

8. Welsford, p. 166, my italics; the letter is calendared in L & P, XX, Part 2, pp. 495–6.

9. *Calendar of State Papers, Foreign, Mary, 1553–58*, p. 52, my italics.

10. *Wilson's Arte of Rhetorique, 1560*, ed. G.H. Mair (Oxford, 1909), p. 201.

11. For Henry's self-identification with this role, see Pamela Tudor-Craig, 'Henry VIII and King David', in *Proceedings of the 1987 Harlaxton Symposium*, ed. D. Williams (Woodbridge, 1989), pp. 195–205.

12. Christopher Lloyd and Simon Thurley, *Henry VIII, Images of a Tudor King* (1990), p. 37.

13. L & P, XXI, Part 2, pp. 400–1.

14. *Documents Relating to the Revels at Court in the Time of King Edward VI and Queen Mary*, ed. A. Feuillerat (Louvain, 1914), p. 49.

15. *Literary Remains of Edward VI* (n. 7), I, p. 381.

16. Feuillerat (n. 14), pp. 67, 73, 77.

17. Ibid., p. 89.

18. Ibid., p. 73.

19. Ibid., pp. 89, 119–20.

20. C.C. Stopes, *Shakespeare's Environment* (1914), pp. 260–3, citing manuscripts in the BL and PRO.

21. *Calendar of Charters and Rolls Preserved in the Bodleian Library*, ed. W.H. Turner (Oxford, 1878), pp. xviii–xix.

22. Leslie Hotson has pointed out (*Shakespeare's Motley*, 1952, reissued New York, 1971, pp. 79–80) that Feste's reply to Maria in *Twelfth Night*, 'for turning away, let summer bear it out' (I.v.20), may contain a similar pun on Will's name. Like Will Somer, Feste can ' "bear out" and even dissipate righteous anger with a jest'. It is doubtful, however, that Feste wore a coat of green motley, as Hotson contends; see Chapter 17, 'The Fools' Motley'.

23. Stopes (n. 20), p. 266.

24. ll. 440, 521–34 in *The Plays of John Heywood*, ed. R. Axton and P. Happé (Cambridge, 1991), pp. 66, 68.

25. Though Heywood was not a jester in the professional sense, he may have shared in the mutual antipathy that characterised relations between clever and innocent fools in the period. Somer himself was not immune to jealousy of this kind; see below, p. 97.

26. Stopes (n. 20), p. 268. I shall have more to say about these Wardrobe entries in

Chapter 17, where I relate them to other evidence of the fools' traditional 'motley'.

27. ll. 262–3 in *Misogonus*, ed. L.E. Barber (New York and London, 1979), p. 142. For discussion of authorship and date, see introduction to this edition.

28. *A Shakespeare Jestbook, Robert Armin's 'Foole upon Foole' (1600)* (with later additions), ed. H.F. Lippincott (Elizabethan Studies, 20, Salzburg, 1973), pp. 120–33. A modernised text of the 1608 edition is given by P.M. Zall in *A Nest of Ninnies and Other English Jestbooks of the Seventeenth Century* (Lincoln, Nebraska, 1970).

29. III.vi.82. As first published in 1600, Armin's account of Somer may have influenced Shakespeare's conception of the Fool, a part that Armin is often supposed to have played. Lippincott, in his introduction to *Foole upon Foole* (n. 28), questions whether Shakespeare, if he read it at all, gained very much from Armin's book; but fails, I think, to appreciate the uniqueness of Lear's fool as an *innocent* among his many other fool characters. If Shakespeare gained anything of value from Armin's account of Somer in his writing of the fool, it was this. See also p. 134 below.

30. Lippincott (n. 28), pp. 119–20.

Chapter 9: The European Dimension

1. M. Domenica Legge, 'John Pecham's Jerarchie', in *Medium Aevum* XI (1934), p. 82. I owe this reference to Dr Bullock-Davies. For early evidence of the division referred to, see Bullock-Davies, *Minstrels*, pp. 15–27.

2. For these, see EMM, especially pp. 83–4, 107–8, 142–3.

3. *Manners and Household Expenses of England* (Roxburghe Club, 1841), pp. lxix–lxx; Bullock-Davies, *Register*, p. 4, citing PRO *Exchequer Accounts* C47/4/5, f. 48r.

4. Vernon J. Harward, *The Dwarfs of Arthurian Romance and Celtic Tradition* (Leiden, 1958), p. 24; Bullock-Davies, *Minstrels*, pp. 71, 80, 67, 146. For the reported death of Adam de la Hale in 1288, see Nigel Williams, *Music in the Age of Chaucer* (Cambridge and New Jersey, 1979), pp. 3–4.

5. *Liber Quotidianus Contrarotulatoris Garderobae, 1299–1300*, ed. J. Nichols (Society of Antiquaries, 1787), p. 166; Bullock-Davies, *Register*, p. 71, citing PRO *Exchequer Accounts* E101/355/17 (sub. *Dona*, one membrane only).

6. Bullock-Davies, *Register*, pp. 167, 171.

7. *Extracts from the Account Rolls of the Abbey of Durham* (Surtees Society, 1898–1901), II, p. 508. This is the only record of Hugo I have found.

8. *Comptes de L'Argenterie des Rois de France au XIVe Siècle*, ed. L. Douët D'Arcq (Paris, 1851, reprinted 1966), pp. 210–11, 207; see also Stella Mary Newton, *Fashion in the Age of the Black Prince* (Woodbridge and New Jersey, 1980), pp. 80–1.

9. *Comptes*, p. 225. A pair of bellows (*soufflet*) was bought for the fire, p. 229.

10. *Comptes*, pp. 223–5.

11. *Comptes*, p. 230.

12. *Comptes*, p. 229.

13. *Comptes*, p. 224. A few months later in London, he was to purchase *un romans du Loherenc Garin*, and *un autre roumans du Tournoiement d'Antecrist*, p. 251.

14. *Comptes*, p. 222.

15. *Comptes*, pp. 241–2.

16. Harward, *Dwarfs* (n. 4), p. 25.

17. Otto Cartellieri, *The Court of Burgundy*, tr. Malcolm Potts (1929), pp. 130–1. Edward's was not the only small person to have featured in the pageant. A bearded dwarf called Master Peter acted as Master of Ceremonies. For accounts of the event as a whole, see Cartellieri, pp. 124–34, and Richard Barber and Juliet Barker, *Tournaments, Jousts, Chivalry and Pageants in the Middle Ages* (Woodbridge, 1989), pp. 121–4.

18. *Paston Letters and Papers of the Fifteenth Century*, ed. Norman Davis (Oxford, 1971), I, p. 539.

19. For this and the following references to Henry's rewards, see (except where otherwise noted), the chronological entries in Sydney Anglo, 'The Court Festivities of Henry VII', in *Bulletin of the John Rylands Library*, 43 (Manchester, 1961), pp. 27–45.

20. See pp. 61–3 above.

21. His fee reduces from 13*s* 4*d* on the first occasion to 10*s* on the second. Dr Anglo (p. 16) describes this as 'an unfortunate promotion'. But in the values of the time, 10*s* was still a considerable sum, and, from Watt's point of view, a most welcome addition to his minstrel's income. There is no suggestion that he was being made a

permanent member of the fool establishment.

22. L & P, II, Part 2, p. 1447.
23. Ibid., pp. 1442, 1447.

Chapter 10: Fools to Jesters

1. For discussion of this terminology and its variations, see MSC VII, pp. x–xv; MSC XI, pp. xvi–xviii; Stanley J. Kahrl, *Traditions of Medieval English Drama* (1974), pp. 100–2.
2. Welsford, p. 114.
3. REED: *York*, I, p. 75; R. Rastall, 'The Minstrels of the English Royal Households', in *Royal Musical Association Research Chronicle*, IV (1967), pp. 33–5, 37.
4. In 1451, a certain William Luter is described as 'luter and mynstrell', indicating both his speciality and that he claimed to be in the service of an unnamed lord; CPR, *Henry VI, 1446–52*, p. 502.
5. Rastall (n. 3), p. 17. Dr Rastall's suggested translation as 'player of a bass shawm' (a kind of pipe) is not supported by other fourteenth-century usages, for which see OED. For Robert IV, see p. 56 above.
6. *Jacob's Well*, ed. A. Brandeis (EETS, 1900), I, p. 136. I am indebted to G.R. Owst (*Literature and Pulpit in Medieval England*, Oxford, 1961 edn, p. 13) for this quotation.
7. REED: *Cambridge*, I, p. 37; HMC, *Fifth Report* (1876), I, p. 551. See also OED under 'bourd' and 'bourder'.
8. Sydney Anglo, 'The Court Festivals of Henry VII', in *Bulletin of the John Rylands Library*, 43 (Manchester, 1961), pp. 28, 33; OED under 'Jocular'.
9. For the harpers, see EMM, chapters 3 and 7.
10. *Confessio Amantis*, Book VII, ll. 2423–4.
11. *Hous of Fame*, l. 1199.
12. *The Great Chronicle of London*, ed. A.H. Thomas and I.D. Thornley (1938), p. 208. For ease of reading, I have added punctuation and omitted capitals.
13. *Shakespeare Jest-books*, ed. W. Carew Hazlitt (1864), II, pp. 144–5.
14. For discussion of date and authorship, see ibid., pp. 38–43; DNB under 'Scogan'; John Wardroper, *Jest upon Jest, A Selection from the Jestbooks* (1970), pp. 198–9. For Archy Armstrong, see Chapter 15.
15. In its long life, the story was told of four

kings: Henry II, Edward II, Edward III and (as probably here) Edward IV. A fifteenth-century text is given in *Middle English Metrical Romances*, ed. W.H. French and C.B. Hale (New York, 1930, one-vol. reissue of 1964), pp. 949–85; *Privy Purse Expenses of Elizabeth of York*, ed. N.H. Nicolas (1830), pp. 53, 87.
16. My quotation is from 'The Image of Ipocrysy', in *The Poetical Works of John Skelton*, ed. A. Dyce (1843), II, p. 418; for authorship, p. 413. For Revels accounts, see A. Feuillerat, *Documents Relating to the Revels at Court in the Time of King Edward VI and Queen Mary* (Louvain, 1914), p. 79.

Chapter 11: 'Jugler' and Jester

1. 'Dramatic Records of the City of London', in MSC. II.3, pp. 286–7.
2. 'Jugler' was also used in a more general sense as 'trickster'. 'Conjuring' had then a more sinister meaning as the raising of the spirits of the dead, such as that of Helen of Troy made to appear before Faustus in Marlowe's play. Henry VIII paid 13s 4d to a man who brought conjurers to Windsor in 1512: L & P, II, Part 2, p. 1458.
3. On attempts by the Musicians' Company to restrict the practice of minstrelsy in the City to their own members, see Walter L. Woodfill, *Musicians in English Society from Elizabeth to Charles I* (Princeton, 1953), pp. 10–13.
4. MSC VII; for Dover, p. 35; Lydd, p. 100; Sandwich, p. 152. For Shrewsbury, REED: *Salop*, I, p. 178, where, however, his reward is given as 11d; but see H. Owen and J.B. Blakeway, *A History of Shrewsbury* (1825), I, p. 331, from which the REED entry is extracted, where the sum of 'xid' in Owen and Blakeway's Latin citation is probably a misprint for 'xld' (i.e. 40d).
5. William More, the blind harper, is often rewarded as a tourist in borough and monastic records of the period. There are references to his wages from the king in L & P, II, Part 2, pp. 1465, 1469, 1473; III, Part 2, p. 1553; V, pp. 303, 748. For his alleged involvement in the so-called 'treason' of the Three Abbots in 1539 (in consequence of which he spent some months in the Tower), see L & P, XIV, Part 2, pp. 194, 216–17; XV, pp. 217, 268, 300. By 1540, he had been exonerated and returned to favour. The last

references to him I have found belong to 1561, when he was still receiving a livery from Queen Elizabeth and hiring out 'V harps and his child for playng' in the Lord Mayor's Pageant of that year: H.C. de Lafontaine, *The King's Musick* (1909, reprinted New York, 1973), p. 16; R.T.D. Sayle, *Lord Mayors' Pageants of the Merchant Taylors' Company* (1931), p. 41.

6. For Thetford, see MSC XI, pp. 110–14. For Worcester, REED: *Hereford and Worcester*, pp. 462(2), 466, 468, 472, 478, 484, 487, 491, 494, 499, 504, 508, 514, 518, 526. Most of the Latin entries I quote from the records appear, and are given here and below, in the dative case.

7. For his return to Shrewsbury, REED: *Salop*, I, p. 193. For Exeter and Barnstaple, REED: *Devon*, pp. 132, 40. For Cambridge, REED: *Cambridge*, I, pp. 105–11.

8. HMC, *Manuscripts of the Duke of Rutland at Belvoir Castle*, IV (1905), pp. 270–322. The references given above to Brandon's touring make no claim to be exhaustive. As further volumes in the valuable REED series are published, they can be expected to throw further light on his travels and activities.

9. *The Discoverie of Witchcraft* (1584), Book XIII, Chapter 13.

10. *The Privy Purse Expenses of Henry VIII*, ed. N.H. Nicolas (1827), pp. 126, 204.

11. *A Shakespeare Jestbook, Robert Armin's Foole upon Foole (1600)*, ed. H.F. Lippincott (Elizabethan Studies 20, Salzburg, 1973), pp. 131–3. I have added some punctuation.

12. L & P, XIX, Part 2, p. 187.

13. For Staney, see REED: *Salop*, I, pp. 84, 204; REED: *Cumb., West. and Glos.*, p. 299.

14. *Records of the Borough of Nottingham*, III (1885), p. 380; IV (1889), pp. 90, 133. REED: *Salop*, I, p. 201. He was preceded briefly by a man referred to as *Master Smyth ioculer domini regis*, who was rewarded at Thetford in 1538/9; MSC XI, p. 114.

15. *Notices Illustrative of the Drama and Other Popular Amusements . . . of the Borough of Leicester*, ed. W. Kelly (1865), pp. 193–204. For Ipswich, 'Players at Ipswich', in MSC II.3, p. 260; for New Romney, MSC VII, p. 137. REED: *Newcastle*, p. 31. For Folkestone, Canterbury, Dover and Lydd, MSC VII, pp. 69, 11–12, 41, 106;

Plymouth and Barnstaple, REED: *Devon*, pp. 230, 233, 41; REED: *Cambridge*, pp. 129, 163, 184; Gloucester, REED: *Cumb., West., and Glos.*, p. 297(2); Faversham, Nichols' 'Progresses', I, p. 352; Shrewsbury and Ludlow, REED: *Salop*, I, pp. 207, 83; Oxford, *Selections from the Records of the City of Oxford*, ed. W.H. Turner (Oxford and London, 1880), pp. 284, 304, 319.

16. *Twelfth Night*, V, stanzas 1, 2 and 5. It is sometimes overlooked that *Twelfth Night* is a Christmas play and Feste a Twelfth-night fool, aiding in the reversals of social hierarchy and gender traditional to that season.

Chapter 12: Jane: a Female Innocent

1. Doran, pp. 62–7; Otto Cartellieri (tr. Potts), *The Court of Burgundy* (1929), p. 162.

2. L & P, X, p. 383; *Miscellanies of the Philobiblon Society*, VII (1862–3), pp. 2, 16.

3. Formally and for financial purposes, the two households continued to be treated as one, under the same controller, initially Sir John Shelton, who described the joint establishment to Cromwell as being 'served on two sides', like that of the king and the queen; but Mary's personal attendants were quite distinct and separate from those appointed to serve Elizabeth, and, to judge by the evidence of the Privy Purse expenses, the two sides rarely came together in any one place. Though highly mobile, Mary was more often at Richmond than anywhere else, Elizabeth at Hunsdon or Hatfield. See David Loades, *Mary Tudor, a Life* (1989, paperback edn 1992), pp. 111–17.

4. *Privy Purse Expenses of the Princess Mary*, ed. F. Madden (1831), pp. 48, 50. The surviving accounts begin in December 1536.

5. Ibid., p. lxxiii. In L & P, XII, Part 2, p. 402, there are payments in October 1537 to 'Thos. Gente, yeoman of the horse to my lady Mary, for hay, litter and oats for her own horse, at Kingston, three of her women's and one of his standing at Ham', and to three 'horse keepers' at 4*d* a day.

6. For the lessons, see *Privy Purse Expenses* (n. 4), p. 26; for Philip and family, ibid., pp. 16, 29, 34, 60–1, 98, 115, 120, 126, 132, 179.

7. Ibid., pp. 62, 104. For Heywood's 'children', see A.W. Reed, *Early Tudor Drama* (1926), pp. 58–61.

8. *Privy Purse Expenses*, pp. 64, 73.

9. L & P, X, p. 494.

10. For Tosso (1513–20), L & P, I, Part 2, p. 1115(27); II, Part 1, pp. 211, 875; III, Part 1, p. 365.

11. *Privy Purse Expenses*, pp. 93, 108.

12. Ibid., for the shavings, pp. 111, 113, 116, 119, 126, 150, 160, 162, 165; for her sickness, p. 123; for the needles and sheets, pp. 130–1.

13. L & P, XXI, Part 1, p. 321.

14. L & P, XIX, Part 2, p. 406.

15. *Privy Purse Expenses*, p. 62.

16. For this identification of place, see Roy Strong, *Gloriana, the Portraits of Queen Elizabeth I* (1987), p. 49.

17. L & P, XXI, Part 1, p. 567.

18. C.C. Stopes, *Shakespeare's Environment* (1914), pp. 261–2, citing *Exchequer Accounts*, 27 April, 1 Mary, 427(11).

19. *Privy Purse Expenses*, pp. 59, 177; Stopes, ibid., pp. 261–2, 266.

20. *Calendar of Charters and Rolls in the Bodleian Library*, ed. W.H. Turner (Oxford, 1878), p. xviii; Stopes, p. 265.

21. Stopes (n. 18), pp. 263–4.

22. Stopes, p. 266.

23. Stopes, p. 268, citing *Exchequer Accounts*, 6 Mary, 427(18).

Chapter 13: Elizabeth's Fools

1. *The Mediaeval Stage* (1903), I, p. 388. In a footnote to *The Elizabethan Stage* of 1923, I, p. 48, he corrects himself with some half-dozen names, mainly culled from the chapter which C.C. Stopes devoted to Elizabeth's fools in her *Shakespeare's Environment* of 1914, pp. 269–75.

2. See S. Schoenbaum, *William Shakespeare, a Compact Documentary Life* (Oxford, 1977), pp. 116–17.

3. For Lockwood, see above pp. 98–9; for Staney, REED: *Cumb., West., and Glos.*, p. 299; REED: *Salop*, I, pp. 84, 204.

4. Janet Arnold, *Queen Elizabeth's Wardrobe Unlock'd* (1988), p. 171. I am indebted throughout the present chapter to this valuable study of Elizabeth's Wardrobe accounts, which cites manuscript sources for this and all my subsequent references.

5. *Calendar of Letters and State Papers Relating to English Affairs . . . at Simancas*, I, p. 465.

6. Arnold, *Queen Elizabeth's Wardrobe* (n. 4), p. 206.

7. Ibid., p. 201.

8. *The Letting of Humours Blood in the Head-Vaine* (1600), Epigram 30, sig. C2^v; quoted by Arnold, p. 206.

9. Arnold, *Queen Elizabeth's Wardrobe* (n. 4), p. 201.

10. TFT (1910), sig. Fii and Fii^v.

11. *Lanthorne and Candle-light. Or the Bellmans second Nights walke* (1608), sig. D1^v.

12. Arnold, *Queen Elizabeth's Wardrobe* (n. 4), pp. 206–7. A *Robert* Grene, described as 'the Queenes Fool', with a servant called Nicholas Knight Smythe, are recorded as receiving 'expenses and chardges' in the queen's Privy Purse expenses for 1559–69 quoted in John Nichols' 'Progresses', I, pp. 270–1. It is possible that Robert was Grene's baptismal name and Jack merely a nickname.

13. Nichols' 'Progresses', I, p. 129.

14. Arnold, *Queen Elizabeth's Wardrobe* (n. 4), p. 107. For the large number of shoes and slippers made for Ippolyta, see ibid., pp. 212–13.

15. Ibid., pp. 107–8. For other references to Thomasina's clothes, see the same author's '*Lost from Her Majesties Back*' (The Costume Society, 1980), pp. 58, 64, 78. A further series of New Year's gifts from the queen are recorded in Nichols's 'Progresses', II, p. 424; III, pp. 12, 455, 464; these were of gilt plate or handkerchiefs. There may be a portrait of Thomasina in the well-known Penshurst Place painting of the queen dancing at court (with Robert Dudley, earl of Leicester, it used to be thought). The small lady seated in the foreground to left of centre of the picture, looking very elegant, appears to be a proportionate dwarf, and, as Thomasina is the only proportionate dwarf known to have been present at court among Elizabeth's ladies, it is almost certainly her.

16. *The Private Diary of Dr John Dee*, ed. J.O. Halliwell (Camden Society, 1842), pp. 7–8.

17. For Heywood's saying, see William Camden, *Remaines of a Greater Worke, Concerning Britain* (1605), p. 234. Pace was dead before 1592 when Nashe, in the foreword to his *Pierce Pennilesse*, complained that the printer's haste had

prevented him from including an epistle he had written to the ghost of 'Pace the Duke of Norfolk's Iester' (*The Works of Thomas Nashe*, ed. R.B. McKerrow, Oxford, 1905, revd edn by F.P. Wilson, 1958, I, p. 153).

18. *The Works of Francis Bacon*, ed. Spedding, Ellis and Heath (1859), VII, p. 125.

19. Nichols' 'Progresses', I, p. 204.

20. Arnold, *Queen Elizabeth's Wardrobe* (n. 4), p. 106.

21. Jonson, Marston and Chapman, *Eastward Ho!*, II.i.54–5 in the New Mermaid edn. I owe this reference to Hotson, p. 129. For the significance of 'gards', see below, pp. 166–7.

22. *Have With you to Saffron-Walden*, in *Works*, ed. McKerrow (n. 17), III, p. 76.

23. Arnold, *Queen Elizabeth's Wardrobe* (n. 4), p. 106. All the warrants quoted in this chapter were signed by Elizabeth. Though she is unlikely to have composed them, she must at least have known what they contained and approved it.

24. *A briefe Discourse of the Spanish State, with a Dialogue annexed, intituled Philobasilus* (1590), p. 39, as cited in the Arden edn of *Love's Labour's Lost*, ed. R.W. David (5th edn of 1956), p. 67n.

25. Book 3, chapter 9.

26. *A pleasaunte labourinth called Churchyardes chance, framed in fancies* (1580), quoted from *New Variorum Shakespeare*, ed. H.H. Furness, XIV (1904), p. 124n.

27. Arnold, *Queen Elizabeth's Wardrobe* (n. 4), for Hoyden, p. 207; for Shenton, pp. 105–6. For more about Shenton's suit, see below, p. 169. Tarlton is pictured playing tabor and pipe on p. 115 below.

28. Nichols, 'Progresses', I, pp. 548–9.

29. Hotson, pp. 10–11; for cloak-bags, ibid., pp. 44ff. For 'motley', see also below, pp. 163–6.

30. *The History of the Worthies of England* (1662), p. 47.

31. Hazlitt's 'Dodsley', VI, pp. 396–7.

32. 'To Sir Ninian Ouzell', in *Thalia's Banquet* (1620), quoted from Edwin Nungezer, *A Dictionary of Actors* (New Haven and Oxford, 1929, reprinted New York, 1968), pp. 362–3.

33. *Worthies of England* (n. 30), p. 47.

34. *Tarlton's Jests and News Out of Purgatory* (1611), ed. J.O. Halliwell (Shakespeare Society, 1844), p. 5. Halliwell and Nungezer give the fullest accounts of Tarlton's life and career.

35. CSPD, *Elizabeth, 1581–90*, p. 541.

36. *Annalles, or a Generall Chronicle of England. Begun by John Stow: Continued and Augmented by Edmund Howes* (1631), p. 698.

37. See n. 35 above.

38. *The Letters of John Chamberlain*, ed. N.E. McClure (Philadelphia, 1939), I, p. 172.

39. *Wit and Mirth*, in *Shakespeare Jest-Books*, ed. W.C. Hazlitt (1864), III, pp. 6–8.

40. CSPD, *James I, 1603–10*, p. 99.

41. For Garret as player, Chambers, ES, II, pp. 236–40; for the epitaph, *Wits Recreations* (1641), epitaph 50, sig. P5.

42. The dedication to *An Almond for a Parrat* (1590), in *Works*, ed. McKerrow (Oxford, 1905), III, p. 341.

Chapter 14: The Player Fools

1. See *European Drama of the Early Middle Ages* (1974), pp. 162–3.

2. For King's Lynn, MSC XI, p. 38; for Mitford, *Household Accounts from Medieval England*, ed. C.M. Woolgar (British Academy, Oxford, 1992), I, p. 419. See OED for 'visor', 2, 3 and 4. For Jakke Travaill, *Foedera, Conventiones, Literae* etc., ed. T. Rymer (1704–17), X, p. 387; Chambers, MS, II, p. 186.

3. Chambers, MS, II, pp. 256, 187. The King's Players (*lusoribus domini Regis*) were at Thetford in 1502/3; MSC XI, p. 105.

4. Sydney Anglo, 'The Court Festivals of Henry VII', in *Bulletin of the John Rylands Library*, 43 (Manchester, 1961), pp. 29–38.

5. Chambers, ES, II, p. 78.

6. *Issues of the Exchequer*, ed. F. Devon (1837), p. 516.

7. L & P, I, Part 1, p. 16. The clerk mistakes Hamond and Scot's first names.

8. Chambers, ES, II, p. 79. The old players are first differentiated in January 1515 (L & P, II, Part 2, p. 1466), when Gibson was also paid for the making of costumes for a disguising on Twelfth Night. For other references to the old players, see L & P, III, Part 2, pp. 1533, 1543.

9. The King's Players were at Dover in 1518/19 and at Lydd in 1520/1 (MSC VII, pp. 35, 101). At Southampton in 1523/4 and at Worcester Priory in 1524/5, they were led by English; at Worcester in 1527 and 1528 by John Slye, who appears to have been leader of the second company (J.T. Murray, *English Dramatic Companies,*

1558–1642 (1910, reprinted New York, 1963), II, p. 395; REED: *Hereford and Worcester*, pp. 485, 494, 499). Other visits in the 1520s were to Exeter and Plymouth in 1526/7, and to Thetford in 1527/8 (REED: *Devon*, pp. 128, 222; MSC XI, p. 112). In the latter year, *interlusoribus domini Regis* were at Shrewsbury (REED: *Shropshire*, I, p. 187).

10. Richard Axton and Peter Happé, in their edition of *The Plays of John Heywood* (Cambridge, 1991, p. 13), 'suspect' that he played the 'vice' roles. My subsequent quotations from the plays (and the line numbers I give to them) follow this edition. Heywood is first mentioned and rewarded as a singer in 1519/20 (L & P, III, Part 2, p. 1543). For his presence at court between 1519 and 1528, see A.W. Reed, *Early Tudor Drama* (1926), pp. 39–42, 50–1.

11. In the Revels accounts of 1552, 'vice' and 'dyssarde' are specifically equated; John Smith, the Lord of Misrule's fool and an interluder by profession, is supplied with a 'vyces dagger', a 'vices coote' and a 'dissardes hood'; and 'disard', as we have seen (Chapter 10, pp. 90, 93), denotes an intermediate stage in the evolution of the jester or clever fool. 'Vice' (in its non-ethical connotation) may derive from 'viser', meaning a mask as often, but not invariably, worn by interluders. In Skelton's *Magnyfycence*, Crafty Conveyance tells Folly, 'In a cote thou can play well the dyser', and Folly replies, 'Ye, but thou can play the fole without a vyser'. See A. Feuillerat, *Documents Relating to the Revels at Court in the Time of King Edward VI and Queen Mary* (Louvain, 1914), pp. 73, 79, 97–8; *Magnyfycence*, ed. R.L. Ramsay (EETS, 1908), ll. 1177–8, p. 37. For the vice, see also Chambers, MS, II, pp. 303–5.

12. *The Plays of John Heywood* (n. 10), p. 13.

13. Palsgrave in 1530 speaks of an 'Elfe or dwarf'. See OED under 'elf', 3(a). The dating of *Witty and Witless* presents an interesting problem. On grounds of style and content, Axton and Happé (*Plays*, pp. 33–5) place it first among Heywood's interludes; but it is the only one not published during his lifetime, and the sole-surviving manuscript, probably dating from the 1540s (not an autograph), has references to Will Somer, who, as we have established, did not come on the scene until

1535. Either the references to Somer are later interpolations or the original play was much later in date than Axton and Happé propose.

14. *Plays* (n. 10), p. 174. Scot is also likely to have played the dwarf part, Fancy, in Skelton's *Magnyfycence*, a court play of the same period. As Crafty Conveyance comments of him, 'A rebellyon agaynst Nature,/So large a man, and so lytell of stature' (ll. 522–3). See also the scene between Fancy and Folly (ll. 1069–79), where Fancy's smallness is referred to again. R.L. Ramsay in his edition of the play (n. 11, pp. xlv–l, xcii–cvi) describes both Fancy and Folly as 'professional court fools' and as equivalent in function to Heywood's vices.

15. *Chronicle of the Grey Friars of London*, ed. J.G. Nichols (Camden Society, 1852), p. 34. Cf. *Julius Caesar*, II.i.186–7: 'If he love Caesar, all that he can do/Is to himself: take thought, and die for Caesar.'

16. J.T. Murray, *English Dramatic Companies* (n. 9), I, pp. 6–21.

17. *Pierce Penilesse* (1592), in *The Works of Thomas Nashe*, ed. R.B. McKerrow (Oxford, 1958), I, p. 188.

18. Henry Peacham, *The Truth of our Times: Revealed out of one Mans Experience, by way of Essay* (1638), pp. 103–5.

19. *Tarlton's Jests and News out of Purgatory*, ed. J.O. Halliwell (Shakespeare Society, 1844), p. 27.

20. Ed. G.B. Harrison (1923), p. 12.

21. Quoted from Edwin Nungezer, *A Dictionary of Actors* (New Haven and Oxford, 1929, reprinted New York, 1968), pp. 355–6.

22. For these references, see ibid., pp. 394–6.

23. *The three Lords and three Ladies of London*, in Hazlitt's 'Dodsley', VI, p. 405. For Wilson's posthumous tribute to Tarlton in this play, see above, p. 114.

24. *The three Ladies of London*, ibid., pp. 363–4. According to a stage direction (p. 358), Love wears a vizard at the back of her head; she is literally two-faced.

25. For biographical data in what follows, I draw mainly from Chambers, ES, II; (for Kempe) pp. 325–7, (for Armin) 299–300. I have also made use of the relevant entries in Nungezer (n. 21).

26. See William J. Lawrence, 'The Practice of Doubling and its Influence on Early

Dramaturgy', in *Pre-Restoration Stage Studies* (Cambridge, MA, 1927), pp. 43–78; David M. Bevington, *From 'Mankind' to Marlow* (Cambridge, MA, 1962), *passim*; and Gerald Eades Bentley, *The Profession of Player in Shakespeare's Time* (Princeton, 1984), pp. 228–33. In most of his plays, Ben Jonson looked more to classical models, and was here an exception.

27. The theatre layman, whether scholar or critic, often assumes that where doubling was required, similar parts were preferred as more likely to lie within the compass of the player's ability; but any actor will tell you that it is easier and more effective to double *contrasting* roles, and that to do so also carries less risk of confusing the audience. An alternation of mode as between one role and another would thus have been of advantage to the player of doubles. It was only by such means that a company of twelve to sixteen players (including apprentices and a few hired men) could cover the much larger number of roles deployed by dramatists of the period. The number of speaking parts in Shakespeare's plays varies between sixteen (*The Two Gentlemen of Verona*) and fifty-five (*Richard III*). In general, the comedies make the least demands and the histories the greatest, with the tragedies falling midway between the two with an average cast of about thirty. See William A. Ringler, Jr, 'The Number of Actors in Shakespeare's Early Plays', in *The Seventeenth-century Stage*, ed. G.E. Bentley (Chicago and London, 1968), pp. 110–34.

28. I am indebted for this suggestion to Brian Gibbons in his Arden edition of the play (1980), pp. 223–4. It allows only fourteen lines for Kempe to make a costume change from Peter to Balthasar between IV.v and V.i, unless there was a pause between the acts, or, as some scholars believe, the scene between Peter and the Musicians (IV.v.100–41) is a later interpolation.

29. From the performers' point of view, a remarkable feature of Shakespeare's plays lies in the opportunities they offer to the players of the smallest parts, and the demands these make of them; with men of the calibre of Kempe and other sharers available through doubling to play them, their author could have confidence that the riches he scattered in the writing of such roles would not be squandered. The practice of doubling would thus have given a consistency of quality and weight to the acting overall which is difficult to achieve in modern productions, however prestigious, where economic factors operate in an opposite direction.

30. The Arden editor of the play, A.R. Humphreys, suggests (1967 edn, p. 186) that the earlier part of the speech (omitted here) belongs to another occasion and another speaker, perhaps the dramatist himself. It is inconsistent with the lines I have quoted and those that follow.

31. Elizabethan performances – even of tragedies – often concluded with a jig, though rarely linked to the play as here. A foreign visitor to the Globe in 1599, Thomas Platter, describes a performance of *Julius Caesar*, after which the actors 'danced according to their custom with extreme elegance. Two in men's clothes and two in women's gave this performance in wonderful combination with each other' (Chambers, ES, II, pp. 364–5).

32. I am indebted for this explanation to J. Dover Wilson (in *The Fortunes of Falstaff*, Cambridge, 1943, pp. 124–5) who, in turn, acknowledges an article by Professor H.D. Gray in *The Modern Language Review*, XXV, pp. 265–7. Though not usually considered as one of Shakespeare's fool characters, it is interesting to find that Falstaff corresponds in every particular to the category of buffoon as previously defined: he belongs to the class of minor gentry, he exploits his familiarity with the prince for personal gain, and is ignominiously dismissed by his patron when he becomes an embarrassment to him. When the newly crowned king describes his former companion as 'fool and jester', he speaks no more or less than the truth.

33. For his complaints of the ballad-mongers, see Kempe's *Nine Daies Wonder* (printed with Chettle's *Kind-Hartes Dreame*), ed. G.B. Harrison (1923), p. 3.

34. *Tarlton's Jests*, ed. Halliwell (n. 19), pp. 22–3.

35. The usual assumption that Armin played the Fool has no evidence of any sort to back it. See William A. Ringler, Jr, 'Shakespeare and His Actors: Some Remarks on *King Lear*', in *Proceedings of the Comparative Literature Symposium*, XII (Lubbock, Texas, 1981), pp. 183–94. The suggestion

that Cordelia and the Fool were doubled by a boy is not new. It was first proposed by Alois Brandl in 1894, and has since been supported by Quiller-Couch, Edith Sitwell (quoting Sir John Gielgud in *A Notebook on William Shakespeare* of 1948, 1962 edn, p. 67), and, most persuasively, by Thomas B. Stroup, 'Cordelia and the Fool' in *Shakespeare Quarterly*, 12 (1961), pp. 127–32. For an opposing view, see W.J. Lawrence, 'The Practice of Doubling' (n. 26), pp. 72–3.

36. Leslie Hotson, *Shakespeare's Motley* (1952, reprinted New York 1971), pp. 102–3; Ringler, 'Shakespeare and His Actors' (n. 35), pp. 189–90. Dr Hotson gives also Menenius in *Coriolanus* and Polonius in *Hamlet* to Armin.

37. Hotson, pp. 71–7; for Armin's death, Nungezer (n. 21), pp. 19–20.

38. Nungezer, pp. 327–8; Chambers, ES, II, pp. 339–40.

Chapter 15: The Last of the Jesters

1. Ll. 357–61; Jonson, III, p. 441.
2. '*Brief Lives*', ed. A. Clark (Oxford, 1898), II, p. 184.
3. *Anecdotes and Traditions Illustrative of Early English History and Literature*, ed. W.J. Thoms (Camden Society, 1839). Lestrange's dates were 1603–54.
4. *Wits Miserie and the Worlds Madnesse* (1596), p. 84.
5. *Table Talk of John Selden*, ed. Sir F. Pollock (Selden Society, 1927), p. 44. Selden's dates were 1584–1654; his *Table Talk* was published thirty-five years after his death so his anecdote of Stone might just have been contemporary.
6. HMC, *Rutland MSS.*, IV (1905), p. 390.
7. *Memorials of Affairs of State in the Reigns of Q. Elizabeth and K. James I Collected (Chiefly) from the Original Papers of Sir Ralph Winwood*, II (1725), p. 52.
8. II.i.53ff. The typically befuddled confidences of Sir Politic that follow this exchange, in which he claims that Stone was actually a spy, receiving intelligence out of the Low Countries and dispersing it in oranges, musk-melons, apricots, etc., are all of course pure fantasy.
9. Sir A.W. [Anthony Weldon], *The Court and Character of King James* (1650), pp. 91–2.

10. Quoted from the introduction by T.H. Jamieson to his edition of the (so-called) *Archie Armstrong's Banquet of Jests* (see n. 39 below) (Edinburgh, 1872), pp. vii–viii. According to Sir Walter Scott, who prints a modern ballad on the subject, Archy's sheep-stealing exploit 'has been preserved, with many others of the same kind, by tradition, and is at this time current in Eskdale' (*Minstrelsy of the Scottish Border*, 5th edn, Edinburgh, 1812, III, p. 487).
11. A Scots source, cited in DNB, gives Langholm in Roxburghshire as his birthplace.
12. [Francis Osborne] *Traditionall Memoyres on the Raigne of King James* (printed for Thomas Robinson, 1658), pp. 121–2.
13. CSPD, *James I, 1611–18*, pp. 31, 46.
14. Ibid., p. 80.
15. *Archaeologia*, XXVI (1836), p. 392.
16. Logan Pearsall Smith, *The Life and Letters of Sir Henry Wotton* (Oxford, 1907), II, p. 18.
17. REED: *Coventry*, pp. 400, 404. On a subsequent visit to Coventry in 1620 (ibid., p. 410), James was accompanied by a man called Starkey, described as 'the Kinges Iester'. Was Archy out of favour in that year, or indisposed? I have found no other reference to Starkey.
18. HMC, *First Report* (Edinburgh University mss) (1870), p. 122.
19. CSPD, *James I, 1611–18*, pp. 523, 566; *The Letters of John Chamberlain*, ed. N.E. McClure (Philadelphia, 1939), II, p. 168. Chamberlain refers to Archy as 'Archie the dizzard'.
20. *The Praise, Antiquity, and commodity, of Beggery, Beggers, and Begging* (1621), sig. Aiii and iv.
21. On first being told of the prince's mission, Archy is said to have 'clapped *his* hat upon the king's head. The king asking him the reason, he answered, *because he had sent the prince into Spain*. But says his majesty, what if he should come back safe? Why then, says Archy, *I will take my cap off from your head, and put it on the king of Spain's*' (Daniel Neal, *The History of the Puritans*, 2nd edn, 1754, I, pp. 499–500). Similar anecdotes are related of earlier fools, and this one is unlikely to be authentic; but it expresses the popular sentiment that Archy shared.
22. CSPD, *James I, 1619–23*, pp. 539–40.
23. CSPD, *James I, 1623–25*, p. 111. The

month is uncertain; it must have been earlier than November, as queried in the Calendar; probably March.

24. *Epistolae Ho-elianae: The Familiar Letters of James Howell*, ed. J. Jacobs (1890), pp. 169–70.

25. *North Country Diaries (Second Series)*, ed. J.C. Hodgson (Surtees Society CXXIV, 1915), p. 11.

26. The pension is referred to again in a letter from Revd Joseph Mead to Sir Martin Stuteville in 1631, where Archy is reported as claiming to have received arrears from Spain of £1,500 – an obviously exaggerated figure. See Thomas Birch, *The Court and Times of Charles the First*, I (1849), p. 104.

27. *Chamberlain's Letters (op. cit. n. 19)*, II, p. 517.

28. Fray Francisco de Jesus, *Narrative of the Spanish Marriage Treaty*, ed. and tr. S.R. Gardiner (Camden Society, 1869), p. 252.

29. There is an intriguing possibility that this fool of Philip IV's was one of those painted by Velasquez in the years that followed. The most likely candidate, perhaps, in being the earliest, is the young Calabazas, shown holding the miniature of a woman in one hand and a pin-wheel in the other. See José López-Rey, *Velasquez*, 1980, pp. 104–8. The painting (now in Cleveland) is reproduced by López-Rey on p. 50.

30. BL *Additional* ms 19402, f. 159. I have made use of transcriptions of the letter by Doran, pp. 199–200, and Welsford, pp. 174–5.

31. *Chamberlain's Letters (op. cit. n. 19)*, II, p. 525. The reference to Archy as Sir Tobie's 'frend' is probably ironical in view of the writer's previous report of their relations in Spain.

32. III.ii.130–3; Jonson, VI, p. 332. Another 'extraordinarie rich suit' was given to Archy by James on the fool's return from Spain; see HMC, *Seventh Report* (Earl of Denbigh mss) (1879), p. 224, col. b.

33. *Neptunes Triumph*, ll. 171–2; Jonson, VII, p. 687. For the elephant, see the prose *Discoveries* of 1640, ibid., VIII, p. 573. In 1623, an elephant and five camels with their keepers had been sent as a present to James by Philip IV.

34. For 'salt Archy', see 'To the Lord Mordant', l. 185, in *The Poems of Richard Corbett*, ed. J.A.W. Bennett and H.R. Trevor-Roper (Oxford, 1955), p. 30. For Osborne, see below, n. 46. The Northampton anecdote is from *Chamberlain's Letters* (n. 19), II, p. 263.

35. Sir Nicholas Lestrange in *Anecdotes and Traditions*, ed. Thoms (n. 3), p. 67.

36. Letter of William Belou to Secretary Conway in CSPD, *Charles I, 1625–26*, p. 526.

37. The fact of the gift emerges incidentally from the report of a court case brought against Archy by his sister and brother-in-law in 1638. See CSPD, *Charles I, 1637–38*, p. 448.

38. Calendared in CSPD, *Charles I, 1628–29*, p. 393. Welsford, pp. 175–6, gives the letter in full.

39. As printed in 'Facetiae Bibliographicae IX' [by Octavius Gilchrist], in *London Magazine* (July to December 1824), p. 407, from the 6th edn of *A Banquet of Jests* of 1640, p. 44. According to Gilchrist, the earliest edition to attribute authorship to Archy was the fifth of 1636, which also included for the first time the portrait reproduced on page 143. The anecdote I have quoted is the only one to relate to Archy in the whole of the book, and appears to have been unique to the 6th edn; it was not included in any earlier edition and is omitted from the edition of 1660, of which the BL has a copy. The fact that it shows the fool discomfited is the strongest indication that Archy had nothing to do with its authorship or publication, though he was probably still alive at the time. For *A Banquet of Jests* and its many editions, see also Jamieson's introduction to his edition of 1872 (n. 10), pp. xxvii–ix, and following note.

40. The earliest source I have found for this well-known anecdote is [Octavius Gilchrist] 'Facetiae Bibliographicae VIII', in *London Magazine* (July to December 1824), p. 287n.

41. *The Earl of Strafforde's Letters and Dispatches*, ed. W. Knowler, II (1739), p. 154.

42. John Rushworth, *Historical Collections, Second Part* (1680), pp. 470–1.

43. *Strafforde's Letters*, n. 41 ibid. The actual Privy Council order is given by Rushworth.

44. CSPD, *Charles I, 1638–39*, p. 220; HMC, *Fifth Report, Part 1* (House of Lords) (1876), p. 50.

45. [D.L.] *The Scots Scouts Discoveries By Their London Intelligencer* (1642), p. 9.

46. Francis Osborn, *Advice to a Son. The Second Part* (1658), pp. 11–12; *Memoirs of the Most Material Transactions in England for the Last Hundred Years* (1700), p. 58.

47. Printed in *Banquet of Jests*, ed. Jamieson (n. 10), pp. 369–74.

48. Daniel and Samuel Lysons, *Magna Brittania; Being a Concise Topographical Account of the Several Counties of Great Britain*, IV (1816), p. 13.
49. Garrard to Wentworth, as cited above in *Strafforde's Letters* (n. 41), p. 154.
50. Doran, pp. 210–11.
51. *Extracts from the Accounts of the Revels at Court in the Reigns of Queen Elizabeth and King James I*, ed. P. Cunningham (Shakespeare Society, 1842), p. xlii.
52. CSPD, *James I, 1619–23*, p. 182; HMC, *Fourth Report* (Earl De La Warr mss), p. 282.
53. CSPD, *Charles I, 1625–26*, p. 526.

Chapter 16: Jeffery Hudson: Court Dwarf

1. It is not clear whether this was before or after the duke's assassination in August 1628.
2. Early accounts are vague as to his exact height. Fuller in his *Worthies* of 1662, pp. 348–9, merely says that 'he never arrived at a full ell' (45 ins). James Wright (*The History and Antiquities of the County of Rutland*, 1684, p. 105) states that at seven years of age he was 'scarce eighteen inches in highth', and that 'between the 7th year of his Age and the 30th he never grew anything considerable'. Cf. Jean (of Eleanor of Provence in 1249, pp. 15–16 above) who at eighteen or nineteen was 'scarcely three feet tall'.
3. The manner of his introduction to the queen was not original; see Doran, p. 211.
4. We know that Henrietta was little more than 5 feet tall. If Van Dyck's drawing is strictly to scale, Jeffery was no more than 30 ins in height at fourteen years of age. It is probable that he exaggerated Jeffery's smallness to make the queen look taller than she really was. In the Mytens portrait of Charles and Henrietta (n. 6 below), Jeffery is shown as ridiculously tiny.
5. CSPD, *Charles I, 1637–38*, p. 49.
6. His involvement in Charles's favourite hobby of hunting is recorded in a painting by Daniel Mytens, *Charles I and Henrietta Maria Departing for the Chase* (*c.* 1630–2), in which Jeffery appears in the left-hand corner holding two dogs on leashes. The only solo portrait of him is by the same artist, dated 1630, and shows him standing alone in a wood. See Oliver Millar,

The Tudor, Stuart and Early Georgian Pictures in the Collection of HM the Queen (1963, 2 vols.), Cat. nos 120, 125, Plates 59, 50.
7. Quoted from Elizabeth Hamilton, *Henrietta Maria* (1976), pp. 144–5.
8. Quoted from Charles Carlton, *Charles I, The Personal Monarch* (1983), p. 136.
9. Revd Joseph Mead to Sir Martin Stuteville (27 March 1630) in Thomas Birch, *The Court and Times of Charles I* (1849), II, pp. 69–70. See also CSPD, *Charles I, 1629–31*, pp. 217–8.
10. Sir William Davenant, *The Shorter Poems, and Songs from the Plays and Masques*, ed. A.M. Gibbs (Oxford, 1972), pp. 37–43, 363–7.
11. Jonson, VII, p. 755.
12. *History of the Worthies of England* (1662), p. 54.
13. Evans and Hudson were also depicted as the 'King's Porter and Dwarf' in a bas-relief over an entry to Bagnio Court in Newgate Street (long since demolished) which may have been the sign of an inn; see Thomas Pennant, *Some Account of London* (1790), pp. 218–19 with illustration.
14. *The Dramatic Works of Sir William D'Avenant* (Edinburgh, 1872), II, p. 318.
15. The BL has two copies. The first (at 1418.i.28, of which I have seen only a photostat) is of the first edition of 1636. The second (at C.40.a.42) has the portrait of Archy with bookplate of 'Mr Horatio Walpole', and is of the later edition of 1638.
16. *Worthies of England* (n. 12), pp. 348–9.
17. *A True and Experimentall Discourse upon the beginning, proceeding, and Victorious event of this last siege of Breda* (1637), p. 45.
18. Hamilton, *Henrietta Maria* (n. 7), p. 173.
19. *Letters of Queen Henrietta Maria*, ed. M.A.E. Green (1857), p. 62. The mistake is understandable. Cf. the portrait of Jeffery in Plate 15 with any of those of the prince by Van Dyck in the royal collection.
20. Carola Oman, *Henrietta Maria* (1936, White Lion edn, 1976), p. 160.
21. Quoted by Green in *Letters*, p. 260. Lord Crofts, the dead man's brother, was later to give a home in Paris, along with his family name, to the illegitimate son of Charles II by Lucy Walter. This was James Crofts who, as duke of Monmouth, was to be executed for rebellion in 1685.
22. Ibid.
23. While Prince of Wales, Charles I had tried to comfort a deputation of women whose

husbands were held in bondage in Algiers; as king, he had written to the pirate chief, Sidi Hamet Laiashi, appealing to him to release English captives, and had issued a proclamation endorsing the collection of money for their ransom and relief. See Carlton, *Charles I* (n. 8), p. 177.

24. Wright, *Rutland* (n. 2), p. 105.

25. On the basis of some verses addressed to him by the poet Robert Heath in his *Clarastella*, in which he is praised as 'the lesser worlds Epitome', a date in advance of the book's publication in 1650 has been accepted; but the lines in question were probably written very much earlier. They make no mention of the Civil War or of Jeffery's exile, and refer to him as 'the Kings dwarfe' (*Clarastella*, 1650, Gainsville fac. edn, 1970, pp. 128–9). Both in style and content, they suggest a composition date more nearly contemporary with the *New Yeares Gift* of 1636 when Jeffery was at the height of his fame.

26. *Moneys Received and Paid for Secret Services of Charles II and James II*, ed. J.Y. Akerman (Camden Society, 1851), pp. 14, 28. The title of these accounts is misleading. The payments listed were simply donations to private persons for services rendered to the crown and extraordinary expenses relating to the king's private estate. They include a generous monthly allowance of £48 to the perjurer Oates.

27. See Oliver Millar, *The Age of Charles I, Painting in England, 1620–1649* (1972), Cat. nos 7 (for Robin) and 28 (for Russell's dwarf); pp. 15, 30–1.

28. Horace Walpole, *Anecdotes of Painting in England*, III (Strawberry Hill, 1763), pp. 64–5; *Poetical Works of Edmund Waller*, ed. R. Bell (1854), p. 119.

29. Revd J.S. Clarke, *The Life of James II collected out of memoirs writ of his own hand* (1816), I, pp. 29–30.

30. *The Diary of Samuel Pepys*, ed. R. Latham and W. Matthews, IX (1976), pp. 66–7 and note.

Chapter 17: The Fools' Motley

1. *Shakespeare's Motley*, 1952, reprinted New York, 1971.

2. See, for one of several examples of this alternative meaning of 'motley' cited in OED (A.1), Caxton's statement in his *Golden Legend* of 1483, 'Israhel lovyd Joseph . . . and made for hym a motley cote'. In Robert Wilson's *The three Ladies of London* (printed 1584, sig. Aiiᵛ), Dissimulation is described as entering with his 'powle [poll] and beard painted motley', which Dissimulation goes on to describe as 'my partie coloured head' (cited by Sidney Thomas in *Shakespeare Quarterly* X (1959), p. 255).

3. For the use of the 'idiot's robe', see Thomas Nashe (quoted by Hotson, p. 53): 'fooles, ye know, alwaies for the most part (*especiallie if they bee naturall fooles*) are suted in long coates' (epistle to *Have With You to Saffron Walden* of 1596, in *Works*, ed. R.B. McKerrow, revised F.P. Wilson, Oxford, 1958, III, p. 17; my italics). The early Shakespeare scholar, George Steevens, in stating that 'petticoats were not *always* a part of the dress of fools, though they were of idiots' (Hotson, p. 14) appears to have been in the right about this, as was another early scholar Joseph Ritson, while Francis Douce, author of the influential *Illustrations of Shakespeare* of 1807, and Hotson himself were mistaken.

4. *A Shakespeare Jestbook, Robert Armin's 'Foole upon Foole' (1600)*, ed. H.F. Lippincott (Elizabethan Studies 20, Salzburg, 1973), p. 57; quoted Hotson, p. 8.

5. Ibid., p. 59.

6. Ibid., p. 93; Hotson, p. 66.

7. REED: *Hereford and Worcester*, pp. 460–83.

8. *Privy Purse Expenses of Elizabeth of York*, ed. N.H. Nicolas (1830), p. 24; see above, pp. 61–2.

9. REED: *Newcastle*, pp. xvii–xix and *passim*; for the references above see pp. 100–1, 104, 129, 142. The many petticoats of white cotton referred to were probably nightshirts. The glossary to this volume interprets 'peticote' as a 'small coat or waistcoat worn by men beneath the doublet', but it does not take 6–8 yards of material to make a waistcoat.

10. *Foole upon Foole*, ed. Lippincott (n. 4), p. 92. The disparity is pointed out by David Wiles in *Shakespeare's Clown* (Cambridge, 1987), p. 186.

11. Doran, p. 210.

12. Shakespeare also uses 'guard' in a figurative sense, as in *LLL*, IV.iii.55–6: 'O! rhymes are guards on wanton Cupid's hose:/ Disfigure not his slop'. (The Q reading of

'shop' adopted in the Arden edition makes little sense.) 'Hose' and 'slop' here refer to the one article of clothing; Berowne is saying that rhymes are as superfluous and demeaning to love poetry as guards would be to wanton Cupid's breeches. For Jack Grene and Tarlton's 'slop', see pp. 108–9 above.

13. I.viii.7–12, 57–62 in Revels edition, ed. G.K. Hunter (1975), pp. 51, 54 and introduction.

14. See above, pp. 56–7; for Robert IV, Bullock-Davies, *Register*, p. 53; Hotson, p. 34; for the Black Prince's list, n. 29 to Chapter 6.

15. For the full text of these specifications, see Janet Arnold, *Queen Elizabeth's Wardrobe Unlock'd* (1985), p. 105 and glossary.

16. *Foole upon Foole*, ed. Lippincott (n. 4), pp. 58, l.53; 56, ll. 3–4.

17. Chambers, MS, I, p. 387.

18. Even here, its adoption by the folk tradition was patchy. Those who played the fool in the more authentically ancient of rural rituals and plays tended to retain (as they still do) their customary wear of animal skins and tails, or to dress themselves in women's clothes as 'Bessies'. See Chambers, MS, I, pp. 142, 192, 196, 210.

19. For an informative study of this popular fool iconography, see Timothy Easton, 'The Fool in Medieval Church and Play', in *The Suffolk Review*, New Series no. 4 (1985), of which I have a revised reprint. For the Betley window, Wiles, *Shakespeare's Clown* (n. 10), p. 184. My italics.

20. REED: *Cambridge*, I, pp. 159, 162.

21. *The English Works of John Gower*, ed. G.C. Macauley (EETS, 1901), II, p. 346; *Magnyfycence*, ed. R.L. Ramsay (EETS, 1908), p. 33.

22. I am drawing here on OED. The earliest use of 'coxcomb' is attributed to Tusser in 1573.

23. *Misogonus*, ed. L.E. Barber (New York and London, 1979), pp. 108–11. For the costuming of fools and vices in the interludes, see T.W. Craik, *The Tudor Interlude, Stage, Costume and Acting* (Leicester, 1962), pp. 66–72.

24. For Shakespeare's association of feathers with folly, see *H8*, I.iii.24–5: 'leave those remnants/Of fool and feather that they got in France'; and *LLL*, IV.i.95 (quoted above,

p. 109): 'What plume of feathers is he that indited this letter?', referring to Armado who, a few lines later, is described as 'a Monarcho'.

25. A similarly bawdy use of 'bauble' is in *Rom.*, II.iv.91–2.

26. For Feste's gaskins, see *Twelfth Night*, I.v.23–4: 'if both break, your gaskins fall' (Maria); and for Shenton's, Arnold, *Elizabeth's Wardrobe* (n. 15), p. 105. There would have been no point in Feste wearing gaskins beneath a long 'idiot's robe' as Hotson proposes (p. 67) since they would not have been seen. For Touchstone's motley, see *AYL*, II.vii.12–61. When, in Sonnet 110, Shakespeare tells us that he has made himself 'a motley to the view', he means that he has made a fool of himself in the eyes of the world.

27. Hotson, pp. 69–70. The stark image of 'unaccommodated man' presented by Tom o' Bedlam in the hovel scenes of the play recalls the frantic fools of the early psalters; cf. Plate 5.

28. *Twelfth Night*, IV.ii.125–32. It is noteworthy that this 'old Vice' with whom Feste associates himself was on the side of the angels. That such a character was vivid in Shakespeare's memory is attested by further references to him: by Falstaff (to Prince Hal) in *1H4*, II.iv.133–6: 'If I do not beat thee out of thy kingdom with a dagger of lath . . . I'll never wear hair on my face more'; Falstaff again (of Shallow) in *2H4*, III.ii.313–4: 'And now is this Vice's dagger become a squire'; and the Boy in *H5*, IV.iv.71–4 (of Pistol): 'Bardolph and Nym had ten times more valour than this roaring devil i' the old play, that every one may pare his nails with a wooden dagger.'

29. For the *targe*, p. 54 above; for Christmas revels, A. Feuillerat, *Documents Relating to the Revels at Court in the Time of King Edward VI and Queen Mary* (Louvain, 1914), pp. 73, 91, 107, and 76–7 above; for the Cambridge 'dagger of wodd', REED: *Cambridge*, I, p. 162.

30. For Rafe Simnel, i. ll. 29–31 in Revels edition; for Devil, I.i.84–5 in Jonson, VI, p. 167 (cited Hotson, p. 58).

31. G.K. Hunter in his introduction to the Penguin edition of the play (Harmondsworth, 1972), p. 11.

Chapter 18: Mr Nobody

1. E.W. Ives, 'Tom Skelton – a Seventeenth Century Fool', in *Shakespeare Survey*, 13 (Cambridge, 1966), pp. 90–105.

2. These not very original verses have been improbably ascribed to Dean Swift, 'who had been Chaplain to Charles Earl of Berkeley, when one of the Lords Justices of Ireland'; see Ralph Bigland, *Historical, Monumental and Genealogical Collections Relative to the County of Gloucester* (1791), I, p. 174; *The Poems of Jonathan Swift*, ed. H. Williams (Oxford, 1958), III, pp. 1131–2.

3. *Illustrations of Shakspeare* (1839 edn), pp. 503–4.

4. J.P. Earwaker, *East Cheshire: Past and Present* (1880), II, pp. 570–1. I am indebted to Sandra Billington, *A Social History of the Fool* (1984), p. 86, for this reference. See also DNB under 'Johnson, Samuel'.

5. Cf., for example, the fool Moros in W. Wager's *The longer thou livest, the more foole thou art* of between 1558 and 1569.

6. R.A. Foakes, *Illustrations of the English Stage, 1580–1642* (1985), p. 94.

7. Ll. 375–92 in *The School of Shakspere*, ed. R. Simpson (1878), I, p. 292.

8. The New (Cambridge) Shakespeare edition of *The Tempest* (1921, glossary, pp. 114–15) adds an interesting gloss to this 'picture of Nobody' in the form of a quotation from Jonson's *Every Man in His Humour* of 1598 (I.iii.58), 'Well, if he read this with patience, I'll be gelt, and troll ballads for Mr John Trundle yonder, the rest of my mortality', noting the parallel between 'troll ballads' and Caliban's 'troll the catch' (*Tp.*, III.ii.115). Trundle was known, not only for his sign, but as a publisher of ballads and broadsides.

9. *The Odyssey*, tr. Richmond Lattimore, Book IX, ll. 360–414; *Hoccleve's Works*, ed. F.J. Furnivall (EETS, 1897), III, p. 54. When asked as to who looked after his fellow clerks, the poet replies that 'Nemo does; save only him, they have but few friends' (ll. 1485–91). For *The three Ladies of London*, see above, p. 128.

10. See Willem Schrickx, '"Pickleherring" and English Actors in Germany', in *Shakespeare Survey*, 36 (Cambridge, 1980), pp. 135–47.

11. Irene Morris, 'A Hapsburg Letter', in *Modern Language Review*, 69 (1974), pp. 12–22.

12. Foakes, *Illustrations* (n. 6), pp. 102–3; Chambers, ES, III, pp. 269–70.

13. G.E. Bentley, *The Jacobean and Caroline Stage* (Oxford, 1956), IV, pp. 861–4.

14. For Cane and Reade, see ibid., II, pp. 398–401, 540–1. For *The Stage-players Complaint* (facsimile of title page), Foakes, *Illustrations* (n. 6), p. 158. For William Robbins (above and below), see Bentley, II, pp. 547–9.

15. Printed in *The Seventeenth-century Stage*, ed. G.E. Bentley (Chicago and London, 1968), p. 32; *The Jacobean and Caroline Stage* (n. 13), IV, pp. 501–5.

16. *The Complete Works of Thomas Shadwell*, ed. M. Summers (1927), IV, pp. 19–20.

17. Sandra Billington, *A Social History of the Fool* (1984), p. 70. In the same year (1679), 'Miss Charke' also appeared at the Haymarket in *The Beggar's Opera*.

18. For the drolls see Foakes, *Illustrations* (n. 6), pp. 160–1; for the fairs, Sybil Rosenfeld, *The Theatre of the London Fairs in the 18th Century* (Cambridge, 1960).

Further Reading

Most of the following books are now out of print but may still be obtained from libraries or through the Inter-Library Loan Scheme.

Sandra Billington in *A Social History of the Fool* (Harvester Press, Sussex; St Martin's Press, New York, 1984) finds evidence for the existence of fools and fool activities in the folk traditions of medieval England. Brief but interesting later chapters on the 'rise of the Fool'.

Dr (John) Doran, *The History of Court Fools* (Richard Bentley, 1858). An expansive, undiscriminating account of fools at the English and other European courts. Contains a mass of fascinating information which, however, is not always reliable and rarely, or only vaguely, sourced. Written to be popular, but its somewhat patronising and archly humorous style may irritate a modern reader.

Leslie Hotson, *Shakespeare's Motley* (1952; reprinted by Haskell House, New York, 1971). A fascinating, if controversial, account of Shakespeare's fools and their costuming, written in the author's characteristically exuberant style.

Barbara Swain, *Fools and Folly during the Middle Ages and the Renaissance* (Columbia University Press, New York, 1932). Scholarly study (originally a doctoral dissertation) of the concept of folly largely from the philosophical and literary points of view, but essential reading for those who wish to pursue the subject at a deeper level.

Enid Welsford, *The Fool, His Social and Literary History* (Faber and Faber, 1935). By far the most scholarly, comprehensive and readable account of fools in a variety of times and cultures to have appeared so far.

David Wiles, *Shakespeare's Clown, Actor and Text in the Elizabethan Playhouse* (Cambridge University Press, 1987) contains accounts of Tarlton, Kempe and Armin. As indicated by the title, the perspective is predominantly literary.

William Willeford, *The Fool and His Scepter, A Study in Clowns and Jesters and Their Audience* (Northwestern University Press, USA, 1969). Primarily a psychological study, drawing on a wide variety of sources. Attempts to answer such questions as, 'Why is the fool such an often recurring figure in the world and our imaginative representations of it? . . . Why are we, like people in many other times and places, fascinated by fools?'

Index

Where surnames are merely descriptive (Roger Follus, Henry Stultus) or preceded by 'of' (*de*) or 'the' (*le*), persons are indexed under their first names. Principal entries are indicated by the use of italics, and illustrations by bold.

Adam de la Hale, alias Adam Le Boscu, 82–3
Adam le Fol, messenger-fool to Henry III, 42
Adelina, entertainer to Earl Roger, 38
Aedh, dwarf to Fergus, 13
Agallamh na senórach (Colloquy of the Ancients), quoted 12
Ager, Mrs, keeper of Jane at Bury St Edmunds, 105
Alcuin, letters from, 19
Alexander the Great, 17–18
Allen, Cardinal, quoted 110–11
Allon, Newcastle fool, 166
Amadas and Ydoine, quoted 49
Anaxarchus, philosopher-fool, 18
Anne of Denmark, queen of James I, 151
    her Players, 119, 181
Anselm of Canterbury, St, quoted 51
Aquinas, St Thomas, 34, quoted 51–2
L'Arbre d'Or, tournament of, 85–6
Armin, Robert, player-fool and author, 79, *133–7*, **135**
    works, 79–80, 97, 133, 134–6, 164, 166, 169
Armstrong, Archibald, fool to James I, 93, *140–51*, **143, 148**
    his *Archy's Dream*, 149
    letters from, 145–6, 147
Arthuret, Cumberland, Archy Armstrong born at and retires to, 149
artificial fools, *5–6*, 8, *17–28*, 29, *32–4*, 35–47, 56, 57, 81–8, 89–93, 94–9, 107, 108–11, 113, 114–20, 121–37, 138–49
Artoys – *see* Calot Jean
Aubrey, John, quoted 138
Augustine of Hippo, St, quoted 39

Bacon, Sir Francis, quoted 111
Baldy Chunyu, Chinese fool, 18–19
Banquet of Jests, quoted 147–8, **143, 148**
Barlow Psalter, 4, **4**
Battle of Hastings, 23–8, **24**
Bayeux Tapestry, **15, 30**
    see also Battle of Hastings

Beden, fool to Queen Mary, 105
Bedyll, Thomas, letter to Cromwell, quoted 70
Bekynton, Bishop Thomas, fool of, **165**
Belou, William, letter from, quoted 151
Berdic, *joculator regis*, 28
Bernard le Fol, fool at Pontoise, 54–5
Bes, dwarf-god of Egypt, 10–11
Betley window, fool of the, 171, **172**
Blakall, Thomas, king's fool to Henry VII, 63
Bláthnait, wife to Cnú dheireoil, 12–13
Blue John, fool described and played by Robert Armin, 134–6, **135**
Boleyn, Anne, queen of Henry VIII, 100
bourders (jokers), 89–90
boy bishops, 52, 53, 84
Brandon, Thomas, 'jugler' to Henry VIII, *94–8*, 101
Brereton, Sir William, quoted 144–5
Bridewell prison, 111, 139
Bright, George, keeper of Will Somer in Elizabeth's reign, 107
Browne, Thomas, fool to Catherine Parr, 103
Buckingham, George Villiers, duke of, 145
buffoons, 19, *31–4*, 42, 138–9
Buhlul-al-Madjnun, fool to Haroun-ar-Rashid, 48
Bussard, Robert
    see Robert Bussard

Calot Jean, dwarf-fool to Count Robert II of Artois, 82–3, **82**
    see also **7**
Cane, Andrew, Caroline player-fool, 182
Careless Shepherdess (*Praeludium*), quoted 182
Carleton, Sir Dudley, quoted 139
Carmen (Song) *of the Battle of Hastings*, quoted 25
Cath Almaine (Battle of Allen), quoted 21
Cath Maige Mucrama (Battle of Mag Mucrama), quoted 12, 21–2
Catherine de Valois, queen of Henry V, 58
Cavendish, George, quoted 66
Cecil, Sir William, quoted 111, **111**
centunculus as worn by Roman fools, 170, **170**

Chamberlain, John, letters from, quoted 117, 142, 146, 147

Chapuys, Eustace, letter from, quoted 68–9

character costumes, 44, 45, **45**, 84 (*à la turque*), 91–2, 126, **127**, 154–6, **155**, 173

   see also clothes

Charles I, king of England, 147–51, 153–61

   as prince, 144–7

Charles II, king of England, 159

Charles VI of France, 58

Charles, prince of Castile (later emperor Charles V), 87

Chaucer, Geoffrey, quoted 90

Chester, Charles, buffoon, 138–9

Chettle, Henry, quoted 126

Chewepayn, William, alias Robert Fol of St Albans (Robert VI), 56

chivalric pageantry, 84–6, **85**

Chrétien de Troyes, quoted 37

Christmas season, significance of, 46, *52–3*, 74–7, 171

Chrysostom, St, quoted 4

Churchyard, Thomas, quoted 112, 113

clever fools – *see* artificial

clothing, fools', 30, 31, 43, 44, 50, 53, 55, 57, 58, 61–2, 63, 67, 68, 70, 71, 73, 76, 77–8, 82, 83–4, 101, 102, 103–5, 106, 108–9, 110, 112, 113, 119, 142, 144, 146, 151, *163–73*, 175

   see also centunculus, character costumes, feathers, *habit de fou*, motley, props

clown, stage, creation of, 178

   see Kempe, Tarlton

Cnú dheireoil, dwarf to Finn, 12–13

Conare Már, Irish king, 20–1

Corbett, Bishop Richard, quoted 146

Crofts, William, killed by Jeffery Hudson at Nevers, 158

Croyland Abbey, young fool at, 70

danga (*dng*), dancing pygmy, 10–11

Davenant, Sir William, works cited 154, 156

David the psalmist, King, 3–4, 7, 51; see also Plates 4b, 6a, 7b, 8b, 9a, 10a, 13b

Death of Fergus, quoted 13

Dego, Spanish fool to Henry VII, 86

Dekker, Thomas, quoted 109

Derry, Tom, fool to Anne of Denmark, **150**, 151

Devers or Devereaux, John, keeper of fools to Henry VIII, 64

Dik, fool to Henry VII, 61

Diogenes, philosopher-fool, 17–18, **17**

disours and disards, 77, *90–2*, 93

   see also vices

Do Déra, fool to Mac Con, 21–2

Dodds, Thomas, Newcastle fool, 166

Domesday Book, cited 28, 38

doubles, fool, 21–2, 63

doubling in plays, practice of, 129–31

Dulcia Withestaf, mother of Robert III, 54

Durham Abbey, fool on tour at, 83

dwarfs, *10–16*, 82–3, 84–6, 100, *110*, 117–19, 123–4, *152–61*

   proportionate,.13, 15–16, 110, 152–61, **152**, **155**, **156**, **160**

Eadmer, quoted 29

Eadwine (Canterbury) Psalter, 5–6

Edgar, king of England, 20

Edmund Ironside, king of England, 23

Edward I, king of England, 43, 54

Edward II, king of England, 41–2, 43 (as prince), *54–5*, 83

Edward IV, king of England, 85, *90–2*, **91**

Edward VI, king of England, 74–7, **76**

Edward the Martyr, king of England, 13–14

Eleanor of Castile, queen of Edward I, 43

Eleanor of Provence, queen of Henry III, 15

Elizabeth I, queen of England, 107–20

Elizabeth of York, queen of Henry VII, 61, 63–4, 93

Emson, keeper of Sexton (with Skinner and Grene), 68

English, John, interluder, 122, 124

Englische Komödianten, 179

epitaphs, 65, 119, 176(2)

Erasmus, quoted 9

eutrapelia, spirit of play, 34

Evans, William, giant porter to Charles I, 156, **156**

Farmor (or Fermor), Sir Richard, 71

farters, 39

Feast of Fools, 52–3

feathers, fools', *108–9*, 151, **162**, 163, 179

female fools, 100–6

Fer Fí, Irish dwarf, 12

Fergal, Irish king, 21

Fergus, Irish king, 13

Ferrers, George (Lord of Misrule), 76–7

Finn, legendary Irish king, 12–13

Folebarba, joker to Miles, earl of Hereford, 38–9

'folyshe Duke of Lancaster', 63

follis/follus, the term, 5, 39, 46, 89

fool bishop, 52

fool characters in plays

   by Shakespeare, 8, 79, 99, 119–20, *130–4*, 136–7, 146–7, 166–7, 173, 174, 183–4

   by Ben Jonson, 136, 138, 154–6, **155**, 174

   by others, 114–16, 126, 134–6, **135**, 156, 167, 174, 179–81, **180**, 182, 183, 184

fool societies, *see Sociétés Joyeuses*

fools – *see under* artificial, female, frantic, innocent, king's, messenger, minstrel, player, psalter, riding, seer, truth-bearer, warrior, wisdom

   see also buffoons, jesters, joculator

Fortunatus de Lucca, knighted buffoon to Henry III, 42

Francis of Assisi, St, 34, 51, 53

frantic fools, 6, *48–52*, 57–8

Fuller, Thomas, quoted 1, 9, 114, 116, 156, 157

Fulsharst, fool committed to Bridewell by Cecil, 111

Gaimar, Geoffrey, quoted 13–14, 25–6

Garrard, letter from Mr, 148

Garret, John, fool to Queen Elizabeth, *117–19*, 136

Gatehouse, Jeffery Hudson committed to, 159

gestour, the term, 89

ghosts, 118, 119, 126

Gibson, Richard, dwarf to Charles I, 159

Gibson, Richard, interluder, 122–3
Globe theatre, **129**, 132, 133
Golet, fool to William of Normandy (later Conqueror), 30–1
Gower, John, quoted 90, 172
Green, John, Jacobean player, 179
Greene, Robert, *Friar Bacon and Friar Bungay*, quoted 174
Greene's Tu Quoque, 179–81
Greenwich, Christmas revels at, 74–7
Gregory the Great, St, quoted 51
Grene, Jack, fool to Queen Elizabeth, 108–9
Grene, keeper of Sexton (with Emson and Skinner), 68
Griscote, Visage and Magote, 43–4
Guillaume, Mantuan fool, 7
Guzman de Silva, quoted 108

habit de fou, 44, *53*, 163–4, 168, *169–71*, **172**
Haincelin Coq, fool to Charles VI of France, 58
Henrietta Maria, queen of Charles I, 153–8
Henry I, king of England, 35
Henry II, king of England, 35, 37–9
Henry III, king of England, 42
Henry VI, king of England, 58. 122
Henry VII, king of England, 61, *62–3*, **62**, 86–7, 122
Henry VIII, king of England, *63–9*, *70–80*, **73**, 87, 94, *96–7*, 122–3
    Henry VIII's Psalter, 72–4
Henry of Huntingdon, cited 26
Henry Stultus, fool to the Count of Savoy, 83
Heywood, John, 78, 101, 110, *123–4*, **125**
    works cited, 65–6, 78, 123–4
Heywood, Thomas, quoted 136
    his *A Maidenhead Well Lost*, 181
Hoccleve, quoted 49, 179
Homer's *Odyssey*, 179
Howell, James, quoted 144
Howes, Edmund, quoted 117
Hoyden, fool to Queen Elizabeth, 113
Hugo de Helmeslaye, fool to Edward II, 83
Hudson, Jeffery, dwarf to Henrietta Maria, 152–61, **152, 155, 156**
huntsman-fools – *see* Roger Follus, John le Fol, Ralph le Fol

innocent fools, 5, 6–8, *48–60*, 61–9, 70–80, 100–6, 111–13, 113–14, 149–51, 175–7
interludes and interluders, 43, *121–4*, 174
ioglere – *see* joculator
Ippolyta the Tartarian, godchild of Queen Elizabeth, *109*, 167
Ipswich, wedding feast at, 43

Jack Puddings, 184
Jacob's Well, quoted 90
Jacomin, king's fool to Henry III, 42
Jakeman, fool to Philippa of Hainault, 57
James I, king of England, 140–7, **140**
James, Prince (later James II), 159
James of St Albans, court painter to Edward II, 42
Jane, fool to Queen Mary, 77, *100–6*, **104**

Jean, dwarf to Eleanor of Provence, 15–16
Jean le Bon, king of France, 83–4
Jehan, Maistre, fool to Jean le Bon, 83–4
jesters, 98–9, 107, 108–9, 110–11, 113, 114–20, 138–49
    the term, 89
Jests of Scoggin, quoted 92–3
jigs, 126, 130–1, 132
joculator, entertainer or joker, 19, 23, 29, 38–9, 90, 188–9 n.6
    for *joculatoris Domini*, 34
    for *joculator regis*, 28
    for *tota joculatorum scena*, 126
    see also jesters
John, king of England, 39–40
John, Mr, fool to Ann Nevill, queen of Richard II, 58
John, Mr, fool to the Archduke Philip of Burgundy, 87–8
John de Blavia, buffoon to Henry III, 42
John Goose, fool to Henry VIII when duke of York, 63–4
John le Fol, huntsman-fool to Henry III, 40–1
John Scot, player-fool to Henry VIII, 122–4
Johnson, Samuel (Maggoty or Fiddler Johnson), 176, **177**
Jonson, Ben, 93, 132, 136, 146, 154–6
    works cited, 112, 136, 138, 139, 146, 174
'juglers', *94–8*, **98**, 107
    the term, 93

Keepers of the King's (Queen's) fools – *see* Worthy, Wise, Devers, Emson, Skinner, Grene, Seyton, Ager, Bright, Mawe
Kempe, William, player-fool, 119, *129–33*, **133**
    his *Nine Daies Wonder*, 132–3
Killigrew, Tom, supposed fool to Charles II, 159–61
King Edward and the Shepherd, 93
king/fool relationship, 1–4, 7–9, 140–1
king's (queen's) fool, 39–40, 42, *43*, 57, 63, 64, 67, 70, 105, 108
    jester, 98–9
    see also joculator regis, riogdruth
kings' idiots, 57
Knight, Roger, fool to Prior William More, 164–6

Langland, William, quoted 44, 51
Laud, Archbishop William, 147, *148–9*
Leane Leonard, fool described by Robert Armin, 166
Leicester, Robert Dudley, earl of, *108*, 114, 116
    his fool, 108
    his Men, 114–16
Lestrange, Sir Nicholas, quoted 138, 147
Lob, fool to Henry VIII, 64–5
    'lob' as synonym for 'clown', 194 n.12
Lockwood, James, jester to Henry VIII, Edward VI, Mary and Elizabeth, 98–9
Lodge, Thomas, quoted 128, 138–9
Lomnae Drúth, Irish fool and seer, 20–1
The longer thou livest, the more fool thou art (W. Wager), quoted 109
Longinus, cited 11
Lords of Misrule, 53, 76–7, *171*

Lucian, quoted 11
Lucretia the Tumbler, servant to Princess Mary, 101–2
Lull, St, quoted 19
Luttrell Psalter, 44, **45**

Mabinogion, 13
Mac Con, Irish king, 12, 21–2
mad fools – *see* frantic fools
Map, Walter, quoted 35
Marshall, Newcastle fool, 166
Marston, John, *The Malcontent*, quoted 167
Martial, quoted 11–12, 19
Martin, Mr, king's fool to Henry VII, 63
Martinet, Gascon fool, 83
Martyn, fool to Edward of Middleham, 58
Mary, Princess, 68–9, 95, *100–3*, **101**
    as queen of England, 77–8, *103–6*
masks, use of, 76, 121, 122, 201 notes 11, 24
Mason, Alexander, minstrl and *geyster*, 89
Matilda Makejoy, acrobat to Edward I, 43
Matthew, Sir Tobie, 145, 146
Mawe, John, keeper of Tom Derry, 151
maypole, 63, 170
Meaux Abbey, Robert II sent in retirement to, 54
Meeres, Francis, quoted 128
Meng, Chinese fool, 18
Merry Andrews, 184
messenger fools, 42
Michael, fool to Isabella, queen of Edward II, 53–4
Middleton, Thomas, with William Rowley, *The Changeling*, 181
mimi et histriones, 34, 35–6, *42*, 184
minstrel fools, 35–47
minstrels, 1, *36–8*, **38**, 42–3, 81
    see also waferers
Misogonus, quoted 78, 172–3
mock combats, 11, 76–7, 117, 142
Monarcho, fool to Queen Elizabeth, *111–13*, 167
More, William, blind harper to Henry VIII, 95, 101
More, William, Prior of Worcester, 95, 164
morris dance, 63, 170, 171
Morris Ken of the kitchen, 41–2
motley, the material, 114, *163–7*
    particoloured, 113, *167–9*, 173
Muckle John, fool to Charles I, *149–51*, **150**, 166
Muncaster Castle, Cumbria, home of Tom Skelton, 173
musical instruments, 36, 58, 72, **73**, 113, 126, **127**, **171**

Nashe, Thomas, works cited 78, 110, 112, 119, 126, 130
natural fools – *see* innocents
nebulo, 1, 32
    see also nobody
Neferkere (Pepi II), pharaoh, 10–11
Newcastle upon Tyne, Corporation of, 166
Newgate, John Scot imprisoned in, 124
New-Yeeres Gift, miniature book, **152**, 157
Nithard, joculator to Edmund Ironside, 23
nobody, 1, 6, 22, 30–1, 65, 128, *178–9*
No-body and Some-body, 178–9, **180**
Northampton, Earl of, 147

Oakham, Rutland, Jeffery Hudson born at, 153
Oates, Jack, fool to Sir William Holles, 164, 169
'old players' of Henry VIII, 122–3
Olivares, Count of, *144–5*, 146
Orderic Vitalis, quoted 29, 31–2
Osborne, Francis, quoted 146, 149

Pace, John, Elizabethan fool, 110–11
Paget, Sir William, despatch from, quoted 72
Paris, Matthew, quoted 16
Parr, Catherine, queen of Henry VIII, 102–3, **102**
Parr, Thomas, an aged man, 156, **156**
Parsons, Sir Thomas, partners Archy Armstrong in mock combat, 142
Paston, John, letter from, quoted 86
Patch, fool to Wolsey, then Henry VIII
    see Sexton
Paul the apostle, St, quoted 51
Peacham, Henry, quoted 116, 126
Pearce, Dicky, fool to the earl of Suffolk, 175–6
Peche (or Pache), fool to Henry VII, 61
Pengelding, Rees, fool to Lord Chancellor Talbot, 176
Pennington, William, of Muncaster, 175
Pepys, Samuel, quoted 159–61
Perron, Cardinal, quoted 7, 8
Peter de Blois, quoted 35
Philip VI of France, fool of, 8–9
Philip of Burgundy, the Archduke, 87–8
Philippa of Hainault, queen of Edward III, 44–6, 57
Phypp – *see* Worthy, William
player fools, 79, 114–16, 119–20, *121–37*, *178–84*
playing the fool, 41–2, 86, 136, 169
    see also player fools
Pleasant History of the Life and Death of Will Summers, 78–9
Privy Chamber of Henry VIII, *65*, *67*
    and garden, 103
props and accessories, fools' (baubles, coxcombs, daggers, etc.), *4–7*, 54 (shield), 76–7 (armour), 91–2 (staff), *169–74*, 175
    see also clothing, feathers, musical instruments
Psalm 52 (53), 3–4, *36–7*, 51, 72–3
psalter fools, 3–4, **4**, 5–6, 6–7, *36–7*, 47, 50, 72–4, **73**, 100, 169–70
    see also Plates

queen's fool, *see* king's fool
Queen's Players (of Elizabeth I), 107, 116, *124–6*

Rahere, *see* Rayer
Raleigh, Sir Walter, 116, *138*
Ralph le Fol, huntsman-fool to King John, 40
Rayer (Rahere), buffoon to William II, later monastic founder, 32–4, **33**
Reade, Timothy, Caroline player-fool, 182
Reading Abbey, Mr John rewarded at, 87
Red Bull theatre, 181
René of Anjou, King, 84
riding fools, *62–3*, 113–14, 142
riogdruth, Irish king's fool, 21–3
Robbins, William, Caroline player-fool, 181, **181**, 182
Robert, 'Horny', fool to William II, 31

Robert, fool to Edward II (Robert III), 54
Robert Bussard, fool to Edward II (Robert II), 54
Robert Curthose, duke of Normandy, 31–2
Robert Fol of St Albans (Robert VI)
    see Chewepayn, William
Robert le Fol, fool to Eleanor of Castile (Robert I), 43
Robert le Fol, fool to Joan of Kent (Robert V), 56
Robert le Fol, fool to Philippa of Hainault (Robert
    IV), 44–6, 56, 90
Robert le Sot, messenger-fool to Henry III, 42
Robert of Cisyle, quoted 49
Robin, dwarf to the earl of Arundel, **160**
Roger Follus, fool and keeper of otter-hounds to
    Henry II, 39
Roland le Pettour, farter to Henry II, 39
Romans d'Alexandre, **55, 56**
Romanus Boilas, Byzantine fool, 3
Rowlands, Samuel, quoted 108–9
Rowley, Samuel, *When you see me, You know me*, cited
    78, 163
Rupert, Prince, 157, 158
Rush, Robin, fool to Lord Bussy Mansel, 176

St Albans Abbey, Robert VI sent in retirement to, 56
St Bartholomew's Priory, Hospital and Fair, 34
    drolls of the fair, 184
St Leonard's, Shoreditch, 78, 117
St Paul's, song school of, 101, 123
St Valentine's Day lottery, 105
Satyrion, Egyptian dwarf-fool, 11
Scogin, apocryphal fool, 92–3
Scot, John – *see* John Scot
Scot, Reginald, *Discoverie of Witchcraft*, quoted 96,
    112
scurrae – *see* buffoons
seer, the fool as, 13, 20–1, 48, 67
Selden's *Table Talk*, quoted 139
Sexton, alias Patch, fool to Wolsey and Henry VIII,
    65–9
'patch' as synonym for 'fool', 194–5 n.17
Seyton, William, keeper of Will Somer, 71
Shadwell, Thomas, *The Woman Captive*, 183
Shakespeare, William, 8, 93, 99, 107, 119–20, *129–37*,
    146–7, 166–7, 173, 183, 184
    plays quoted, 8, 79, 93, 99, 106, 108, 109, 111–12,
    131, 132, 134, 136, 137, 166–7, 173, 179, 183
Shenton, William, fool to Queen Elizabeth, 113, 169
Shepherd, Anne, dwarf to Henrietta Maria, 159
shout, fool's (of laughter), 21
Sibelot, frantic fool to Henri III of France, 6
Sima Qian, Chinese historian, quoted 8, 18–19
Singer, John, Elizabethan player-fool, 136
Skelton, John and imitators, quoted 65, 93, 172
Skelton, Tom, fool to the Penningtons of Muncaster,
    175
Skinner, keeper of Sexton (with Emson and Grene),
    68
Smith, John, player to Henry VIII, 77
Sociétés Joyeuses, 53, *54–5*, **55, 56**
Somer, William, king's fool to Henry VIII, *70–80*, **73,
    75**, 97, 105, 107–8, **162**, 163, 166–7
Somerton Castle, Lincs., Jean le Bon at, 83–4

Song of Roland, quoted 26–7
Stage-Players Complaint, 182
Staney or Stanway, Thomas, 'jugler' to Philip and
    Mary and Elizabeth, 97–8, 107
Starkey, jester (possibly riding fool) to James I, 203
    n.17
Stone, early Jacobean fool, 139–40
Stow's *Annales*, quoted 126
Suffolk, fool of the duke of, **64**

Taillefer, Norman joculator, 23–8
Tale of Tristan's Madness, quoted 50–1
Tarlton, Richard, jester and player to Queen
    Elizabeth, 108–9, *114–17*, **115**, *124–6*, **127**,
    133, 169
    his *Seven Deadly Sins*, 126–8
Tarlton's Jests, quoted 116, 126
Taylor, John, quoted 118–19, 142–4
theatre, origins of professional, 121–2
Thetford Priory, visited by Thomas Brandon, 95
Thomas, jester to Henry VIII, 97
    see also Brandon, Thomas
Thomasen, Mrs, alias Thomasina or Tomasina de
    Paris, dwarf to Queen Elizabeth, 110
Togail bruidne Da Derga (Destruction of Da Derga's
    Hostel), quoted 20–1
Tom Fole, fool to John Howard, duke of Norfolk, 58
Tom le Fol, king's fool to Edward I, 43–4
tonsure, fools', 21–2, *49–50*
Tosso, Stephen, tumbler and footman to Henry VIII,
    102
trickster, the, 2–3, 6, 10
truth-bearer, the fool as, *7–9*, 17–18, 68–9, 92, 137
    see also wisdom
Túatha Dé Danand (People of the Goddess Danu), 12
Tulchaine, fool to Conare Már, 21
Turold, dwarf of the Bayeux Tapestry, *14–15*, **15**, 27,
    188 n.16
Twisty Pole, Chinese dwarf-fool, 8
Tyler, William, disour rewarded by Elizabeth of York,
    93

Úa Maigleine, *riogdruth* to Fergal, 21–2

Van Wilder, Philip, leading musician to Henry VIII,
    67, 68, 101
Vergilius Maro, Gaulish dwarf-poet, 13
vices, 77, *123–4*, 128, 136–7, 174
    see also disours

Wace, quoted 26, 30–1, 37
waferers, 36, 39, 40–1, **41**, 44
Walter the Jester, riding fool to Queen Elizabeth, 114
Walworth, Surrey, Nithard's gift of, 23
wardrobe, fools' – *see* clothing
Warin, entertainer to Roger de Mowbray, 38
warrior fools, 20–8
Watt, minstrel and fool to Henry VII, 86
weapons, fools' – *see* props and accessories
Welwood, James, quoted 149
Westminster Abbey, Archy discovered in, 149
wild men – *see* wodwoses

Will, riding fool to Queen Elizabeth, 114
William II (Rufus), king of England, 31, 32, 34
William, duke of Normandy (the Conqueror), 14–15,
    30–1
    see also Battle of Hastings
William, fool to Elizabeth of York, 61–2, 166
William, king's fool to Henry V (William II), 57–8
William Fool, fool to Richard II (William I), 57
William of Malmesbury, quoted 20, 26–7, 31
William Picol, fool to King John, 39–40
William Taberer, wait and *bourder*, 90
Wilson, Robert, player-fool and playwright, 114–16, *128*
    plays quoted, 114, 128

Wilson, Thomas, quoted 72
Windsor Great Park, 79, 108
wisdom, fools', 5, 9, 51–2, 72, 80, 163
    see also truth-bearer
Wise, Rauf, keeper of Sexton at Greenwich, 61
wodwoses (wild men), 49, **50**
Wolsey, Cardinal, 65–7
Wolstanet, dwarf-fool to Edward the Martyr, 13–14
Woodhouse, 'sage dyzour' to Edward IV, *90–2*, 168
Worcester Priory, visitors to, 95
Worthy, William, alias Phypp, keeper of the king's
    fools to Henry VII, 61–2, 63
Wotton, Sir Henry, letter from, quoted 142